Collaborative Production in the Creative Industries

Edited by
James Graham and Alessandro Gandini

UNIVERSITY OF
WESTMINSTER
PRESS

University of Westminster Press
www.uwestminsterpress.co.uk

Published by
University of Westminster Press
101 Cavendish Street
London W1W 6XH
www.uwestminsterpress.co.uk

First published 2017
Cover Design: Diane Jarvis

Printed in the UK by Lightning Source Ltd.
Print and digital versions typeset by Siliconchips Services Ltd.

ISBN (Paperback): 978-1-911534-28-0
ISBN (PDF): 978-1-911534-29-7
ISBN (EPUB): 978-1-911534-30-3
ISBN (Kindle): 978-1-911534-31-0

DOI: https://doi.org/10.16997/book4

The full text of this book has been peer-reviewed to ensure high academic
standards. For full review policies, see: http://www.uwestminsterpress.co.uk/
site/publish/

To read the free, open access version of this book
online, visit https://doi.org/10.16997/book4 or
scan this QR code with your mobile device:

Competing interests

The editor and contributors declare that they have no competing interests in publishing this book

Contents

Acknowledgements

The editors would like to thank the Media and Performing Arts Research Fund at Middlesex University for enabling this project and Andrew Lockett of the University of Westminster Press for his support in preparing this book for publication.

CHAPTER ONE

Introduction: Collaborative Production in the Creative Industries

James Graham* and Alessandro Gandini†

*Middlesex University

†King's College, London

Collaboration has always functioned as the kernel of creative work. Yet from the artisanal workshops of the Renaissance masters to the globally networked start-ups of the twenty-first century, the character, context and consequences of creative collaboration have been mythologised and mystified in equal measure. Consider for example how, in the latter half of the twentieth century, high-profile success stories contributed to the building of an aura of around the magic that happens when popular artists collaborate. Think about Andy Warhol's collaborations with Jean-Michel Basquiat in the visual arts, or David Bowie's in music; about the way The Velvet Underground came together as a band through the addition of Reed to Cale, and then, at Warhol's suggestion, of Nico as singer. Or, more pertinently, think about how these collaborations catalysed a large-scale production process, through Warhol's Factory, that in conjunction with broader socio-economic transformations would play a part in reconfiguring creative production as an increasingly business-oriented process and influence trends in popular culture for decades to come (Berger, 2014).

How to cite this book chapter:

Graham, J. and Gandini, A. 2017. Introduction: Collaborative Production in the Creative Industries. In: Graham, J. and Gandini, A. (eds.). *Collaborative Production in the Creative Industries*. Pp. 1–14. London: University of Westminster Press. DOI: https://doi.org/10.16997/book4.a. License: CC-BY-NC-ND 4.0

In contrast to the aura that pervades these iconic collaborations, consider for a moment those who dwell in the shadows cast by the limelight. How many unheralded individuals will also have played some kind of role in the work produced through the headline collaborations, nestling in the wings or noodling in studios? In the case of Bowie alone the list would include a bewildering array of producers and publicists, session musicians and sound engineers, fans and fashionistas. But even that list would overlook the socio-technical dimension of collaboration, for instance in how the qualities of Bowie's music also derive from the relationship between the spaces where collaboration occurs and the technologies and techniques through which it is afforded. Michel Callon (2005) describes such phenomena as the *agencement* of human and non-human agents, a concept that Antoine Hennion further develops in his discussion of 'the material organization of co-production' (Hennion and Farías 2015, 74) in the music studio. In his 1982 book *Art Worlds*, Howard Becker described the human actors involved in these processes as 'support personnel', with the named artist (or indeed artists) occupying the central node of 'a network of cooperating people, all of whose work is essential to the final outcome' (25). Although Becker's primary concern was the socio-aesthetic function of 'art worlds', the examples he uses range across the fields that comprise what are now known popularly and in cultural policy as the 'creative industries', from jazz musicians to film makers. In recent years research into creative labour and cultural work has tended to address the politics of production in these fields, but the socio-technical and aesthetic dimensions of collaborative creative work that Callon, Hennion and Becker draw to our attention have not been subject to the same kind of sustained enquiry.

This book aims to address this gap. Through case studies that range from TV showrunning to independent publishing, this collection develops a critical understanding of the *integral* role collaboration plays in contemporary forms of cultural production. It draws attention to the kinds of creative collaboration afforded through digital platforms and networked publics. It considers how these are incorporated into emergent market paradigms and investigates the complicated forms of subjectivity that develop as a consequence. But it also acknowledges historical continuities, not least in terms of the continued exploitation of Becker's 'support personnel', but also the resulting conflicts, resistance and alternative models that attend the precarious nature of contemporary cultural work. Finally, it attempts to situate developments in the cultural sphere in broader social context and economic contexts, where not just the ideal of artistic creativity, but more specifically the idea of artistic *collaboration* has come to assume central importance.

•   •   •

As Fredric Jameson (1984) once observed, the boundaries between high art and popular culture have become porous in late capitalism. The technological acceleration, cultural globalization and economic stagnation that hallmark late capitalism paved the way for a new model of capital accumulation and governance. In the neoliberal 'creative economy' that emerged from this conjuncture, culture would seem in all places and all ways to be commodified and subject to the logic of the market, and so comes to occupy a pivotal role in economic and political as well as social affairs (McGuigan, 2016). Conversely, the ideal type of the artist has evolved toward that of the 'creative', a hybrid socio-economic actor who carries the romantic ideal of the artist into the fragmented ecosystem of the market – where the individual is entrepreneurialised (Gandini, 2016) and the social relations around collaboration commodified, as Angela McRobbie (2015) amongst others has argued. The promise of creative autonomy that attaches to this figure functions in a similar way to what Sarah Brouillette (2016, np) describes as the 'ameliorate social balm' of culture and the arts for a generation born into a precarious world, where work is increasingly defined by competition, risk and individualization. This kind of work is doubtless fun and fulfilling for many, but the reality is that in the creative economy labour is casualised and its sociality divested of political purchase. It gives rise to a promotional culture that both fuels and normalises these transformations – not least by occluding the intensification of the racial, gendered and international divisions of creative labour and cultural work (Curtin and Sanson, 2016). Nonetheless, the ethos and practices of artistic collaboration have flooded into the everyday practices and micro-politics of diverse industries across a global geography. Consequently this ethos, these practices and, perhaps most significantly, their much-hyped non-monetary payoffs, have become a feature of many different professions; yet they have also been thoroughly managerialised in the process. As Brouillette (2016) puts it:

> The impetus against routine work has been brought into even the least apparently creative workplaces, in the form of a management commitment to crediting every employee's interest in self-realization and personal wellness. In certain industries, for instance the "cool" tech sector, attracting the best employees involves telling people that in their work they will experience the artist's unique "freedom."(np)

This scenario will be all too familiar to a great many young people today doing a job they 'love' yet struggling to make ends meet. So what is the appeal and nature of 'the artist's unique "freedom"' to the 'creative', exactly? In a listicle that appeared on the popular digital newsite *Buzzfeed* in 2014 (Rebolini) detailing 10 habits of creative people, 'collaborating' sits at number four – after 'moving', 'taking naps' and 'daydreaming'. The listicle is designed to be consumed tongue-in-cheek. Bite-size self-improvement literature packaged as an ironic joke that will be shared instantly by acutely self-aware 'creative types' – the legions who spend so much of their lives in what Mark Banks (2014) calls 'the zone of cultural work', they are left (or rather, they are presumed to be left) with precious little time to engage more thoughtfully and critically with the culture they make as well as consume. Nonetheless, the appearance of collaboration on the list is substantiated by an anecdote starring one of the most renowned creative personalities of our times, the late Steve Jobs. It recounts the way in which Jobs redesigned the Pixar Studio campus in 1999 in order to better foster creative collaboration, based on the insight that 'human friction makes the sparks'(Lehrer, 2012).

For all the listicle's playfulness, the Jobs anecdote captures the auratic allure and affective pleasures of creative work that make it so appealing to young professionals – whilst simultaneously adding to the mysticism surrounding what it actually entails. Indeed, the listicle encapsulates the kind of reflexive irony that serves as the leitmotif of creative work in the era of neoliberalism more generally. The creative worker not only has to negotiate multiple dispositions simultaneously (autonomous artist and exploited labourer, and in many cases much more besides, parent, carer etc.), but to survive, let alone thrive, in this world they have to embrace, with stoic good humour, the doublethink necessary for living with the contradictions this entails. This paradoxical mode of subjectivity is addressed in this collection by a number of our contributors, who variously characterise it – from a state of 'ambivalence' strategically cultivated to negotiate socio-economic realities (Gandini, Bandinelli and Cossu), to a more abject condition of 'schizophrenia' (Wong) in thrall to the logic of late capitalism.

That such contradictions have emerged and come to define all manner of contemporary forms of work without great resistance[1] is in no small part due to the way the ideas around collaboration derived from the arts have been appropriated by business schools and management gurus and subsequently filtered into practice and policy-making since the 1990s (Brouillette, 2014, O'Brien, 2014). Writing in the *Harvard Business Review*, for example, Ben Hecht (2013) argues that 'what we're seeing around the country is the coming together of non-traditional partners, and a willingness to embrace new ways of working together' (Hecht, 2013, np). Collaboration today is a multi-faceted beast, and collaborative production is undoubtedly an asset for many industries in information-based economies where, as Hecht argues, collaboration is seen as 'the new competition' (Hecht, 2013, np). Here, collaboration is figured as the primary driver of economic growth in a post-crisis world seemingly straight out of Jonathan Swift, that is, where governance has so successfully been captured by transnational corporations that the oligopolies they maintain at all costs can be construed as an exemplary model of creative collaboration at work on a global scale (Baird, 2016).

What happens, then, to an artistic notion of collaboration production in the fields from which the practice originated – Becker's (1982) art worlds – now that boundaries between 'art' and 'business' are blurred and these terms are no longer the oxymorons that sustained the traditional (if always already mythical) dichotomy? How has work in the creative industries been reshaped by the *managerialised* emphasis on collaboration that characterises the current land-scape? In what ways might cultural production, conventionally understood, be transformed by the convergent dynamics of digital intermediation and con-sumption in the contemporary creative economy? This book originates from a symposium held at Middlesex University on November 2015 which gathered academics from media and cultural studies, sociology, literary and publishing studies, to address these questions and discuss the scope, nature and future of collaborative production in the creative industries.

In the contributions collected in this volume we highlight the two most prominent strands of discussion that emerged from this event. The first of these concerns the growing body of work which investigates the diverse forms and functions of media production. A number of recent studies have evidenced how, at the heart of production practices in the creative industries, lies the managerialised coordination of a number of people who come together in the expectation that their creative collaboration will amplify their self-worth, in all senses, as well as simply provide some form of financial remuneration. In a sig-nificant body of academic and also non-academic work, punctuated by the *Pro-duction Studies* reader (Mayer, Banks and Caldwell, 2009) and its recent *Sequel!* (Banks, Conor and Mayer, 2015), the work of media producers in creative and cultural industries has been extensively dissected and analysed. In parallel with empirical research into the consumption of media content exemplified in *audi-ence studies* (Brooker, 2003), production studies research has brought to the surface complex sets of micro- and macro-production practices that charac-terise the professional work of creatives in industries such as television, film, radio and publishing. In both the *Production Studies* collections collaboration emerges as a definitive aspect of creative labour across a range of disciplines. To quote from the preface of *Production Studies: The Sequel!*:

> Media production is an imbricated and prolonged process, one that can simultaneously be highly individualized and fully collaborative. Even labor that practitioners conduct while working alone is not produced in a vacuum: directors have producers, artists have grants from founda-tions or organizations, and journalists have a community of sources – who now also tweet their own news-bytes (Banks, Conor and Mayer, 2015, pp. ix–x).

The second strand concerns the political economy of creative labour. An extensive body of research has looked at creative work in the media indus-tries in relation to market devices and logics. This work has largely criticised the increasingly casualised and precarious nature of creative labour, unveiling notions of value, autonomy and self-realisation as serving the imperatives of neoliberalism (Curtin and Sanson, 2016). This kind of work is associated with a range of aesthetic pleasures and affective dispositions; yet these are invariably compromised through various forms and to varying degrees of co-option. As

Hesmondhalgh and Baker (2010) put it, they offer the aspirant creative worker 'a complicated version of freedom'. Studies by, amongst others, Angela McRobbie ('Everyone is Creative', 2004, *Be Creative*, 2015), Andrew Ross (*No-Collar*, 2004, *Nice Work If You Can Get It*, 2009), David Hesmondhalgh and Sarah Baker (*Creative Labour*, 2011), as well as issue number 25 (7-8) of the journal *Theory, Culture and Society* (2008), hosting essays by Rosalind Gill and Andy Pratt, Susan Christopherson, Ned Rossiter amongst others, have paved the way in shifting this field into a broader perspective of inquiry. By framing creative work as one of the many forms of knowledge work that needs to be subject to critical analysis – i.e., without brandishing creativity as a lifestyle trend instrumental for capital accumulation and vice versa, as in the work of Richard Florida (2002) – these studies reveal how the attractions but also the problems with creative labour have become embedded in professions not traditionally thought of as being 'creative'.

Yet, the tendency within much of the literature that emerged out of these pivotal contributions has been to focus on the extent to which individual action in a networked context has become integral to the enactment of creative work, whilst implicitly taking for granted its highly competitive nature as a natural process in a context of flexible employment relations. Put differently, whilst casting light on the controversial evolution of work in the creative industries, this very same literature has simultaneously overlooked, to a large degree, the extent to which a networked individual has to engage in collaboration with others in order to be a recognised actor in such networked scenes, and how in this currency collaboration is one side of the coin – networking – where competition is the other side. A closer focus on collaborative practices therefore appears to be particularly timely in that it not only addresses an aporia within the literature on creative industries – concerning all the disciplines listed above – but also focuses attention on the rise of 'collaboration' as *the* buzzword of the creative economy. It is notable that, whilst the creative economy was arguably flourishing as a research topic to a greater degree than its much-vaunted role as a catalyst for innovation and prosperity, the term 'collaboration' has gained an ever-increasing emphasis. Together with its often sibling buzzword 'sharing', the term 'collaboration' has become the fashionable shorthand for describing a socio-economic scenario that fosters individualised practices whilst at the same time demands 'compulsory' interaction with others in order to complete the individual projects that, ironically, cannot be achieved in isolation (Gandini, 2016). Here one encounters the rise of the terms 'collaborative consumption' (Botsman and Rogers, 2010) and 'sharing economy' (Slee, 2016) for describing the neoliberal logics of access for consumers of shared services – cab rides, home rentals, etc. – or the increasing relevance of a start-up culture founded on a shared belief in the complementarity of technological advancement and social innovation (Murray, Caulier-Grice and Mulgan, 2010) up to the coterminous rise of 'making', envisaged to be no less than a 'third industrial revolution' (Anderson, 2013).

This collaborative turn in the creative economy is evidenced by the notable efforts of many funding bodies to finance and support research projects that investigate collaborative practices at various levels (O'Brien, 2015, McGuigan, 2016). The all encompassing role played by digital media, which in what Robin Millar (2016) calls a 'cybertarian' discourse is understood as the pre-eminent catalyst for new forms of production practices but also their depoliticisation, makes even more central the necessity to scrutinise how collaborative production takes place in contexts where personal branding melds with socialisation, cooperation with competition. Social media provide platforms that enable these new modes of collaborative production, which vary from typical market-based endeavours, such as apps or social networking sites, to processes which find their roots in the ethos of peer production (Bauwens, 2006; Benkler, 2006) and assume free access to common resources for the creation and distribution of content which escapes the logic of the market. Similarly, the nature of collaborative work is being transformed by the intermediation processes afforded by social media and platforms. For one example, in a context where new forms of untethered work, that may or may not rely on the access to a shared space in order for collaboration to occur, develop (Johns and Gratton, 2013), we witness the rise of Online Labour Markets where conventionally commercial modes of creative production – graphic design, copywriting, illustration, filmmaking, etc. – become algorithmically governed labour transactions with concerning implications (Gandini, Pais and Beraldo, 2016). In response to this fragmented scenario, and with the aim of mapping the more media-based collaborative practices that live within it, this collection plots a course through the multi-disciplinary aspects of collaboration across a range of creative industries. The chapters that follow challenge some of the key assumptions that characterise the understanding of the sector as a whole, and its framing in the contemporary socio-economic context.

• • •

The opening chapter, co-authored by Alessandro Gandini, Carolina Bandinelli and Alberto Cossu, presents a framing discussion of the fractured subjectivity that characterises the three main social actors who have been long typically portrayed, from various perspectives, as the main protagonists in the collaborative turn in the creative industries: freelancers, social entrepreneurs and artists. The authors draw from different empirical research projects to offer a comparative discussion of these subjects, their practices and ways of making a living, investigating the common aspects that characterise their subjectivity. The authors argue that the working stance of these subjects entails a mix of collaboration and competition, solidarity and market logic, including a somewhat frustrated potential to coalesce as a collective subject as a result of their inability of the same subjects to recognise themselves as one.

The example of freelancers, social entrepreneurs and artists discussed in this chapter illustrates a general phenomenon that this collection as a whole begins to map. In the new geography that is charted here, the role of collaboration within the diverse forms of cultural work that characterises the creative industries emerges as a key driver through which the economic is being re-embedded in the social – a process initiated after the economic crisis, in many sectors of the economy, as value is reformulated (Arvidsson and Peitersen, 2013). This process is ongoing and challenges established notions of production and consumption, work and play, profit and social impact, with the aim of reconciling the often dichotomous views these terms convey.

This theoretical framing is further expanded in chapter two, where Jacob Matthews investigates the political economy of collaboration in a paper largely inspired by the notion of 'digital labour' (Fuchs, 2014), offering a critique of what he terms 'collaborative economy discourse'. With the emergence of the so-called 'web 2.0', the 'collaborative economy', Matthews argues, has been object of a discourse at the centre of which lies the role of platforms operating across diverse fields of cultural and creative production. By discussing the concept of 'digital intermediation' by platform and its 'collaborative' nature, this chapter unpacks a few of the most relevant theoretical propositions with regards to cultural capitalisation and production as usually mobilised within the political economy of culture industries, and questions the extent to which this brings changes in the relations of production within them.

In the chapters that follow immediately after, authors address in more detail the constituency of what Adam Arvidsson (2013) calls 'collaborative publics'. In chapter three, Rosamund considers the impact on publishing of the 'productive consumer publics' (Arvidsson, 2010) afforded by the Wattpad platform. Davies begins by situating Wattpad in the context of emergent peer-to-peer (P2P) collaborative production before discussing its specific features: how it provides a launch pad for fledgling writers, an audience development opportunity for established writers, and a marketing service for brands. Wattpad offers its users a community but also a marketplace, and as such articulates with the transformations in traditional publishing, as well as with the wider field of platform-enabled commerce described by Matthews. Having considered these aspects, Davies argues that Wattpad's predominantly young female fan community represents a 'productive consumer public' that might exercise significant social and political as well as economic influence, and that the platform as such provides a potentially game-changing model for collaborative production in publishing.

The publishing angle developed by Davies brings the reader to chapter four, where James Graham considers the spectre of auteurship in neoliberal cultural economies. Graham uses the example of *Ponte City*, the 2015 Deutsche Börse Photography Prize prize-winning photobook by Mikhael Subotzky and Patrick Waterhouse, to examine the role of collaborative production in book publishing in a 'post-digital age' – a term deployed by Alessandro Ludovico (2013) to account for contexts in which print is being revitalised rather than replaced. Graham argues that *Ponte City* provides an example of how the independent publishing sector resists certain aspects of digital transformation in the wider creative industries, but also of how it struggles to escape complicity with the governing neoliberal imperative for such transformations. By fully crediting all those with creative input, the book provides a platform from which its contributors are able to recoup their collective creative investments in the form of symbolic capital. Similar to the workings of the film industry that this in some ways comes to resemble, however, these returns are not evenly distributed. This niche sector of the publishing industry projects collaborative production as the kind of 'art world' Howard Becker (1982) described. Yet this model of networked collaborative production remains largely in thrall to a neoliberal cultural economy dominated by promotional authorship, evidenced in this discussion by the *auteur* roles played by the book's editor and publisher.

Following Graham's discussion of independent publishing, Leora Hadas's chapter examines how collaborative production in the US TV industry is organised, and to a large extent overshadowed, by the promotional authorship of the showrunner. Focusing on the work of Bad Robot, the production company of 'quality TV' doyen J. J. Abrams, the chapter traces a range of collaborative practices in the context of authorship as a promotional device and of the auteur as brand. While the creation of a television show is a complex collaborative endeavour, Abram's promotional authorship obscures the logic of production in the process of legitimation. Drawing on comparisons with the historical workshop model of the Italian Renaissance, in which corporate creative work would be validated and branded by the signature of the master, Hadas argues that the Abrams-Bad Robot model as a significant development in a media landscape in which the demand for authorship exceeds possible supply. In this scenario the showrunner's 'position of absolute author … takes on the cast of property manager'.

Chapter six, authored by Jamie Clarke, develops this enquiry into the evolving function of the auteur-figure in the context of collaborative production through a discussion of the 2015 Oscar nominees for best cinematography. Clarke begins by discussing how digital workflows have displaced the collaborative axis of director-cinematographer as author of the final look of the film. As control has shifted towards postproduction, the craft boundaries previously policed by union jurisdiction are blurred and the autonomy of the cinematographer challenged. In close readings of *Mr. Turner* (directed by Mike Leigh, cinematography by Dick Pope), *The Grand Budapest Hotel* (directed by Wes Anderson, cinematography by Robert Yeoman) and *Ida* (directed by Paweł Pawlikowski, cinematography by Lukasz Zal and Ryszard Penczewski), Clarke identifies a common trope of 'digital naturalism' and argues that it serves a strategic function. The elegiac portrayal of superannuated artistic craft in *Mr. Turner* is taken to encapsulate the contemporary situation of the cinematographer. Just as the artful use of 'digital naturalism' serves to commemorate Turner's genius, it also promotes and protects that of the cinematographer. The dominance of 'digital naturalism' at the 2015 Oscars therefore testifies to the resistance of a community of cinematographers to their usurpation by digital post-production – by reasserting the primacy of a neo-traditional workflow, but in the process also reinforcing the concomitant divisions of labour.

This trilogy of chapters paves the way for contributions that delve into more specific case studies where collaboration and collaborative productions are observed 'at work' across the digital domain. Chapter seven, authored by Dinu Gabriel Munteanu, discusses the microblogging and social networking site Tumblr, showing how the 'curatorial' collaborative authorship practice within a community of Tumblr users evidences an autonomous cultural practice that rows against the currents of the neoliberal cultural economy described by other contributors. Notwithstanding the anomalous position of Tumblr in the current social network ecosphere – it originally adopted a 'freemium' commercial model whereby it neither served advertising nor sold its users' data. Munteanu shows how the circulatory dynamics of the platform challenge conventional understandings of originality, authorship and commodification. The content shared and curated among the community of 'young nostalgics' destabilises the three conventional sites of an image (production, image, audience), and in so doing enables individual agency and autonomy *through* the practice of creative collaboration.

In chapter eight, Karen Patel offers a reflection on the way artists engage in reciprocal forms of digital-based interaction and collaboration across social media for purposes of mutual recognition in the scene. Patel argues that this is illustrative of a logic that may be described through Pierre Bourdieu's concept of *illusio*, as associations and consensus are crucial for performing expertise via public endorsement from other people and institutions on social media, which thus contribute to artists' performance of expertise. Patel demonstrates that on social media, artists negotiate their expertise construction by engaging in a dialectical relationship between competition and collaboration, which contributes to their overall performance of expertise.

This is followed by chapter nine where Miranda Campbell offers a feminist perspective on collaborative production and analyses Girls Rock Camp in Canada as a 'community of practice' (Lave and Wenger 1991; Wenger 1998, 2010). Using participant observation and examining the camp's pedagogies and cultural norms, the chapter evaluates the notion of a community of practice in a context of music collaboration and learning. Campbell argued in favour of the instrumental role of collaboration in widening access to the usually male-dominated music scenes, while at the same time warning that collaborative modes of production alone cannot intervene against systemic barriers to entry to creative work or lack of equity in the creative industries at large.

In the final chapter, creative professional and arts activist Ashley Wong discusses the collaborative turn of the creative economy as evidence of the schizophrenic condition of capitalism in the digital age. The chapter provides an auto-ethnographic account of the struggle to reconcile the demands of a day job in a digital start-up with longstanding investment in independent creative projects and arts activism. By reflexively exploring the conditions of surviving in a post-crisis neoliberal economy where creative workers are forced to take on multiple roles and professional identities at the same time, Wong warns us of the inner conflicts as well as the social struggles such an economy carries with it, which often go largely overlooked by those within this same scene.

• • •

If we are effectively witnessing a *structural* transformation in the cultures of work and in the morphology of the workforce in the contemporary cultural economy (see Rifkin 2014, 1996; Moretti 2012), then the key insights offered by this collection are that the role of collaboration in creative and cultural work is key to this transformation, but that the experience and outcomes of such work are contradictory to say the least. Some contributions highlight how platforms and paradigms have emerged in recent years which aim to facilitate creative collaboration, spreading value across individuals and organisations. Yet in these and other contributions there is also evidence that this value is not equally distributed. The buzz around collaborative production also serves to mask exploitation, as cultural and creative workers have little choice but to embrace individualisation and self-exploitation in undertaking work that increasingly revolves around the production of author-brands that function as the primary currency of the cultural economy. This being the case collaborative production in the creative industries looks set to continue to prove as contradictory as it is enabling, enmeshed as it is in politics and policies, practices and publics

Notes

[1] This is not to discount the significance and success of resistance from within the creative sector as such – witness internationalist arts activism, the social art movement, or the resistance to corporate control central to the films analysed by Jamie Clarke. Rather, the observation is that in almost all cases the effects of such resistance, whilst real, have tended be been contained within their respective fields, while the transformations in general employment and in the more specific subjectivities and dispositions attending so-called 'creative work' described here have developed relatively unchecked.

References

Anderson, C. (2013). *Makers: The New Industrial Revolution*. New York: Crown Books.

Arvidsson, A. and Peitersen, N. (2013). *The Ethical Economy: Rebuilding Value After the Crisis*. New York: Columbia University Press.

Arvidsson, A., Malossi, G. and Naro, S. (2010). Passionate work? Labour conditions in the Milan fashion industry. *Journal for Cultural Research*, 14(3): 295–309.

Baird, V. (2016). Smiley-faced monopolists. *New Internationalist*, July/August: 12–16.

Banks, M. (2014). 'Being in the Zone' of cultural work, *Culture Unbound*, 6: 241–62.

Banks, M., Conor, B. and Mayer, V. (2015). *Production Studies: The Sequel! Cultural Studies of Global Media Industries*. New York: Routledge.

Bauwens, M. (2006). The political economy of peer production. *Post-autistic Economics Review*, 37(28): 33–44.

Becker, H. (1982). *Art Worlds*. Berkeley, CA: University of California Press.

Benkler, Y. (2006). *The Wealth of Networks*. Princeton, NJ: Princeton University Press.

Berger, D. (2014). *Projected Art History: Biopics, Celebrity Culture, and the Popularizing of American Art*. Trans. Brigitte Pichon and Dorian Rudnytsky. London: Bloomsbury.

Botsman, R., and Rogers, R. (2010). *What's Mine is Yours: The Rise of Collaborative Consumption*. New York: HarperCollins.

Bourdieu, P., & Johnson, R. (1993). *The Field of Cultural Production: Essays on Art and Literature*. New York: Columbia University Press.

Brooker, W. (2003). *The Audience Studies Reader*. New York: Routledge.

Brouillette, S. (2014). *Literature and the Creative Economy*. Standford, CA: Stanford University Press.

Brouillette, S. (2016, June). *On the Creative Economy: An Apostate Thesis*. Retrieved from http://www.humag.co/features/on-the-creative-economy.

Callon, M. (2005). Why virtualism paves the way to political impotence: A reply to Daniel Miller's critique of *The Laws of the Markets*. *Economic Sociology*, 6(2): 3–20.

Curtin, M., & Sanson, K. (2016). *Precarious Creativity: Global Media, Local Labor*. Oakland, CA: University of California Press.

Florida, R. (2002) *The Rise of the Creative Class*. New York: Basic Books.

Fuchs, C. (2014) *Digital Labour and Karl Marx*, London, Routledge.

Gandini, A. (2016). *The Reputation Economy: Understanding Knowledge Work in Digital Society*. Basingstoke: Palgrave Macmillan.

Gandini, A., Pais, I., & Beraldo, D. (2016). Reputation and trust on online labour markets: The reputation economy of elance. *Work Organisation, Labour and Globalisation*, 10(1), 27–43.

Hecht, B. (2013). Why collaboration is the new competition. *Harvard Business Review*. Retrieved from https://hbr.org/2013/01/collaboration-is-the-new-compe.

Hennion, A and Farías, I. (2015). For a sociology of *maquettes*: An interview with Antoine Hennion. In Farías, I. and Wilkie, A. (Eds.) *Studio Studies: Operations, Topologies & Displacements*. Abingdon and New York: Routledge.

Hesmondhalgh, D. and Baker, S. (2010) A very complicated version of freedom: Conditions and experiences of creative labour in three cultural industries. *Variant,* 41. Retrieved from http://www.variant.org.uk/pdfs/issue41/complicated41.pdf.

Hesmondhalgh, D. and Baker, S. (2011). *Creative Labour: Media Work in Three Cultural Industries.* Abingdon: Routledge.

Jameson, F. (1984). Postmodernism, or, the cultural logic of late capitalism. *New Left Review,* 146 (July-August): 59–92.

Johns, T. and Gratton, L. (2013). The third wave of virtual work. *Harvard Business Review,* 91.1: 66–73.

Lave, J., & Wenger, E. (1991). *Situated Learning: Legitimate Peripheral Participation,* Cambridge: Cambridge University Press.

Lehrer, J. (2012). *Imagine: How Creativity Works.* Boston, MA: Houghton Miffin Harcourt.

Ludovico, A. (2013). *Post-Digital Print: The Mutation of Publishing since 1894.* Santa Monica, CA: Ram Publications

Mayer, V., Banks, M., and Caldwell, J. (2009). *Production Studies: Cultural Studies of Media Industries.* London: Routledge.

McGuigan, J. (2016). *Neoliberal Culture.* Basingstoke: Palgrave Macmillan.

McRobbie, A. (2002). Clubs to companies: Notes on the decline of political culture on speeded-up creative worlds. *Cultural Studies* 16(4): 516–31.

———. (2002). Everyone is creative: Artists as pioneers of the new economy. In E. Silva, T. Bennett, *Contemporary Culture and Everyday Life,* Durham: Sociology Press, 186–99.

———. (2015). *Be Creative. Making a Living in the New Culture Industries.* London: Wiley.

Millar, R. (2016). Cybertarian flexibility – when prosumers joint the cognitariat, all that is scholarship melts into air. In M. Curtin & K. Sanson (2016), *Precarious Creativity: Global Media, Local Labor* (p. 336). Oakland, CA: University of California Press, pp. 19–32.

Moretti, E. (2012) *The New Geography of Jobs.* Boston, MA: Houghton Mifflin Harcourt.

Murray, R., Caulier-Grice, J., & Mulgan, G. (2010). *The Open Book of Social Innovation.* London: National Endowment for Science, Technology and the Art.

O'Brien, D. (2014) *Cultural Policy: Management, Value and Modernity in the Creative Industries.* Abingdon-on-Thames: Routledge.

Platman, K. (2004). 'Portfolio careers' and the search for flexibility in later life. *Work, Employment & Society,* 18(3): 573–599.

Rebolini, A. (2014). 10 habits of highly creative people. *Buzzfeed*. Retrieved from https://www.buzzfeed.com/ariannarebolini/habits-of-highly-creative-people?utm_term=.si8xWg2w3#.bn0LXZR7o

Rifkin, J. (2014). *The Zero Marginal Cost Society: The Internet of Things, The Collaborative Commons, and the Eclipse of Capitalism*. London: Macmillan.

———. (1995). *The End of Work: The Decline of the Global Labor Force and the Dawn of the Post-Market Era*. New York: Putnam Publishing Group.

Ross, A. (2004). *No-Collar: The Humane Workplace and Its Hidden Costs*. New York: Basic Books.

———. (2009). *Nice Work If You Can Get It. Life and Labor in Precarious Times*. New York: New York University Press, 2009.

Slee, T. (2016). *What's Yours is Mine: Against the Sharing Economy*. New York: OR Books.

Theory, Culture and Society. Vol. 25 (7–8), December 2008. Retrieved from http://tcs.sagepub.com/content/25/7-8.toc.

Wenger, E. (1998). *Communities of Practice: Learning, Meaning and Identity*. Cambridge: Cambridge University Press.

_____. (2010). Communities of Practice and Social Learning Systems: The career of a concept. In C. Blackmore (Ed.) *Social Learning Systems and Communities of Practice*. London: Springer Verlag, pp. 179–98.

CHAPTER TWO

Collaborating, Competing, Co-working, Coalescing: Artists, Freelancers and Social Entrepreneurs as the 'New Subjects' of the Creative Economy

Alessandro Gandini*, Carolina Bandinelli*
and Alberto Cossu[†]

*King's College, London
[†]University of Milan

More than a decade after the enthusiastic call for the rise of a 'creative class' (Florida, 2002), the conditions of today's creative economy appear to be quite different from the expectations that accompanied its acclaimed surge as a propeller of economic development in the late 1990s and early 2000s. The frenzy around creativity that has characterised cultural economies as a whole since then has evolved into a context that is now largely animated by a casualisation and entrepreneurialisation of work, with project-based employment rising to an unprecedented scale (McRobbie, 2015).

How to cite this book chapter:
Gandini, A., Bandinelli, C. and Cossu, A. 2017. Collaborating, Competing, Co-working, Coalescing: Artists, Freelancers and Social Entrepreneurs as the 'New Subjects' of the Creative Economy. In: Graham, J. and Gandini, A. (eds.). *Collaborative Production in the Creative Industries.* Pp. 15–32. London: University of Westminster Press. DOI: https://doi.org/10.16997/book4.b. License: CC-BY-NC-ND 4.0

Within this context, the recent popularisation of a 'hip' discourse around innovation, collaboration and sharing, particularly across those once labelled as 'creative cities' (Landry, 2000), has involved many working subjects. Among them, three social actors seem to be particularly involved: freelancers, social entrepreneurs and artists. Freelancers have been repeatedly advocated as trail-blazers of an on-demand economy based on distributed forms of work (The Economist, 2015); similarly, social entrepreneurs have risen to prominence for epitomising the attempt to pursue more 'ethical' forms of business in and for society after the economic crisis (Bandinelli and Arvidsson, 2013); whilst artists are reclaiming a newly central role in their experimentation with new forms of critique against late capitalist modes of accumulation stemming from the digital realm (Sholette, 2011). These characters, in their own specificities, provide us with three peculiar forms of subjectivity worthy of a closer look, as too the fashionable but also quite contradictory traits that characterise their role in the present conjuncture.

This chapter is concerned with offering an understanding of the main traits that characterise the subjectivity of these social actors, and assess their emergence and significance. Building on individual ethnographic fieldwork conducted in various contexts between 2011–2014, we offer an *ex post* reflection that draws from each author's empirical research to provide a better understanding of the role these subjects play in the meeting of collaboration and creativity. These, we will argue, represent – each with its own peculiar features – an accurate illustration of the process of reshaping the creative economy in the shift towards collaboration and sharing – a shift one encounters in the confluence of emergent 'alternative' economic perspectives in the aftermath of the financial crisis and the rise of forms of economic valorisation that are increasingly rooted in the social (Arvidsson and Peitersen, 2013).

Within this scenario, freelancers, social entrepreneurs and artists have intervened in the social fabric by operating in peculiar, but somewhat analogous ways, blending collaboration, entrepreneurship and creative practice in an original manner. Each from their own standpoint, they now reclaim a central role in an urban collaborative scene that they commonly consider the space for the enactment of their creative, (self)entrepreneurial endeavours. Their subjectivity, as we are about to observe, is similarly characterised by a political attitude towards change and an ideological disposition to 'newness', that is made explicit in the attempt to combine economic with what may be seen as forms of 'aest-ethical' action – and is nonetheless frustrated in the capacity to coalesce as a collective subject within and beyond the fragmented scene they inhabit. By operating in a milieu largely determined by a market economy, yet nonetheless experimenting with forms of commons-based peer production, we argue that freelancers, social entrepreneurs and artists are manifestations, in their own peculiar ways, of that process of 're-embeddedness' of the economic into the social (Pais and Provasi, 2015) that seems to characterise the current socio-economic conjuncture.

Setting up the context: the creative economy
in the age of austerity

In *Be Creative*, Angela McRobbie (2015) gives an account of the evolution of the creative economy on a global scale in the last decade, from post-New Labour Britain to the post-crisis scenario. McRobbie argues that the creative economy represents the political packaging of a neoliberal vision of work founded on entrepreneurialism and organised on project work and flexible employment relations. Today, she maintains, a set of varied phenomena characterise this context, from social entrepreneurship to hipsterism, all marked by the realisation of the artist as economic pioneer she had earlier predicted (McRobbie, 2002).

The most recent employment figures available on the creative sector in the UK seem to support this interpretation. Similar to what happened with the DCMS reports in 1999 and 2002, recent government-issued data on the creative economy convey the picture of a growing economic scene where a variety of jobs are up for grabs in a job market that includes a broad range of industries, from architecture to marketing, for a 'scene' that is depicted as being constituted by highly qualified workers, mostly male and white (DMCS, 2015). However, what these representations do not adequately account for or explain is what kind of jobs are those at stake, whether secure or precarious, economically satisfying or scarcely paid, and especially what kind of 'quality' intended as the sociology of work (Kalleberg, 2011; Hesmondhalgh and Baker, 2011) characterises it. This is an important issue, considering that the creative labour market has largely been described as one made of 'lousy and lovely' jobs (Goos and Manning, 2007; Ross, 2009) whereby, beyond high level skill requirements, it is the capacity to network and brand one's passion and talent, often in exchange for scarce or no economic remuneration, that makes the real difference (Gandini, 2016b; Arvidsson et al., 2010; McKinlay and Smith, 2009).

Recent data confirm how creative workers today have a higher-than-average likelihood of being self-employed or working on a freelance basis, as a result of an environment that induces them into developing independent and resilient subjectivities (Prospects, 2015). An eminently project-based structure characterises this highly-skilled labour market, where a mere 1 per cent of the creative workforce gets permanent jobs through an apprenticeship route, and 48 per cent of workers engage in unpaid work at some point in their career. Yet, the rate of diffusion of freelance-based employment varies consistently from one industry to another, from 9 per cent in VFX (Visual Effects) to 90 per cent in film and television (CreativeSkillset, 2015). What is common to all these sectors is that job seeking practices rely ever more on the capacity of workers to navigate across personal contact networks, something that has historically characterised creative work (Gandini, 2016b; Blair, 2001).

Put differently, despite being culturally constructed around the idea of a creative class of workers who actively valorise their talent and skills (Florida, 2002), the actual nature of this labour market in practical terms is exemplary of an eminently neoliberal, strategically-pursued logic of flexibilisation of work relations and entrepreneurialisation of the workforce (Bonini and Gandini, 2016; Christopherson 2008; Neilson and Rossiter, 2008). The rapid diffusion of social media has further amplified the more controversial aspects of this condition. While allowing workers to showcase their skills, develop a personal brand and network more efficiently, at the same time social media enabled a refinement of the managerial processes of flexibilisation, with technological infrastructure affording remote working and social interaction in new and unprecedented ways (Gandini, 2016b).

Nonetheless, within such a complicated scenario, we are witnessing today a rejuvenated version of an already hyper-enthusiast discourse, that is rooted within the premises and promises of a 'sharing economy' that magnifies the opportunity for workers to collaborate with others across creative, (self)entrepreneurial endeavours (Botsman and Rogers, 2010). The rise of such discourse calls for a necessity to put into question the dialectical relationship between the economic and the social within this context, and to investigate what features this nexis possesses insofar as collaboration and sharing become relational *dispositifs* of power (Foucault, 2008; Lazzarato, 2009) that serve to purposes of socially-conceived value production (Arvidsson and Peitersen, 2013).

Within this framework, three anomalous creative subjects have come to stand out. We say anomalous here as a result of their comprehensively multi-dimensioned subjective dynamic, that we are about to observe in detail. Freelancers, as noted, are vital to today's vision of the creative economy; it may be said, as Barley and Kunda (2006) envisaged, that the diffusion of managerial visions of knowledge work built around distributed models of work was inevitably destined to put freelancers in a prominent position. Today, this idea has even led *The Economist* (2015) to advocate the surge of an 'on-demand economy' made of 'workers on tap' who offer contract-based work to various service providers, mainly digital-based ones, at various levels. Collaborative practice is a natural component of the professional subjectivity for freelancers, as a result of the well-known emphasis on networking that characterises their working practice, and blends with the ambivalent social and economic nature of their action, which stands at the interface of entrepreneurialism and precarity (Arvidsson et al., 2016; Gandini, 2016b). Similarly, social entrepreneurship has been a recently growing phenomenon involving a variety of actors across a range of fields including politics, civic society, business and academia. According to a 2013 survey published by Social Enterprise UK, it is estimated that 70,000 social enterprises currently exist in the UK, employing around a million people. The sector's contribution to the economy has been valued at over £24 billion (Social Enterprise UK, 2013).

Lastly, the position of artists in this renewed encounter of the economic and the social is also of peculiar interest. Alongside other cultural workers, artists today are increasingly engaged in the reclamation of social and political space, broadly defined. As demonstrated by a series of recent events, artists participate in broad social movements (such as Occupy and Gezi Park) or create movements of their own (such as the Network of Occupied Theaters in Italy and Greece). They protest against the structures and dynamics of the art world (e.g. Liberate Tate), experiment with alternative economic models and currencies (e.g. Macao and D-CENT), and host or co-produce public art at a time when the budget for culture and independent projects in this field is generally shrinking (Faccioli et al., 2014). They undertake social research, partner up with institutions and various entities, support neighbourhoods and sometimes also fill the void left by nation states in social and cultural action that results from their neoliberal-driven disinterest in intervening in society unless this intervention is economically-oriented (which means turning a profit for the private sector).

Building on the ambivalent centrality of these subjects, we argue that the literature on creative work has so far been unable to fully account for the existence of a peculiarly strong dialectical relationship between the economic and the social, that is distinctive of the processes of subjectification that characterise creative, cultural and knowledge workers, and that is now coming to further prominence. Creative workers have long engaged in forms of collaborative work that enable them to explore the possibilities of a performative re-articulation of their social standing through creativity, and its re-signification into forms of economic action. Today, as a result of the current logics of creative work and the discursive regimes of collaboration and sharing deploying around them, their subjectivity finds new and multiple forms of expression that call for a closer observation.

Hence, in this chapter we read some of the most recent social forms of collaboration that characterise social actors in the creative economy as the manifestation of a greater process of re-embeddedness of the economic in society. The concept of a 're-embeddedness' of the economic in society draws on the work by sociologist Karl Polanyi and his analysis of the Great Transformation wrought by the Industrial Revolution ([1944] 2001). As Pais and Provasi (2015) have argued, today's rise of initiatives orientated around collaboration and sharing may be read, potentially, as a phenomenon that is able to completely re-embed economic relations within social ones, after a century characterised by a 'dis-embedding' of economic action from its eminently social resonance, favoured by the diffusion of hierarchies and markets as dominant organisational forms (Williamson, 1973).

In the following sections, using thick ethnographic description based on each author's field research, we will look more closely at the similarities and differences that characterise freelancers, social entrepreneurs and artists and how they come to prominence now as protagonists of the current social and economic transition. In so doing, we offer an account and a critical understanding of their subjectivities, to illustrate the main traits of the dialectical relationship between the economic and the social here argued, and to discuss the extent to which they incarnate a form of re-embeddedness of the economic into the social that is peculiar to the creative economy. In each section, we will question the extent to which the idea of collaboration produces, and is produced by, processes of subjectivisation that peculiarly characterise these social actors. Central questions are: what does collaboration mean for them? How does it stand in relation to the more economic aspects of their societal action? To what extent can we envisage the possibility that new forms of collective organisation or coalition can be experienced in this scenario? With this in hand, we will conclude by offering a reflection that takes these actors as exemplary subjects of such process of re-embeddedness of the economic into the social in the emergent collaborative economy of creativity – and further highlight the contradictions this entails, pondering on the extent to which these might turn out to be substantially unsolvable in the present socio-economic context.

The market subjectivity of freelancers

As anticipated, freelancers have long been at the heart of a vision that set independent workers as the protagonists of a shift towards decentralised and distributed work models in the rising economy of new media (Malone and Laubacher, 1998). Yet, the growth of distributed models of work has been accompanied by a concomitant rise in precarity and project-based work (McKinlay and Smith, 2009), which has rendered this vision very much a controversial one.

The insights provided here on freelancers build on a study of the network cultures and practices of freelance work in London and Milan, conducted in 2012–213 by one of the authors through an ethnographic framework, and consisting of 80 interviews (38 in London, 42 in Milan) with a variety of independent professionals working in various contexts in the creative and cultural industries – especially communication-based and digital media industries. Freelancers emerge in this study as a comprehensively young and highly-skilled workforce, well-educated and networking-obsessed in their professional disposition. Although their earnings would leave them unable to live in the urban centres of high-rent cities such as London and Milan, they are very much urban subjects who approach the city as the environment where their work may find appropriate recognition – insofar as this depends on the access to relevant professional networks (see Gandini, 2016b). The presence of such a trait is somewhat inevitable in a labour market built on a logic for which 'you are only good as your last job' (Blair, 2001), that is taken for granted by the same workers.

The forms of subjectification freelancers exhibit are deployed as a response to such a context – a response which, nevertheless, takes two distinct forms. A first one consists in the embodiment of entrepreneurialism as a discursive device and logic of action. This includes a conception of social media as a terrain for self-branding, and of freelancing as a professional condition whereby the practice of free labour represents a form of 'investment' with expectation of economic and reputational return (Gandini, 2016a). The 'other side' of this form of subjectivity is the existence of a condition of endemic professional uncertainty that many – although not all – respondents relate to instances of precariousness and exploitation. This showcases an ambivalent scenario, epitomised by the contrasting meaning that freelancers attach to the words 'competition' and 'collaboration'. In spite of the highly competitive work that freelance professionals experience, collaboration for them ostensibly outperforms competition, through a logic of action that is deeply economic *as well as* social – given that the most important aspect a freelancer must look after is always, first and foremost, one's contacts and reputation within the professional network.

This is not to say, however, that freelance scenes are non-competitive environments – actually, the opposite is true. In fact, it may be argued that a freelancer's subjectivity is eminently a market-orientated one, insofar as one's market coincides with one's social sphere – the personal network of contacts – and, in tandem, social relations represent the object of a process of marketisation that takes place with various degrees of ideological adherence. To some extent, this can be described as somewhat of analogous to the concept of *illusio* (Bourdieu, 1996) also described in this collection by Patel (2017), being a process akin to the gamification of social status that keeps together the logics of cultural work and the construction of one's expertise – in this case, however, an elaborately constructed social status, curated through the management of reputation via social networks.

This process seems to be deeply entrenched with the framing of a notion of collaboration as a discursive device that keeps together two opposing forms of subjectification in a comprehensively market-oriented subjectivity. For some, this consists in a discursive recoding of their ethos into a narrative of 'liberation' and release from the constraints of office work. For others, on the other hand, this fully reflects their condition of 'immaterial workers' (Lazzarato, 1996), characterised by exploitation, alienation, long hours of work and a need to comply with the anxiety over the unpredictability of work-related duties that completely redefine working times. Put differently, we may see the existence of a 'fracture' in the subjectivity of freelancers, that makes them a textbook example of the market-oriented side of the dialectical relationship between the economic and the social that is under discussion in this chapter.

This ambivalent positioning of the freelance subjectivity renders freelancers a comprehensively plural and heterogeneous set of subjects with limited political subjectivity, and – in addition – a frustrated potential to coalesce into a collective subject. The entrepreneurial aspects of freelance work are in fact often so strongly attractive that the option to coalesce against the precarious and exploitative side of this working condition fails to be perceived as such by freelancers themselves, and sometimes comes to be explicitly refused. The diffusion of co-working spaces evidences this aspect. Despite the existence of accounts that envisage a role for co-working spaces as places where a potential coalition and re-collectivisation of individualised working subjects can take place (de Peuter, 2014), within co-working spaces freelancers more typically work independently rather than collaboratively, and pursue socialisation mainly for entrepreneurial rather than communitarian purposes (Gandini, 2015). In short, freelancers are a hybrid social group whose subjectivity is at present very far from being capable of building a political collective consciousness around their professional condition. This is further supported by the widespread presence of freelancers in both the other categories of 'collaborative' creative workers considered here, starting with social entrepreneurs.

The ethical subjectivity of social entrepreneurs

To explore the subjectivity of social entrepreneurs, this section builds on qualitative, ethnographic fieldwork conducted by one of the authors at two branches of the most important global co-working franchise for social entrepreneurs in Westminster, London and Milan: Impact Hub (see Bandinelli, 2016). The research methodology involved participant observation, interviews, events ethnography and action research in the period November 2011 to March 2012 (London, Westminster) and April to June 2012 (Milan).

As in most ethnographies, the majority of the data comes from informal interaction between the researcher and the participants. In terms of demographics, the vast majority of the social entrepreneurs encountered in this research are white, well-educated men and women in their late twenties/early thirties. Many work in the knowledge and creative industries as freelancers or independent professionals on a contract-basis, or as entrepreneurs (mostly a one-person company). They usually have a background in disciplines across media and communication, consultancy, architecture and design, and work on projects in a variety of fields in the creative industries and beyond, such as consultancy, finance, technology and innovation.As a result, such a picture prevents us from seeing clearly the relationship of social entrepreneurs to a specific economic sector. In fact, it may be argued that what defines social entrepreneurs is a specific subjectivity characterised by a specific world vision that is marked by a certain set of beliefs. The core of the social entrepreneurial subjectivity is the belief that entrepreneurial means can be used effectively to pursue the common good, and improve the conditions of society. This goal is encapsulated in the widespread formula 'change the world', and represented by the trademark term coined by Ashoka (one of the largest organisation supporting social entrepreneurship): *changemakerTM* (Bandinelli and Arvidsson, 2013).

In spite of how hyperbolic and vague these expressions may be – indeed they leave unanswered a series of key questions about the nature of this 'change' – they nonetheless signal the presence of a strong dimension concerning ethics. The term 'ethics', as we use it here, has two main connotations. The first one points to a very general notion of ethics, that is a system of values and action directed towards collective happiness (as summed up by the Aristotelian concept of *eudaimonia*). Therefore, to use a Ricoeurian parlance, we can define ethics here as a mode of thinking and feeling that exceeds the limits of individual interests to embrace the responsiveness towards the other than itself (Ricoeur, 1992). The second draws on Foucault's conception of ethics as a process of 'self-fashioning' that concerns 'the kind of relationship you ought to have with yourself, *rapport a sòi*' (Foucault, 2000, p. 263). In this respect, ethics is a form of continual work on the self, a perennial activity of 'self bricolage' (Rabinow, 2000, p. xxxix). These two meanings of the term are closely interrelated for social entrepreneurs, insofar as they constitute their identity by engaging in a process of self-fashioning in relation to the objective of 'changing the world', and in the belief of acting for the good of others.

It must be noted that the simple fact that young and well-educated people want to 'change the world' is not actually new in itself. What characterises social entrepreneurs is the claim to effect this change by means of entrepreneurial tools. In this respect, in analogy with the freelancers discussed earlier, social entrepreneurs emerge as highly ambivalent subjects for they mark a difference in relation to both traditional forms of political subjectivation (i.e. those articulated in party politics and activism), and embody the individualistic ethos of the neoliberal subject par excellence, i.e. the entrepreneur of the self, who is by definition concerned only with her or his private interest and wealth (Bauman, 2002; McNay, 2009; Lazzarato, 2009; Donzelot, 1991). Yet, this ambivalence does not determine a 'fracture' as in the case of freelancers seen above – it is in fact a reconciliation. Social entrepreneurs bridge the gap between entrepreneurial individualism and ethical responsiveness by putting their virtues and values at work in a way that is entirely similar to the valorisation of talents and passions by creative and cultural workers (McRobbie 1998, 2002; Ross, 2004; Arvidsson et al., 2010; Arvidsson et al., 2016)

Social entrepreneurs, nonetheless, also act in, and contribute to, the attempt to establish an 'alternative' kind of economy that is collaborative and commons-based in logic. Consistently, they promote values of cooperation, collaboration and sharing often expressed and represented by the signifier 'community', a term widely used across the scene and particularly so at Impact Hub. For instance, at Impact Hub Westminster, this signifier is also physically distributed throughout the space – a sign giving instruction on how to use the kitchen facilities reads 'Welcome to the Community Kitchen!'; a glass house used for meetings is decorated with big capital letters claiming 'This is Community'; on leaving the space users are reminded that 'Together We Make Community'. As in most co-working environments, the community is here not to be understood in its traditional sociological significance, rather as a discursive translation of the 'open source approach to work' intended to facilitate collaborative practice that ultimately seeks to establish social relations among the member-workers (Gandini, 2015). Despite not being a social group bounded by a common background and narrative, there is still evidence of the need to establish social relations in the context of a collaborative approach to work.

Yet, social entrepreneurs also enact a form of collaborative economy and sociality beyond the co-working space's walls. They organise and participate in workshops, conferences, and – more generally – events (e.g. pop-up think tanks, innovation camps, business clinics, etc.) whose main purpose is the sharing of knowledge, skills, experiences and contacts. In this regard, the social entrepreneurial subjectivity is surely oriented towards practices of collaboration and sharing. Yet, their modes and objectives may reveal, again, an ambivalent character.

On the one hand, social entrepreneurs' discourses and practices imply and, to an extent, demand the creation of human relationships alongside the display of ethical values and virtues. This combination of social relationships and ethical values is due to the fact that one of the requirements to establish relationships in the scene is exactly to display and prove the will to have a 'positive impact' – in other words, to be a changemaker (or, at the very least, a changemaker wannabe), therefore to show a virtuous character. The barriers of inclusion and exclusion from the scene revolve around the embodiment of a number of ethical principles that are thought to characterise and distinguish social entrepreneurial subjects (Bandinelli and Arvidsson, 2013).

On the other hand, the very embodiment and display of such ethical virtues, and the related engagements in collaborative relations, is ultimately instrumental to the acquisition of the necessary capital (social, cultural and economic) to further one's career. Virtually every social entrepreneur observed made clear that establishing friendships, and collaborating on projects, even with no immediate financial reward, was part of a strategy to eventually 'find a paid job'. It could thus be argued that, for these subjects, collaboration and ethics assume a somewhat opportunistic character. According to Paolo Virno (2005), opportunists are those whose socialisation is characterised by 'a flow of ever-interchangeable possibilities, making themselves available to the greatest number of these, yielding to the nearest one and then quickly swerving from one to another' (p. 86). To be an opportunist, Virno continues, is a professional quality, a skill which is acquired in a mode of socialisation that is increasingly connected with work (Virno, 2005, p. 86). Far from pretending to solve the inherent contradiction between individualism and social responsibility, collaboration and opportunism, it may be argued that social entrepreneurs are exemplary of a subjectivity that combines individualism and entrepreneurialism with the political will to 'change the world', and with the articulation of values and virtues that exceed the boundaries of private wealth and interest. Whilst their economic positioning puts them in coherence with the forms of subjectification that characterise freelancers, as illustrated above, the more social nuance of their subjectivity aligns them with the political intent towards change that characterises artists, who are the focus of the analysis in the next section.

The radical subjectivity of artists

The reflections offered here on the subjectivity of artist and cultural workers originate from research on Macao, the 'New Center for Arts, Culture and

Research' in Milan, conducted by one of the authors in 2012–2013 during an 18-month ethnography comprising of 35 semi-structured interviews, surveys and digital methods (see Cossu, 2015). Active since 2012, Macao started as a project led by artists and curators that aimed at raising awareness on the conditions of cultural workers, and quickly spread through the social fabric of Milan, the Italian city with the highest density of this kind of workforce (Arvidsson et al., 2010; Bonomi, 2008). The project originated from the occupation of an abandoned 33-storey building in the heart of the financial district of Milan, which gathered thousands of people to reclaim the skyscraper for the city. Macao can be viewed as many things: a hub, a brand, a space, a process, a group of activists, a venue for concerts, a number of rooms bookable for free for seminars or exhibitions, an alternative innovation centre, a partner of EU-funded projects, or an illegal squat. To pin down its unique artistic voice it is necessary to contextualise Macao within a broader – and renewed – wave of art activism. In the words of Boris Groys:

> Current discussions about art are very much centered on the question of art activism, that is, on the ability of art to function as an arena and medium for political protest and social activism. The phenomenon of art activism is central to our time because it is a new phenomenon – quite different from the phenomenon of critical art that became familiar to us during recent decades. Art activists do not want to merely criticize the art system or the general political and social conditions under which this system functions. Rather, they want to change these conditions by means of art – not so much inside the art system but outside it, in reality itself. (Groys, 2014, p. 1)

Concerning Macao's composition, their rank-and-file participants are highly engaged with this endeavour and represent many subjects at the same time. According to a self-inquiry conducted by Macao on its base in winter 2012 (Macao, 2012) participants in the mobilization were 'working' for Macao a staggering 35 hours a week on average, on top of their day jobs – many of these on a freelance basis. To provide a snapshot, the average Macao activist is in her mid-thirties, highly skilled, usually with a degree and more than one job, and is both dissatisfied with her income and work life. Data also reveal that the top third of Macao's participants are relatively well off, earning €2,000/month on average, whilst the bottom third is under the relative poverty threshold. This means that whereas the top tier is able to afford a relatively decorous life and pay the rent of a non-shared house – owning a house, in some cases – thanks to high-added-value collaborations, freelancing and publicly-funded projects (outside Macao), on the contrary those in the lower tier often live with their families and report unsuccessful careers in the creative industry.

This brief breakdown evidences some of the complexities inherent to a body of subjects whose subjectivity is shaped around the deploying of events. Events for Macao are a means to communicate the unexpected, through a carefully planned artistic performance. At the same time, the event may also be seen as an attempt to tune in with the language spoken by the city itself, Milan (Cossu and Murru, 2015), in which societal functioning is largely articulated through a grammar of events, from the most informal ones (the Aperitivo or happy hour) to the largest imaginable (the Expo). The economy of a city like Milan is itself deeply entrenched with social events, and oddly enough, the sustainment of the illegal occupation of Macao is based on a number of events that attract publics of consumers. Macao events vary considerably in qualitative terms, from hosting experimental and avant-garde forms of art (e.g. poetry readings), to organising music gigs (e.g. a concert of a famous Italian folk singer) or cultural events (e.g. a talk by software freedom activist Richard Stallman) that are capable of gathering large crowds. Their own political action, since its inception, is at risk of being subsumed by capitalist logics as of the potential gentrification of the working class area they currently inhabit; yet, the urban administration felt even more compelled to tackle the issue of abandoned spaces in Milan after their action, and has since promoted a top-down urban regeneration program. However, revealing of their political stance is the widespread awareness of being already subsumed, and the recognition of the inability of their action to solve the contradictions of capitalism well before this took place. A lively debate on the economy of Macao has been present since its start. Currently, a partnership with the EU-funded project D-CENT is engaged with the experimentation of a cryptocurrency (CommonCoin) that might offer a basic income and forms of exchange based on communities' own (political) values.

Macao directly organises, co-organises or hosts hundreds of events, often in partnership with other subjects – institutions, associations, or single individuals – or directed and managed entirely by 'external' actors. This demonstrates the know-how possessed by Macao activists in terms of event organisation and the need for such a space in Milan. For instance, out of a total of 270 events in 2013, around 60 per cent were produced by Macao itself, while 40 per cent were co-organised with external actors. In addition, the public is involved at different levels in these events, as a traditional audience or with greater involvement as participants in workshops, up to the co-creation of performances. In the case of an event organised by external actors, Macao often acts as curator, with a particular attention to guarantee not just the mere artistic quality of the artwork, but also the quality of the process.

Alongside a strategy for economic sustainability based on the organisation of a diverse range of events, Macao is characterised by an emphasis on the relations implied in the artistic production process. In the business world, relations are often framed within a notion of 'organisation'. However, in the case of Macao the notions of 'organisation' and 'relation' actually refer to different schemes and political sensibilities. Whereas the notion of organizing entails a structured and structuring activity aimed at efficacy and goal-attainment, the notion of relation constitutes a looser and wider concept that embraces both general human relations and the abstract ideas that shape groups and communities together. In this sense, relations are intended in Macao as sites of political investment that are not leveraged to maximise an individual's reputation – as is the case, for instance, with freelancers. Rather, they are conceived as forms of struggle to redefine relations themselves and, ultimately, the search for a different (and better) life, in analogy with the notion of change brought forward by social entrepreneurs.

However, to capture the specificity of Macao's political action as well as the radical posture embodied by the subjectivity of its members as political innovators, we need to consider the political role they play in the dialectical relationship between the economic and the social. If activists have traditionally used their own political subjectification to resist being corrupted by capitalism, and social innovators (such as the social entrepreneurs discussed above) are using capitalist tools to some extent against it, and in the absence of an explicit political subjectivity, then we could interpret Macao as a case of militant imagination striving to combine the two – thanks to the enactment of a political attitude and its application to and through cultural and social innovation.

Put differently, what we are confronted with in this case are subjects whose idea of change, that is deeply at the heart of the subjectivity and the collective recognition of Macao itself as an entity, is empirically based on 'making together' (Sennett, 2013) and strongly anchored to the belief that social relations precede and even supercede production – an idea that, despite inherent differences, has much in common with the ethos of social entrepreneurs. Similar to the sort of 'post-political' subjectivity inherent in the notion of change advocated by social entrepreneurs, the notion of change that characterises Macao and the subjects participating in it consists of an attempt to move beyond the dialectical relationship between the economic and the social, towards a more collective direction. As subjects who have always felt uneasy identifying themselves in initiatives deemed to be too 'political' and potentially identitarian, artists are seemingly witnessing a political turn in a yet to be defined post-ideological field that shares traits with the social entrepreneurial attempt to marry profit with social good.

Discussion and conclusion

This chapter has offered a discussion of the subjectivity of freelancers, social entrepreneurs and artists using an original weaving of three different empirical ethnographic research projects. Despite peculiar differences in research design, the juxtaposition of these 'thick descriptions' offers an otherwise unavailable variety of insights which provides existing research on the creative economy with a better sense of how the bigger picture of creative work and the creative economy as a whole might look like in the unfolding of what should be seen as a 'collaborative turn' in the economy and in society. To begin with, it may be argued that these subjects seem to share a kind of subjectivity that is under-pinned by ambivalent notions of newness and change. This is realised through an analogous tension with/within the social that re-articulates processes of collectivisation in different ways. Their rising relevance as protagonists in the current scenario comes along with, and to some extent as a consequence of, the experience of processes of political subjectification that are based on stronger (artists), more ephemeral (social entrepreneurs) or comprehensively fragmented (freelancers) collective self-perceptions. The new element here is the attempt to try and combine the economic with what we can describe as a sort of 'aest-ethical' action with the aim to find themselves in an 'other' space where the social is put to work and re-embedded in the economic.

This comes about in three distinct ways that span across varying degrees of reflexivity and critique. Freelancers, for instance, put to work their social relations in an explicitly market-based logic, with a degree of critical interiorisation that varies consistently among them. Social entrepreneurs, on the other hand, put to work their 'ethical' virtues with the aim of a somewhat vague notion of the common good, seeing themselves as a kind of social movement that finds its roots in the same economic-oriented milieu that entrepreneurial freelancers populate – in fact some of them are, as discussed, professional freelancers in the creative industries. Finally, artists more explicitly articulate this subjectification in a collectivised approach that nonetheless struggles to become a comprehensive body. This vision represents an ideal progression from fragmentation to coalition, and in spite of internal fragmentation openly aims at being a social movement that might overcome the argued dialectical relationship by means of togetherness.

Taken as a whole, the study of the subjectivity of these peculiar social actors indicates that these subjects are intervening onto the social fabric in the post-crisis creative economy by enacting different forms of 're-embeddedness' of the economic into the social - with varying degrees of collaboration, redistribution and reciprocity. The social logic of action that characterises freelancers, social entrepreneurs and artists locates these subjects at the crossroads of the economic and the social, as social actors that tend towards the development of proto-collective forms of consciousness but still fluctuate between forms of cooperativism that might foster solidarity and the individualised nature of neoliberal subsumption. Their action inhabits a hybrid socio-economic space whereby their personal stories, their cultural, social and economic capital come together in the form of a shared ethos they are ultimately unable to recognise as such, as with the ambivalent blend of collaboration with (self-) entrepreneurship. These processes are activated in response to the relative employment challenges they face, and the difficulty in getting collective representation in the more complex political arena.

The space we wanted to map by taking these subjects together is one that is created via practices that are by no means new – freelance work, social entre-preneurship and artist-based social movements were there, in various ways, well before contemporary ideas of 'collaborative' forms of production were fashionable. Yet, what is new in this picture is that such practices, contoured by a discursive framework that legitimises economic action as an eminently social endeavour, seems to determine forms of 'integration' between the economy and society (Pais and Provasi, 2015) that are characterised by a re-embeddedness of the economy within eminently societal relations of production. Still, this is a contradictory mix that on the one hand revises processes of collectivisation typical of social movements in the absence of adequate political and trade union representation, and on the other hand operates a misleading rebranding of economic action through a new lexicon. Moreover, the social actors discussed in this chapter illustrate the existence of an organisational form that is not merely networked, i.e. principled on social relations, but actually built on the social relation itself. We believe the acknowledgment of these actors as central, and the understanding of their contradictory positioning in the bigger picture of an emerging economy based on collaboration, is the necessary step to found a political economy of creative work that moves beyond the – still necessary – critique of exploitation and precariousness and develops an intellectual and critical approach that is capable of not only making sense of the existing criticalities, but also dismantling its discursive rhetoric.

References

Arvidsson, A., Gandini, A., and Bandinelli, C. (2016). The ethics of self-branding among freelance knowledge workers. In Crain, M., Poster, W., & Cherry, M.A. (Eds.), *Invisible Labour: Hidden Work in the Contemporary World*, Oakland, CA: University of California Press, pp. 239–56.

Arvidsson, A. and Peitersen, N. (2013). *The Ethical Economy: Rebuilding Value After the Crisis*. New York: Columbia University Press.

Arvidsson, A., Serpica, N., Malossi, G. (2010). Passionate work? Labour conditions in the Milan fashion industry. *Journal for Cultural Research*, 14(3): 259–309.

Bandinelli, C. (2016). Social entrepreneurship: Sociality, ethics and politics. Unpublished PhD dissertation, PhD in Cultural Studies, Goldsmiths College, University of London.

Bandinelli, C. and Arvidsson, A. (2013). Brand yourself a changemaker! *Journal of Macromarketing*, 33 (1): 67–71.

Banks et al. Eds. (2014) *Theorizing Cultural Work: Labour, Continuity and Change in the Cultural and Creative Industries*. London: Routledge.

Barley, S. R., & Kunda, G. (2006). Contracting: A new form of professional practice. *The Academy of Management Perspectives*, 20(1): 45–66.

Bauman, Z. (2002). Individually Together. Preface to U. Beck, and E. Beck-Gernsheim, *Individualization: Institutionalized Individualism and its Social and Political Consequences*, pp. xiv–xix. London & Thousand Oaks: Sage.

Blair, H. (2001). 'You're only as good as your last job': The labour process and labour market in the British film industry, *Work, Employment & Society*, 15(1): 149–69.

Bonini, T. & Gandini, A. (2016). Invisible, solidary, unbranded and passionate. Everyday life as a freelance and precarious worker in four Italian radio stations. *Work Organisation, Labour and Globalisation, 10* (2): 84–100.

Bonomi, A. (2008). *Milano ai tempi delle moltitudini*. Milano: Bruno Mondadori.

Bourdieu, P. (1996). *The Rules of Art: Genesis and Structure of the Literary Field*, translated from French by S. Emanuel. Cambridge: Polity Press.

Botsman, R., and Rogers, R. (2010). *What's Mine is Yours: The Rise of Collaborative Consumption*. New York: HarperCollins.

Christopherson, S. (2008). Beyond the self-expressive creative worker:An industry perspective on entertainment media. *Theory, Culture & Society*, 25(7–8): 73–95.

Cossu, A. (2015) *Mobilizing art. An inquiry on the role of art in social movements: The case of Macao.* Unpublished PhD dissertation, PhD in Sociology, University of Milan.

———. (2015). *Mobilising Art: An inquiry into the role of art in social movements: The case of Macao – Milano.* Unpublished PhD Dissertation, University of Milan, Graduate School in Social and Political Sciences.

Cossu, A. & Murru, M.F. (2015). Macao prima e oltre i Social Media: la creazione dell'inatteso come logica di mobilitazione, *Studi Culturali 3*: 353–372, DOI: https://doi.org/ 10.1405/81912 (English Trans. *Macao before and beyond Social Media: The creation of the unexpected as a logic of mobilization*).

Creative Skillset. (2015). Workforce survey calls for fairer access to creative media industries. Retrieved from: http://creativeskillset.org/news_events/press_office/3412_workforce_survey_calls_for_fairer_access_to_creative_media_industries.

DCMS. (2015). Creative Industries: Focus on Employment. Department for Culture, Media and Sport, UK, London. Retrieved from: https://www.gov.uk/government/uploads/system/uploads/attachment_data/file/439714/Annex_C_-_Creative_Industries_Focus_on_Employment_2015.pdf.

DCMS. (2001). 'Creative Industries Mapping Document'. Department of Culture, Media and Sport, UK, London. Retrieved from: https://www.gov.uk/government/publications/creative-industries-mapping-documents-2001.

DCMS. (1998). Creative Industries Mapping Document. Department of Culture, Media and Sport, UK, London. Retrieved from https://www.gov.uk/government/publications/creative-industries-mapping-documents-1998.

de Peuter, G. (2014). Beyond the model worker: Surveying a creative precariat. *Culture Unbound: Journal of Current Cultural Research 6* pp. 263–284.

Donzelot, J. (1991). Pleasure in Work, in G. Burchell, C. Gordon & P. Miller (Eds.), *The Foucault Effect: Studies in Governmentality*. Chicago IL, University of Chicago Press, pp. 251–80.

Economist, The. (2015). Workers on tap. Retrieved from: http://www.econo-mist.com/news/leaders/21637393-rise-demand-economy-poses-difficult-¬questions-workers-companies-and.

Faccioli, F., Gallina, M., Iaione, C., Leon, A. and Melotti, M. (2014). Rapporto sul futuro del Teatro Valle. Retrieved from: http//www.academia.edu/7825873/Rapporto_sul_Futuro_del_Teatro_Valle.

Florida, R. (2002). *The Rise of the Creative Class*. New York: Basic Books.

Foucault, M. (1994). *Ethics, Subjectivity and Truth*. New York: New Press.

———. (2000) *Ethics. Essential Works 1954–1984*, Vol. 1. London: Penguin

———. (2008) *The Birth of Biopolitics. Lectures at the Collège de France 1978–1979*. Basingstoke: Palgrave Macmillan.

Gandini, A. (2015). The rise of coworking spaces: A literature review, *Ephemera*, 15(1): 193–205.

Gandini, A. (2016a). Digital work: Self-branding and social capital in the freelance knowledge economy, *Marketing Theory*, 16(1): 123–41

———. (2016b). *The Reputation Economy. Understanding Knowledge Work in Digital Society*. Basingstoke: Palgrave Macmillan.

Goos, M., & Manning, A. (2007). Lousy and lovely jobs: The rising polarization of work in Britain, *The Review of Economics and Statistics*, 89(1): 118–33.

Groys, B. (2014). On Art Activism, *E-Flux*, 1/2014. Retrieved from: http://www.e-flux.com/journal/on-art-activism.

Hesmondhalgh, D. and Baker, S. (2011). *Creative Labour: Media Work in Three Cultural Industries*. London: Routledge.

Kalleberg, A. (2011) *Good Jobs. Bad Jobs: The Rise of Polarized and Precarious Employment Systems in the United States, 1970s to 2000s*. New York: Russell Sage Foundation.

Landry, C. (2000). *The Creative City: A Toolkit for Urban Innovators*. London: Earthscan.

Lazzarato, M. (1997) *Lavoro immateriale: Forme di vita e produzione di soggettività*. Verona, Italy: Ombre Corte.

Lazzarato, M. (2009). Neoliberalism in action: Inequality, insecurity and the reconstitution of the social. *Theory, Culture & Society*, 26(6): 109–33.

Macao. (2012). *69300 ore. La produzione artistica e culturale nella città fabbrica: sistemi di cattura e pratiche di lotta*. Retrieved from https://issuu.com/macaomilano/docs/69300_ore.

Malone, T.W. and Laubacher, R.J. The dawn of the e-lance economy. *Harvard Business Review* 1998, 76(5):144-52

McKinlay, A., & Smith, C. (eds). (2009). *Creative Labour: Working in the Creative Industries*. Basingstoke: Palgrave Macmillan.

McNay, L. (2009). Self as enterprise: Dilemmas of control and resistance in Foucault's The Birth of Biopolitics, *Theory, Culture & Society*, 26(6): 55–77.

McRobbie, A. (1998). *British Fashion Design: Rag Trade or Image Industry?* London, New York: Routledge.

———. (2002). Clubs to companies: Notes on the decline of political culture in speeded up creative worlds. *Cultural Studies*, 16(4): 518–31.

———. (2015). *Be Creative: Making a Living in the New Culture Industries*. London: Wiley.

Neilson, B., & Coté, M. (2014). Introduction: Are we all cultural workers now? *Journal of Cultural Economy*, 7(1): 2–11.

Neilson, B., & Rossiter, N. (2008). Precarity as a political concept, or, Fordism as exception. *Theory, Culture & Society*, 25(7–8): 51–72.

Pais, I., & Provasi, G. (2015). Sharing Economy: A step towards the re-embeddedness of the economy? *Stato e mercato*, 105: 347–78.

Patel, K. (2017). Expertise and collaboration: Cultural workers' performance on social media. In J. Graham, A. Gandini (Eds.), *Collaborative Production in the Creative Industries*, London: University of Westminster Press.

Polanyi, K. [1944] (2001). *The Great Transformation: The Political And Economic Origins Of Our Time*. Beacon Press.

Prospects. (2015). *Overview of the creative arts sector in the UK*. Retrieved from http://www.prospects.ac.uk/creative_arts_design_sector_overview.htm.

Rabinow, P. (2000). The History of Systems of Thought, in Foucault, M. *Ethics. Essential Works 1954–1984*, Vol. 1. London: Penguin

Ricoeur, P. (1992). *Oneself as Another*. Chicago and London: University of Chicago Press.

Ross, A. (2004). *No-Collar: The Humane Workplace and its Hidden Costs*. Philadelphia, PN: Temple University Press.

———. (2009). *Nice Work If You Can Get It: Life and Labor in Precarious Times*. New York: New York University Press.

Sennett, R. (2013). *Together: The Rituals, Pleasures and Politics of Cooperation*. New Haven, CT: Yale University Press.

Sholette, G. (2011). *Dark Matter: Art and Politics in the Age of Enterprise Culture*. London: Pluto Press.

Social Enterprise UK. (2013). *The People's Business: State of Social Enterprise Survey 2013*. Retrieved from: http://www.socialenterprise.org.uk/uploads/files/2013/07/the_peoples_business.pdf.

Virno, P. (2003). *A Grammar of the Multitude*. Los Angeles, CA: Semiotext(e).

Williamson, O. (1973). Markets and hierarchies: Some elementary considerations. *American Economic Review* 63(2): 316-25

CHAPTER THREE

Beyond 'Collaborative Economy' Discourse: Present, Past and Potential of Digital Intermediation Platforms

Jacob T. Matthews

Cemti / Paris 8 University

Introduction

This paper draws on research looking into the hypothesis of a new stage in the historical process of cultural industrialisation – increased rationalisation, commodification and integration with external economic sectors – prompted by the expansion of digital intermediation devices (or *dispositifs*),[1] in particular 'collaborative' web platforms and mobile applications (Bouquillion and Matthews 2010, 2012; Matthews 2014). The key proposal advanced in these works is that of a greater systemisation of the culture industries,[2] simultaneously affecting both structural and ideological dimensions – the first pertaining to reconfigured ties between economic players and the relations of production and organisation of labour these industries rest upon; the second to the contributions they make to 'superficial' legitimisation of contemporary capitalism, and potentially to the effective redesigning of real processes of exploitation and domination.

How to cite this book chapter:
Matthews, J. T. 2017. Beyond 'Collaborative Economy' Discourse: Present, Past and Potential of Digital Intermediation Platforms. In: Graham, J. and Gandini, A. (eds.). *Collaborative Production in the Creative Industries*. Pp. 33–49. London: University of Westminster Press. DOI: https://doi.org/10.16997/book4.c.
License: CC-BY-NC-ND 4.0

While reinforced structural ties between so-called 'content' industries and communication industries (IT, electronic equipment and network players, tele-communications) developed to the advantage of the latter during the 1990s, the recent period has seen a simultaneous surge in the financialisation of culture industries and their increased articulation with consumer goods and service industries (Bouquillion, 2008, pp. 195–238, Hesmondhalgh 2013, pp. 185–99). The 'collaborative' web consolidates the culture and communication industries system, opening up a vast electronic marketplace (Bouquillion and Matthews, 2012, p. 8). Cultural 'content' appear to become mere consumer incentives, fully integrated into the capitalisation process of external sectors. This phenomenon has been interpreted as a 'culturisation of economy' (Lash and Lury, 2007), but as with the proposals of other 'digital optimists' (Hesmondhalgh, 2013 pp. 313–20), this thesis fails to take into account intensified rationalisation and commodification; in this respect, it would be more appropriate to speak of a further 'economicisation of culture'.

Considering the production of 'content', it has been noted that these evolu-tions are contributing to a polarisation between, on the one hand, premium offers (which still represent a direct source of capitalisation for major opera-tors) and, on the other, so-called 'semi-pro', 'pro-am', or 'user-generated' goods, generally elaborated and distributed without any financial contribution from traditional industry players. Directly linked to this phenomenon is the grow-ing significance of digital intermediation platforms. These last few contrib-ute, of course, to the circulation of premium content ('legal' or otherwise), but their mode of capitalisation mainly proceeds from the direct or indirect exploitation of user production – whether in the shape of actual cultural or informational 'content', promotional elements such as prescriptions, or *simply* data. In any case, the key point is that these platforms allow for a significant transfer of costs towards user-consumers (Matthews and Vachet, 2014a, p. 36).

This brings us to the superstructural or ideological level of this systemisa-tion. Indeed, the demand for increased participation of user-consumers within the capitalisation process cannot be without consequence with regard to the elaboration of culture in the anthropological sense, as theorised by Raymond Williams – i.e. culture as a set of symbolic and material productions, beliefs and practices, as a *whole way of life* (Williams, 2014 [1958], p.3). Side-stepping the enchanted discourse of empowerment and increased cultural diversity, my research questioned web and mobile application usage as vectors of ideological concentration, stressing nonetheless that such a tendency was perhaps not so much dependent on an inflation of intelligible representations, manifest ideo-logical productions, but rather at work in 'the repetitive gestures of adhesion that the system requires of users' (Matthews, 2014, pp. 50–1). This hypothesis has been further explored with regard to what can be seen as an 'agglomera-tion of actions that individuals perform unreflectively to sustain the status quo', i.e. 'the banal repetition of the tasks that are assigned by the trusted networks, which seem to have little or no connection to the determination of political practices – opening one's laptop, logging onto a network, sending a phone message, etc.' (Gak and Karatzogianni, 2015, p. 137)

If the ideological construction of a new 'collaborative economy' around the web clearly contributes to the legitimisation of contemporary capitalism (Bouquillion and Matthews, 2010, pp. 51–76), I have since suggested that digital intermediation platforms might be considered as an 'avant-garde' of this new extended system of culture industries (Matthews, 2014, pp. 51–2). This implies that these *dispositifs* constitute models which can be applied to a variety of human activities. In enthusiastic accounts, the 'sharing economy' is based on a worldwide market, open to a multitude of player of all sizes, linked together by digital networks. The regular emergence of new markets and conversion of users into economic players gives this project an allure of realisation – as long as one ignores the fact that a powerful oligopoly has emerged, and that even fringe players objectively dominate individual users. Moreover, we have shown that web platforms innovate mainly by reducing costs and allowing for an 'alteration of perceptions' that the various players have of the capitalisation process and the internal organisation of economic sectors (Matthews and Vachet, 2014b, p. 50). These elements point to significant cracks in the system, which are all the more apparent as the 'collaborative' web is still in many respects a socio-economic experimentation zone (Bouquillion and Matthews, 2010, p. 21).

The present chapter aims, firstly, to reassess two notions used in much of the aforementioned analyses and which continue to fuel significant interrogation and debate. The first is 'collaboration'. What objects and socio-economic processes does the notion of a 'collaborative' web refer to? What are its flaws? The second, frequently employed in both institutional/media discourse and in academic work, yet rarely defined, is the notion of intermediation platforms. How can this help describe and analyse socio-technical devices (*dispositifs*) having emerged over the past 15–20 years, as well as social constructs pertaining to earlier stages of capitalism? Secondly, I offer a contribution to deeper theoretical discussions about what 'collaborative' web platforms and mobile applications are doing to the culture industries in particular, but also to far broader areas of social and economic activity. This question cannot be seriously addressed without considering what relations of production these *dispositifs* command and what forms of labour they promote. It is one that we cannot shy away from, at a time when so many public discourses put forward the creative and democratic potentials of so-called 'social media' (Jenkins, 2006); the political and cultural promises attached to digital intermediation platforms oblige us to consider not only their infrastructural and superstructural 'attributes' (i.e. what they potentially change with regard to the production of economic value and cultural forms), but more fundamentally, the way they articulate these two realms.

The limits of the 'collaborative' web

First of all, let us recall with Bernhard Rieder (2010) that in the notion of a 'collaborative' web, the second term refers to a particular technical structure:

> In order to add a new functionality to the Internet all that is needed is to distribute to users the software that implements it; no infrastructural adjustment is required. On the web – which is also a software innovation – this logic has been pushed to the extreme (…). New functionalities, activities and contents are offered each day and despite the conventions and tendencies that structure it, the space of possibilities is immense (Rieder, 2010, pp. 36–7).

This evocation points to the highly adhesive and extensive character of this 'web' – its ability to stick to a quasi-infinite number of human activities. In their characteristically euphoric style, Tim O'Reilly and John Battelle (2009) write: 'The web is no longer an industry unto itself – the web is now the world' (p. 12). Although this is clearly an attempt at self-realising prophecy, it is interesting to observe how their pamphlet *Web Squared* promotes a vision of socio-economic systemisation in which capitalisation opportunities would be exponentially multiplied. Their enthusiastic descriptions of quasi-universal, real-time, data management tools illustrate their affiliation with the wider discourse of ubiquitous computing (Pucheu, 2014).

As is well known, the 'web 2.0' label popularised by the same O'Reilly after the explosion of the dotcom bubble in the early 2000s was first and foremost a story-telling tactic designed to reassure investors who had been momentarily disorientated by the extent of speculative losses (Allen, 2007; Rieder, 2010). By identifying 'web 2.0' with the bubble survivors, the notion came to represent Internet-based economic activities which had placed their users at the heart of the value creation process (Bouquillion and Matthews, 2010, pp. 5–7). Despite its obvious ideological undertones, elements of this discourse remain relevant, for instance when these authors declare that 'the web as a whole is a marvel of crowdsourcing' (O'Reilly and Battelle, 2009, p. 2), explicitly acknowledging its imperious need of user-consumer 'participation'. If the web's potential to expand can seem unlimited, it's precisely because the notion associates the aforementioned technical characteristics with supposedly boundless reserves of capital and labour.

A second level where one encounters the question of the limits of the 'collaborative' web is that of the actual activities and sectors concerned. From a structural point of view, how far does the web stretch out, when 'the only true obstacle to the propagation of a new application is to be found in the meanders of the attention economy' (Rieder, 2010, p. 37)? As a provisional answer to this key question, I suggest employing a broad definition, including all commercial and non-commercial entities whose activities are dependent on web interface and who integrate significant user contributions into their revenue model and/or mode of capitalisation. This definition implies that the 'collaborative' web is not restricted to niche and small- or medium-sized players, as we have previously suggested (Bouquillion and Matthews, 2010, pp. 17–26). Philippe Bouquillion has since pointed out that:

> the collaborative web represents a new stage in the history of links between marketing industries and culture industries, as there is no opposition between the participative and cultural dimensions, on the one hand, and marketing, on the other, since the second – in particular the production of marketing data and targeted advertising – is 'fed' by the cultural exchanges of Internet users. (Bouquillion, 2013, p. 8).

If one follows this reasoning to its logical conclusion, it can be said that the 'collaborative' web does not replace any existing sectors (any more than it constitutes a new sub-sector in its own right). It simply integrates existing industries, *enriching* them both through its ability to articulate and intermediate, and by the 'collaborative imperative' that it propagates.

The semantic problem posed by this notion constitutes its third limit. At a primary level, the idea of collaboration implies a certain degree of reciprocity and recognition. Despite the negative connotation associated with the term in certain contexts, due to specific historical events (cooperation with the enemy), it is typically taken to refer to the freely consented participation to a common task.[3] The hypothesis of collaborations between users, and *a fortiori* between users and industrial players, can only be examined taking into account the relations of production that underlie these activities and *dispositifs*: who is collaborating with who, and how? (i.e. with what relations of subordination?) Previous research addressing these questions has focused on platforms supposedly designed for funding, producing and distributing cultural goods and services, in the absence of relations based on either waged or freelance labour. For instance, on video sharing or cultural crowdfunding platforms, how do the different types of usage allow industrial players to generate surplus value? Interesting insights have been provided by the analyses of 'immaterial' or 'digital labour'; critiques of the 'attention economy' have attempted to illustrate the importance of generalised and automated data production (Andrejevic, 2009; Comor, 2010; Fuchs, 2014; Hesmondhalgh, 2010; Peters and Bulut, 2011; Scholz, 2013; Terranova, 2000). My investigations into the management of user contributions or of intermediation processes which users take part in – for example, in the isolated 'consumption' of music via YouTube (Matthews, 2014, pp. 49–50), or in the uploading of a project to Kickstarter (Matthews and Vachet, 2014b, pp. 44–7) – show that a significant part of the so-called 'collaboration' takes part without user-consumers being aware if it. That a minority deposits 'contents' knowing that the platform is legally entitled to use them to generate advertising revenue, and having thoroughly examined the site's terms of agreement, is one thing. But it is a wholly different matter when a majority of users access goods and services with the illusion of 'free' usage and without having the slightest understanding of the function they occupy within the complex threads of capitalisation spun with care by the owners and managers of web platforms.

Whatever their level of understanding of these last, 'collaborating' users are objectively in a position of subordination with regard to players who determine these capitalisation strategies, by virtue of their appropriation of the means of production and communication. In this respect, fully in line with the neoliberal-inspired evolutions of capitalism, the 'collaborative' web operates a cost transfer towards 'persons who do not have the capacity to propose or realise their own vision of the social order' (Schoenberger, 1997, p. 202). With the exception of consumer rights organisations, web users are bereft of representative institutions that might allow collective action and find themselves in a situation comparable to that of the least organised workers. In contemporary public debates, in France, the rare critiques of web players are centred around issues such as the 'right to be forgotten' or 'tax evasion'. *Blablacar*, *Adopteunmec* and others like *Kisskissbankbank* are almost unanimously applauded as French success stories, brilliant contributions to the 'collaborative economy', whilst the issue of property is never addressed (despite significant public financing of start-ups). This shows the prevalence of the 'creative industries' discourse, where protecting intellectual and industrial property rights is axiomatic.

In sum, it appears that the recurrent and positively connoted representations of 'collaboration' (and 'sharing') conceal specific processes of exploitation. I argue that these should not only be precisely analysed, but also countered, *a minima* with the proposal of new social rights, based on the model of intervention powers acquired by workers' committees in various European countries, in the mid twentieth century.

On the versatility of intermediation platforms

The idea that intermediation platforms occupy a key function in the present evolution of culture industries has been discussed in a series of recent works. In their book, *L'industrialisation des biens symboliques*, Philippe Bouquillion, Bernard Miège and Pierre Mœglin (2013) draw up a critical synthesis of three key paradigms which are attempting to legitimise and encourage current industrial, cultural and social shifts. All three share this idea. Firstly, in what the authors name the 'convergence paradigm', the key players are 'those who develop a downstream command of sub-sectors via platforms integrating cultural and informational contents and services (...).' These players are in charge of extracting and redistributing collected resources (Bouquillion, Miège and Mœglin, 2013, p.40). Secondly, in the 'collaborative paradigm', the central players are those that 'occupy dominant – and even compulsory – meeting points for Internet users, contents and advertisers or other funders'. The authors add that this strategy is adopted by the most successful players of the web (*ibid*: 46–8). Thirdly, with the 'creative paradigm', intermediation platforms are again in a pivotal position due to their ability to articulate goods and service offers downstream, either by directly capitalising from these products, or to reinforce the capitalisation of external offers (*ibid*: 56). Although the origin of the surplus value extracted by these players is not explicated (a question we will come back to later in this chapter), it is clear that all three paradigms share an 'intuition' that these authors' more critical conclusions cannot dismiss: that of the growing importance of agents who 'interpose within sub-sectors and collect part of the generated value, to the detriment of creators, producers and not necessarily to the advantage of consumers' (*ibid*: 144).

In a recent publication Vincent Bullich and Thomas Guignard attempt to provide a clear definition of intermediation platforms and raise a significant question, suggesting that these might constitute a 'specific sector' in their own right. This proposition deserves further examination; for the while though, let us consider the five criteria identified by these authors. Firstly, intermediation platforms are described as 'distribution systems for goods and services that find their existence solely on networks' (Bullich and Guignard, 2011, p.2). Secondly, they carry out 'economic functions which are both informational (research and prescription tools) and transactional (securing transactions, logistic management, etc.)' (*ibid*: 3) Thirdly, referring to the works of economists Jean-Charles Rochet and Jean Tirole, platforms operate multi-sided markets, bringing together a variety of different players which are nonetheless interdependent for the exchange; doing so, they 'capture positive externalities produced by the interactions between the different sides, the setting up and management of the platform by no means being an aim *per se*.' (*ibid*: 5) Fourthly, the authors underline that although this model appears to be widely applied in sub-sectors linked to ICTs, it is not fundamentally innovative, either for the cultural sector or for other economic areas, such as finance and retail (*ibid*: 6). Lastly, they recall a decisive characteristic that Pierre Mœglin (2011) has already associated with these *dispositifs*: the value that these players (supposedly) add, and the profits they make, are not linked to an activity of 'content' production of their own.

Evidently the new web oligopoly players encompass these criteria (despite eg. *Apple*'s historical core business of hardware and software production), sharing this key characteristic of being positioned 'above' production cycles, attempting to canalise transactions between diverse agents through their control over digital networks. But what is true for the 'big four' (Google, Amazon, Facebook, Apple) is also relevant to the strategies of thousands of web platforms struggling to poise themselves – in a blatantly parasitical manner – 'on top of' activities as varied as car-pooling, romantic relations, retail, accommodation, personal care, etc. (not to mention 'content' production). Their revenues are dependent on their ability to directly or indirectly 'monetise' cultural and informational flows. For these new intermediaries, surplus value extraction is not so much based on private appropriation of 'contents' via intellectual property rights and/ or sale of goods and services (although these streams do remain significant for some players). Digital intermediation platforms mainly rely on a model stemming from the fields of advertising and finance; 'commissions' are justified by their ability to link up individuals and/or groups with commercial entities, brands or investment opportunities. As Jeremy Vachet and I have pointed out, using the example of cultural crowdfunding and crowdsourcing sites (2014a), the platform constitutes a locus of transaction and *translation* – an instrument of ideological convergence. Presenting themselves as mere 'tools' which can be used in order to diversify cultural production, these platforms simultaneously engage with players of very diverse dimensions and rationales (from amateur to fully professional cultural producers, fans and individual funders, institutional funders, corporations, public institutions and agencies, charitable organisations, NGOs and so-called 'third sector' players). Intermediation is all about bringing these different agents to speak a common language.

Vincent Bullich and Thomas Guignard (2011) correctly point out that there is nothing profoundly novel in the model of digital intermediation platforms. An early study by Bernard Miège (1974), analysing the role played in the 1950s and 1960s by French 'comités d'entreprises' (CEs) in response to workers' demand for cultural goods and services, offers an historical example of what truly alternative intermediation platforms might look like. Although their existence is obviously prior to the advent of digital communication networks, three factors demonstrate this negative connection.

Firstly, Miège's study shows that – analogous to web players busy capturing the positive externalities produced by interactions between different sides – CEs constituted, in a specific historical context, established 'meeting points' for a range of players. In this respect, one can speak of an intermediation platform linking together: workers (and their families) as cultural users/consumers; capital, i.e. the corporations contributing part of their revenues, and culture industry players; mutualist organisations (often linked to trade unions) operating leisure equipment, ticketing and cultural goods procurement services; and public and para-public institutions. Secondly, Miège's analysis of CEs show that they carried out clear socio-economic functions, of both informational and transactional nature – and unlike contemporary web-based players, the setting up and management of the platform did appear to constitute an end *per se*.[4] Thirdly, as with contemporary digital intermediation platforms, resources diverted to CEs may constitute a form of rent; but unlike web players, this is not based on the parasitical straddling of external production cycles or on the collecting and commercialisation of data or *attention*: the actual running of CEs was dependent on the voluntary work of employees and on a percentage of turnover deducted prior to the remuneration of both labour and capital.

These historical reminders are useful to question the supposedly ineluctable character of the socio-economic model which contemporary digital intermediation platforms rely on. Like Trebor Scholz's platform cooperativism, they suggest a potential for truly collaborative platforms and demonstrate the possibility of a viable and efficient alternative model (vulnerable precisely because of the obstacles it laid before capitalisation in this field and others). It is worthwhile envisaging what sets us apart from the era in which Bernard Miège conducted this study, but also persisting factors. One place to start is the author's conclusion that collective consumption of cultural goods and services was bound to increase significantly. A posteriori, this hypothesis is certainly one of the work's most surprising propositions, and appears to be in sharp contrast with the findings of much subsequent research pointing to increasingly individualised cultural practices. It is tempting to ask whether this individualisation has encountered its limits – or, perhaps, its logical outcome – with the advent of so-called 'social media'. In fact, one must acknowledge that cultural consumption has always had a collective dimension and implied a degree of productive activity on the part of supposed 'end-receivers'.

This observation is of course not new; it is central to the 'encoding/decoding' model of communication formulated by Stuart Hall in the mid-1970s (and developed in much subsequent research in the field of cultural studies). It is also a key element of the work of Brice Nixon, which re-examines the notion of audience labour and analyses the transformation of social communication into a process of capital circulation and accumulation (Nixon, 2013, 2014). Using a series of historical case-studies spanning from the emergence of the US publishing industry in the mid-nineteenth century to the advent of Google, Nixon attempts to demonstrate the continuity of a model where 'capital's ownership of the object of audience labour, culture, creates audience labour by creating a class relationship between those who own culture and those who do not' (Nixon, 2014, p.729). In order to illustrate this model, the author suggests an analogy with landed capitalism: in the same way that the landowner collects rent from the peasants who work his land, the culture industrialist owns the property of resources, and often tools, which allow user-consumers to produce cultural goods (or 'complete' their production): 'The copyright holder is a cultural "landlord" who does not accumulate capital through the sale of commodities by rather through the granting of access to a privately owned cultural resource in return for payment, i.e. through rent.' (Nixon, 2014, p. 731).[5]

These theoretical propositions allow us to reformulate the fundamental questions that this text seeks to address. Firstly, what material processes are representations of 'participatory' culture, or of 'collaborative' economy/society, attempting to account for? And how do digital intermediation platforms actually exploit so-called 'participative' or 'collaborative' usages? Secondly, can one consider that the production of culture is fundamentally modified by these phenomena – in the sense that the culture industries' modus operandi may be radically transformed? In other words, what do so-called 'collaborative' usages of web platforms do to the culture industries?

Back to the notions of capitalisation and cultural production

Firstly, let us return to the question of shifts in relations of production within the culture industries – in particular to the broad segments that have been contaminated by the 'collaborative' web. The aim here is not to look at modifications in paid labour conditions: these are well documented, as well as the fact that these sub-sectors are characterised by the relative absence of waged labour (Baker and Hesmondhalgh, 2013; Deuze, 2007; McRobbie, 2015; Neff, 2005). The fact is that today, private appropriation of means of production and communication remains the dominant model (despite exceptions and the remnants of certain historical compromises). This evidently implies a class relation between user-consumers and owners of what Nixon names 'means of communicative production'. Enchanted representations of collaboration can only endeavour to conceal, embellish or justify this objective material contradiction. As Christian Fuchs (2013) remarks, 'scholars who suggest that today's Internet is participatory advance an ideology that simply celebrates capitalism without taking into account how capitalist interests dominate and shape the Internet.' He adds: 'Web 2.0 is not a participatory system, and it would be better understood in terms of class, exploitation, and surplus value' (p. 215). The analysis of the exploitation of 'participative' usages by digital intermediation platforms implies an understanding of the capitalisation processes they allow, and in particular that stemming from the automated production of data, which has been perceived by many researchers as a central component of their 'business models'. This leads us to question the hypothesis of renewed/modified relations of production deriving from 'positive externality capture' strategies (Bullich and Guignard, 2011, p. 5) bringing together numerous industrial players and user-consumers, without 'opposition between the participative and cultural dimensions, on the one hand, and marketing, on the other.' (Bouquillion, 2013, p. 8)

In the model proposed by Brice Nixon, communication and culture industries deploy three generic modes of capitalisation. Firstly, rents ensuing from the direct exploitation of cultural labour ('digital' or otherwise). Secondly, rents collected in exchange for the access to goods or services (cultural or otherwise), which entails direct exploitation of audience labour. Thirdly, interest from the leasing of 'fictive capital' to external players (advertisers, sponsors, etc.), which requires the indirect exploitation of audience labour. The first two cases imply a priori possession of intellectual property rights – although the author rightly points out that this is not the case with most web platforms, including Google (Nixon, 2013, pp. 233–6). Ancillary commercial activities, such as the sale of data produced by/on users, complete these three modes; however, although 'the data gathered through online surveillance can be, and often is, sold as its own commodity' it does not constitute the principal source of value (Nixon, 2013, p. 237). According to this thesis, capitalisation is based first and foremost on the exploitation of digital audience labour, and therefore on the control that web platforms are able to achieve of 'the means of audience communicative production' (Nixon, 2013, pp. 214–15). His analytic model nevertheless fails to specify whether automated data production is best considered as a mere opti-mising element for the interest that can be collected on the leasing of 'fictive capital' or as a form of payment 'in kind', by users, of the access rent, notably in the case of platforms providing 'free' services and products. Moreover, it is worth pointing out here that these three modes of capitalisation are being extended and applied in a variety of areas far beyond the recognised perimeter of the culture industries.

Secondly, let us observe how Nixon's propositions shed light on the hypoth-esis of a new stage in cultural industrialisation, induced by the proliferation of digital intermediation platforms. For this, it is useful to go back to some of the answers provided by the authors of *Capitalisme et industries culturelles* in the late 1970s, when faced with the key question: how does capital accumulate in the sphere of cultural production?

> Cultural production (…) essentially consists of integrating artistic labour into a process of material reproduction. The specific character-istics of this articulation do not necessarily imply waged labour. On the contrary, submission of labour to capital rests upon the *preservation of forms and frameworks of artistic labour which belong to pre-capitalist organisation*: amateurism, free-lance labour, craft and cottage indus-try. These conditions allow the training and maintenance of the artistic workforce at a lower cost [and] limit the risks that capital faces due to the nature of use-values, leaving a significant part of those risks to those who create use-values, the artists; lastly, they provide capital with the most favourable means of making and distributing profits and potential rent. (Huet et al. 1978: 178)

I've reproduced several terms here in italic, as I wish to raise the following question, based on the model put forward by Brice Nixon: have these authors implicitly relied on a restrictive definition of 'artistic workforce'? In the same period, Nicholas Garnham (1979) set out to 'examine the specifically capitalist mode of media production (…), the ways in which capital uses the real process of media production in order to increase its value' (p. 139). David Hesmond-halgh (2013) points out that 'the cultural industries are concerned, fundamen-tally, with the management and selling of a particular kind of work' (p. 6) which he chooses to name 'symbolic creativity'. This author is careful to stress his dif-ferences with cultural studies perspectives such as those advanced by Paul Wil-lis, who does indeed use the same term to praise the empowerment of cultural consumers (while refraining from analysis of the question of property of means of cultural production). When Paul Willis writes that 'symbolic creativity is essential to ensure the daily production and reproduction of human existence' (1990: 207) this can of course be read as yet another culturalist mantra. But if one relates this to Nixon's proposition suggesting that audience labour is an integrated component of the process which generates the use value that allows capital to reproduce, the formula takes on a wholly different meaning. One might then ask whether the authors of *Capitalisme et industries culturelles* were neglecting a crucial implication of their observation of the 'preservation of forms and frameworks of artistic labour which belong to pre-capitalist organisation' within what Garnham designated as 'the specifically capitalist mode of media production'. How might the amateurism that these authors refer to be intrinsically distinct from pre-industrial, authentically participative popular cultural forms? This interrogation concurs with the hypothesis that cultural products are not *contained* in commodified and industrially reproduced cultural 'contents'. From amateur dramatic production to the 'symbolic creativity' of game show audiences, to the contributions of web user-consumers, audience labour does appear to be one of the uncharted – or at least underestimated – sources of capitalisation in culture and communication. This perspective offers a secure base to counter the assumptions of the 'collaborationist' discourses that Henry Jenkins promotes, which tell the story of a sudden resurgence of audiences from the ghettos of fandom in the 1970s. It also resonates with the conclusions of a study looking into consumer labour on crowdsourcing platforms which aptly remind us that the 'functional differentiation of society into two dichotomous spheres of "production" and "consumption" is an artefact of early industrial society.' (Kleemann, Voss and Rieder, 2008, p. 6) In this respect, we have now reached the end of a parenthesis during which cultural production and consumption were conceptually separated – including within the framework of political economy of communication.

Several observations must now be made. Firstly, if one must push aside the notion of a 'happily concluded' parenthesis (with 'participatory culture' atoning for the original sin of the culture industries), the hypothesis of a new stage of cultural industrialisation may however not be the most useful way of understanding what digital intermediation platforms are the name of. Let us go one step further and assume that if the category of audience labour was formerly the quasi-exclusivity of the culture industries, it is now effectively being extended to vast swathes of social activity via web platforms and mobile apps, in the same broad sweep that dissolves borders between professional and laymen, and transforms both amateurs and waged workers alike, into legions of freelance 'entrepreneurs'.

Nixon's analyses of Google are worth considering from this point of view, insofar as they firstly suggest a fundamental continuity with the culture industries:

> While Google's users are relatively empowered as digital cultural laborers, as digital audience laborers they are no more empowered, or any less exploited, than any other audience laborers in other eras of the capitalist mode of communicative production. Even in the digital era, processes of communication are also processes of capital accumulation specifically because communicative capitalists control audience activities of

cultural consumption and exploit audience laborers (either directly or indirectly). (Nixon, 2013, p. 237)

Here, the author refers to a distinction between, on the one hand, Google's strategy as an owner of platforms whose 'free' usage affords the generation of 'content' via the contributions of 'digital cultural labourers', and on the other hand, its more parasitical strategy, as a tool controlling access to 'content' that it does not own. Combined, these two strategies make for an apparent empowerment of user-consumers, while exploiting *in fine* digital audience labour to accumulate capital (Nixon, 2013, p. 249).

Secondly, Nixon's case study of Google illustrates three indicators of deep shifts which are being stimulated by intermediation platforms in the field of cultural production, and beyond. First he points out that this corporation has been able to amplify its impact as a 'communicative capitalist' by covering more and more aspects of digital communication, extending its control over an ever broader range of digital audience activities (ibid. p. 241). Google continues to create new devices for the exploitation of audience labour, not because it is forced to (as with numerous 'traditional' culture industries), 'but because these were relatively inexpensive ways for it to grow as a communicative capitalist' (ibid.). Finally, like other platforms, 'it produces none of the digital culture over which it assumes control, while that control is what enables it to extract surplus-value from the consumption of that digital culture, i.e. to exploit digital audience labor.' (ibid.p. 216)

Lastly, one cannot help wondering whether the proliferation of web platforms effectively marks the disappearance of the culture industries as we have 'understood' them for the past hundred odd years. What if this 'new stage in the historical process of cultural industrialisation' was in fact the end of these industries *per se*? And at the same time, what about the proliferation of discourses and (often extremely mundane, semi-automatic) practices which escort these new intermediation platforms in very diverse fields: are they to be 'understood' as a formidable expansion of ideological production far beyond the frontiers of the former culture industries?

Conclusions

The consecrated expressions of 'collaborative' web or 'social' media echo like an unconscious avowal of the intensification and diversification of user-consumer exploitation. Such expressions are poor attempts to conceal the contradictions of what I've earlier referred to as an extended system of culture and communication industries – which can hardly be envisaged as a sum of economic subsectors, but rests upon 'social engineering *dispositifs*' (Rieder, 2010) interfering in a previously unseen range of human activities and experiences. Platforms demand the 'collaboration' of user-consumers, yet doing so they reflect the key role that these last play in the production of both cultural and economic values, and in their capitalisation to the advantage of a minority of proprietors. Given the antagonisms that lie at the very core of this system, there are reasons to think that socialisation of means of cultural and communicative production, opening a pathway towards authentic forms of collaboration, can become a widely shared political aim.

Our task as critical intellectuals is to contribute to the emergence of concrete demands. For this, I suggest leaning on the gains of prior socio-economic and political struggles, such as the 'fixed forms of class struggle' (Miège. 1974, p. 269) that the CEs embodied in France between the 1950s and 1970s, and of which little is known by the younger generations that are so fiercely targeted by web platforms. The articulation between praxis and theory must not however be sacrificed in favour of the 'perversion of spontaneity' that Adorno rightly condemned in the late 1960s: 'The transition to a praxis without theory is motivated by the objective impotence of theory and exponentially increases that impotence through the isolation and fetishization of the subjective element of historical movement, spontaneity.' (Adorno 2005, p. 266) This is why I stress the importance of reassessing the question of *mediations* between relations of material production and cultural forms – that of the potential of autonomy, and inversely, of effectivity (Garnham 1979, p. 129) of cultural productions in regard to the dominant relations of production. The apparently low autonomy of 'collaborative' ideological production may be linked to the fact these cultural forms 'mime' their conversion into effective social forms.

'Collaborative' web platforms exist as real parasites on a fundamental material productive process, which their subsistence relies on *in fine*. But on a secondary level, their strength lies in their ability to coordinate and motivate labour, via 'collaborative' cultural forms – ideological discourse and practice – and therefore to *effectively* contribute to the relative stability of relations of production. When Brice Nixon challenges us to radically extend the perimeter of what we have traditionally 'understood' as cultural labour, is he suggesting an underlying equation between the production of cultural forms (using resources and tools belonging to 'communicative capitalists') and the extraction of surplus value by the latter? Does this perspective point towards increasingly effective false collaborative cultural forms, which in turn may stimulate and/or consolidate shifts in relations of production that have decorously been called the 'uberisation' of economy? It would be foolish for theory to overlook this question.

Notes

[1] This notion refers to the work of Michel Foucault, for whom the *dispositif* is fundamentally a socio-technical construct constituted by a set of internal, mobile parts, whose layout is precisely normative in the sense that it influences the environment, inducing certain social and ideological

dispositions (Raffnsøe, 2008). Giorgio Agamben expands this definition to include 'that which, one way or another, has the ability to capture, guide, determine, control and ensure gestures, behaviour, opinions and discourses of living beings' (Agamben, 2007, p. 31).

[2] The term 'culture industries' is used here in preference to that of 'creative industries' due to my contribution to previous works which deconstruct the latter, from the point of view of its heuristic viability and with regard to public policy implications (Bouquillion, Miège and Mœglin, 2013; Matthews, 2015). However, this preference does not signify that the notion of creativity cannot be used within a critical analysis framework – as other chapters included in this volume fully illustrate.

[3] http://www.cnrtl.fr/lexicographie/collaboration, accessed 15/05/2015.

[4] This point could be questioned if one considers the ideological function of CEs to have been a showcase for 'pre-socialist' satisfaction of cultural needs, in the same way that web platforms now contribute to legitimising a 'post-political' capitalism.

[5] Here it must be noted briefly that Nixon does not deny the validity of the 'traditional' cultural labour exploitation model theorised by political economists of communication since the 1970s.

References

Adorno, T. (2005). *Critical Models*, New York: Columbia University Press.

Agamben, G. (2007). *Qu'est-ce qu'un dispositif?* Paris: Rivages.

Allen, M. (2007). Web 2.0: Discursive entrapment, empowerment or both? Vancouver: AOIR annual conference.

Andrejevic, M. (2009). Exploiting YouTube: Contradictions of user-generated labor. In P. Snickars and P. Vonderau (Eds.) *The YouTube Reader*, Stockholm: National Library of Sweden, pp. 406–24.

Baker, S. and Hesmondhalgh, D. (2013). *Creative Labour: Media Work in Three Cultural Industries,* London: Routledge.

Botsman, R., and Rogers, R. (2010). *What's Mine Is Yours: The Rise of Collaborative Consumption.* New York, NY: HarperBusiness.

Bouquillion, P. (2008). *Les Industries de la Culture et de la Communication. Les Stratégies du Capitalisme,* Grenoble: Pug.

———. (2013). Socio-économie des Industries Culturelles et Pensée Critique: le Web Collaboratif au Prisme des Théories des Industries Culturelles, *Les Enjeux de l'Information et de la Communication,* 2013 supplement.

Bouquillion, P., Matthews, J. (2010). *Le Web Collaboratif, Mutations des Industries de la Culture et de la Communication,* Grenoble: Pug.

———. (2012). Collaborative Web and the Cultural Industries System: a Critical Appraisal. Retrieved from http://www.observatoire-omic.org/fr/art/497/collaborative-web-and-the-cultural-industries-system-a-critical-appraisal.html

Bouquillion, P., Miège, B., Mœglin, P. (2013). *L'Industrialisation des Biens Symboliques: les Industries Créatives en Regard des Industries Culturelles*, Grenoble: Presses Universitaires de Grenoble.

Bullich, V. and Guignard, T. (2011). Les Plates-formes d'Accès aux Contenus : des Dispositifs au Cœur de la Reconfiguration des Filières Communicationnelles, Paper presented at the Médias 011 conference, Université Aix-Marseille 3, 8–9 December 2011.

Comor, E. (2010). Digital Prosumption and Alienation, *Ephemera*, 10(3/4): 439–54.

Deuze, M. (2007). *Media Work*, New York: Polity.

Fuchs, C. (2013). Class and exploitation on the internet. In T. Scholz (Ed.) *Digital Labor: the Internet as Playground and Factory*, London: Routledge, pp. 211–24.

Fuchs, C. (2014) *Digital Labour and Karl Marx*, London, Routledge.

Gak, M and Karatzogianni, A. (2015). Hack or be hacked: the quasi-totalitarianism of global trusted networks. *New Formations*, 84(84): 130–47.

Garnham, N. (1979). Contribution to a political economy of mass-communication. *Media, Culture & Society*, 1(2): 123–46.

Hesmondhalgh, D. (2010). User-generated content, free labour and the cultural industries. *Ephemera*, 10(3/4): 267–84.

———. (2013). *The Cultural Industries*, London: Sage.

Huet, A., Ion, J., Lefebvre, A., Miège, B., Peron, R. (1978). *Capitalisme et Industries Culturelles*. Grenoble: Pug.

Jenkins, H. (2006). *Convergence Culture: Where Old and New Media Collide*, New York: New York University Press.

Kleemann, F., Voss, G. and Rieder, K. (2008). Un(der) paid innovators: the commercial utilization of consumer work through crowdsourcing. *Science, Technology & Innovation Studies*, 4(1): 5–26.

Lash, S. and Lury, C. (2007). *Global Cultural Industry: The Mediation of Things*, New York: Polity.

———. (2015). Like a fraction of some bigger place – the "creative industries" in a peripheral zone: reflections from a case study, *TripleC*, 13(1): 144–62.

Matthews, J. (2014). *Un Parcours de Recherche au Croisement de la Théorie Critique et des Approches Socio-économiques des Industries Culturelles. Bilan et Perspectives*. Habilitation à Diriger des Recherches, Université Toulouse Jean Jaurès.

Matthews, J. and Vachet, J. (2014a). Le Crowdsourcing et le Crowdfunding Culturels dans le Web Collaboratif. In J. Matthews, V. Rouzé, J. Vachet, *La Culture par les Foules? Le Crowdfunding et le Crowdsourcing en Questions*, Paris: MKF Éditions, pp. 28–39.

———. (2014b). La Production et le Financement Collaboratifs : vers une Extension de l'Industrialisation Culturelle? In J. Matthews, V. Rouzé, J. Vachet, *La Culture par les Foules? Le Crowdfunding et le Crowdsourcing en Questions*, Paris: MKF Éditions, pp. 40–55.

McRobbie, A. (2015). *Be Creative: Making a Living in the New Culture Industries,* Cambridge, Polity.

Miège, B. (1974). *Les Comités d'Entreprises, les Loisirs et l'Action Culturelle,* Paris: Cujas.

_____. (1987). The logics at work in the new cultural industries. *Media, Culture & Society,* 9(3): 273–89.

Mœglin, P. (2011). Vers une Redistribution des Cartes entre Opérateurs de Télécom, Fournisseurs de Contenus et Acteurs du Web? Paper presented at the THD Symposium, Université Paris 13, 28–9 April 2011.

Neff, G. (2005). The changing place of cultural production: The location of social networks in a digital media industry. *The Annals of the American Academy of Political and Social Science,* 597(1): 134–52.

Nixon, B. (2013). *Communication as Capital and Audience Labor Exploitation in the Digital Era,* Ph.D. thesis, University of Colorado.

Nixon, B. (2014). Toward a political economy of 'audience labour' in the digital era. *Triple C,* 12(2): 713–34.

O'Reilly, T. and Battelle, J.(2009). *Web Squared: Web 2.0 Five Years on,* Sebastopol, CA: O'Reilly Media.

Peters, M. and Bulut, E. (Eds.) (2011). *Cognitive Capitalism, Education, and Digital Labor,* New York: Peter Lang.

Pucheu, D (2014) L'altérité à l'épreuve de l'ubiquité informationnelle. *Hermés, La Revue 68,* 2014/1

Raffnsøe, S. (2008). Qu'est -ce qu'un dispositif? *Symposium,* 12(1): 44–66.

Rieder, B. (2010). De la Communauté à l'Écume: Quels Concepts de Sociabilité pour le 'Web Social'? *Tic &,Société,* 4(1): 34–53.

Schoenberger, E. (1997). *The Cultural Crisis of the Firm,* Oxford: Blackwell.

Scholz, T. (ed.) (2013). *Digital Labor: The Internet as Playground and Factory,* New York: Routledge.

Smythe, D. (1977). Communications: Blindspot of western Marxism, *Canadian Journal of Political and Social Theory,* 1(3): 1–27.

Terranova, T. ([2000] 2013). Free Labor. In T. Scholz, *Digital Labor: The Internet as Playground and Factory.* New York: Routledge, pp. 33–57.

Williams, R. ([1958] 2014). Culture is Ordinary. In J. McGuigan (Ed.), *Raymond Williams on Culture and Society, Essential Writings.* London: Sage.

Willis, P. (1990). *Common Culture: Symbolic Work at Play in the Everyday Cultures of the Young,* Milton Keynes: Open University Press.

CHAPTER FOUR

Collaborative Production and the Transformation of Publishing: The Case of Wattpad

Rosamund Davies
University of Greenwich

Collaborative production is another way to describe what Bauwens terms peer-to-peer (P2P) production, whereby P2P collaborators work together to construct a shared commons and use value (Bauwens, 2005). This approach to production has been enabled on a large scale by the widespread availability, low cost and connectivity of digital technologies (Bauwens, 2005, Benkler, 2006). Examples of such practices might include the open software movement, crowdsourcing and crowdfunding initiatives, MMOGs (massively multiplayer online games) and fandoms, among others. Although the core aims and values of collaborative production and its products are generally understood to be non-market based, many of its manifestations are interdependent with the market-based economy (Bauwens, 2005, Benkler, 2006, Jenkins, 2013, Arvidsson, 2013), as we shall go on to examine.

The social reading and writing platform, Wattpad, offers a fairly recent example of such collaborative production. Wattpad is a digital enterprise, founded in

How to cite this book chapter:
Davies, R. 2017. Collaborative Production and the Transformation of Publishing: The Case of Wattpad. In: Graham, J. and Gandini, A. (eds.). *Collaborative Production in the Creative Industries*. Pp. 51–67. London: University of Westminster Press. DOI: https://doi.org/10.16997/book4.d. License: CC-BY-NC-ND 4.0

2008 in Canada, but with a global user base of 40 million at the time of writing (Wattpad, 2016a). Around 80 per cent of this user base is 30 years old or under (around 40 per cent 13-17 and 40 per cent 18-30 year olds) (Wattpad, 2016f). At the time of writing, Wattpad is free to join and offers its members a digital platform for both reading and writing. Although it does offer conventionally published works that are out of copyright, Wattpad users mainly read and con-tribute to stories written by other users. Ninety per cent of interaction with the site is through mobile use (Wattpad, 2016a). Common practice on the site is for writers to serialise their stories, uploading one or two chapters at a time and inviting comment and discussion on each chapter. New users are encour-aged to follow this practice (Wattpad, 2016b). 'Wattpaders', as they are known, can also follow each other's profiles and join clubs (discussion forums) focused on particular genres or other aspects of reading and writing. There are also forms of collaborative writing, such as role-playing games. Some readers set up curation profiles, offering curated selections of works in a particular genre or otherwise defined category, e.g. short stories, YA, fan fiction, diversity, literary fiction. Wattpad has become particularly well known as a source of fan fiction, of which 13 million hours worth was read by users in 2014 (Anderson, 2015).

In the following pages, I will consider Wattpad as a community of readers and writers engaging in a process of creative dialogue and collaborative pro-duction of a shared commons and also as a transactional marketplace in which these readers and writers engage in the creation and circulation of value and exchange of services. In doing so, I will draw on existing debates relating to collaborative production.

These debates return frequently to the relationship and tensions between the potential social, political and economic roles of collaborative production. Bauwens explicitly distinguishes P2P commons-based exchange from market exchange, which is concerned with exchange value and individual profit. How-ever his analysis of the contemporary situation is that the two are currently interdependent. 'Netarchists' (Bauwens, 2005, n.p), such as Amazon and eBay, profit from peer collaboration by building platforms to enable it and monetize the value created in various ways. It is not currently possible for P2P produc-ers to earn a living from P2P production independently of these structures, although Bauwens' hope is that P2P production may ultimately transcend mar-ket capitalism. Benkler (2006) identifies non-market collaborative production as a rising force within the 'networked information economy' (Benkler, 2006, p. 4), which is 'reshaping the market conditions under which businesses operate' (Benkler, 2006, p. 24). At the same time, he cautions that concerted social and political action will be needed (and is yet unforthcoming) to fully realise the social, political and economic possibilities opened up by these new material conditions of production (Benkler, 2006).

Writing half a decade later, Rachel Botsman is a passionate advocate of the transformative potential of what she terms the rise of 'Collaborative Consumption'. Botsman and Rogers (2011) enumerates multiple examples of how a new relationship between market and community values has been successfully forged in new types of organisation that have emerged, based on the model of peer-to-peer collaboration and sharing. Citing both large commercial companies such as Airbnb and non-commercial and small initiatives, such as time banks and barter-based community markets, the authors identify a 'socioeconomic groundswell' in which 'the old stigmatized C's associated with coming together and sharing – cooperatives, collectives, and communes – are being refreshed and reinvented into appealing and valuable forms of collaboration and community.' (Botsman and Rogers 2011, n.p) Botsman envisages collaborative consumption markets as offering a contemporary version of the kind of trust-based exchange characteristic of traditional communities.

Jenkins (2013), however, problematises the relationship between market and community values in contemporary networked culture, focusing particularly on media production. Drawing on the idea of a 'moral economy', based on wider social norms, which governs business transactions within a particular society (E. P. Thompson, 1971, in Jenkins, 2013), Jenkins suggests that the digital networked economy has caused a crisis in the contemporary moral economy, creating new contexts in which goods and services are produced and exchanged, such as peer-to-peer sharing and production (Jenkins, 2013). Uncertainty and disagreement over the extent to which such contexts assign market or non-market values to these goods and services has eroded established bases for trust and mutual understanding. This uncertainty relates both to the activities of companies whose business model is based on monetizing collaborative production and consumption and also to the ways in which traditional media producers are starting to engage with fans. When value creation is shared between producers and consumers, those very terms are called into question, as is our understanding of the separation between commodity and gift economies (Jenkins, 2013). We are at present still developing a language with which to discuss and understand these new conditions of production and exchange.

As Botsman's account demonstrates, a term that has come to the fore, as we try to develop such a language, is 'community'. Corporations and marketers across all sectors of the economy have seized on the concept of 'community building' as a strategy they need to embrace, in order to encourage consumer loyalty and monetise consumer attention (Jenkins, 2013). However, while 'brand communities' have become a valuable commercial asset, they are not actually owned by the brand in any straightforward way, since their value is created through the autonomous participation of the members of the community. As the networked economy becomes more and more dependent on this process of shared value creation, there is the potential for such communities to exert significant economic pressure (Jenkins, 2013, Arvidsson, 2013, Balaram, 2016) and, furthermore, to function as 'productive consumer publics' – exerting not only economic but wider social and political influence (Arvidsson 2013).

This chapter will explore the ways in which these kinds of tensions and potentials in the interrelations between market and non-market values and activities, between communities, markets and publics, characterise the operations of Wattpad. The aim will be to understand more about the nature of collaborative production on Wattpad and also to consider the model it might offer for the transformation of creative and business practices within writing and publishing.

According to Wattpad's Head of Content, Ashleigh Gardner, 'Wattpad is a social network and not a publishing platform.' (Gardner, 2014) She points out that 90 per cent of Wattpad's users are readers, compared to 10 per cent who are writers (Gardner, 2014). As outlined above, these readers use the site not only to access content to read, but to engage in discussion with the writers they read and also with other readers. Thus, as a platform, Wattpad's aim, similar to that of Facebook, YouTube and others, is to facilitate the creation of content in order for that content to generate interactions between users and so build a community.

Although the terms 'social network' and 'community' are often used interchangeably, Owens (2014) draws a distinction between an online community as a virtual place 'in which people come together around shared interests' and a social network in which the individual user is 'a node, as an object, that is networked and connected to other users based on features of their profile.' (Owens, 2014, p. 94) One key implication of this distinction is a greater emphasis on collective experience in the community and on a customised individual experience in the network. In the social network, the status of the individual is increased by the number of links he or she has with other individuals in the network (Boltanski and Chiapello, 2005), rather than by his or her contribution to the common aims and objectives of a community as a whole.

In contemporary online culture most of what are referred to as communities are in fact structured as social networks. This fact is closely linked to the network's ability to function as a market and to the monetization opportunities it offers to the organisation that hosts it. Individual profiles linked in a network can be quantified, analysed and leveraged not only by the individuals themselves, but also by the host organisation, which is able to sell both their community's attention and their data to advertisers and other third parties.

Wattpad would seem in fact to offer both versions. It is a community of interest focused on writing and reading and its clubs offer a version of old style online community engagement as defined by Owens: where Wattpaders raise and discuss ideas and concerns of common interest to the community. At the same time, Wattpad's structure of individual user profiles provides the basis for a social network.

Before going further into an analysis of how Wattpad's social network structure enables its function as a marketplace and as a monetisable asset for its owners, I want to bring the concept of the 'public' into the discussion, turning first to boyd's (2014) discussion of teenage networked publics.

Beyond spending time with their friends in private spaces, such as each other's homes, teenagers feel the need to gather together in public. In the physical world, spaces such as shopping malls and public parks continue to attract teens as places to gather. Social media offer them a further public space in which to congregate. According to boyd (2014) 'teens engage with networked publics for the same reasons they have always relished publics; they want to be a part of the broader world by connecting with other people and having the freedom of mobility... social media services like Facebook and Twitter are providing teens with new opportunities to participate in public life.'(p. 10)

boyd stresses that, in seeking public spaces in which they can appear and express themselves, teenagers are looking for more than a chance to socialise with their peers. Although social networks may work by linking one individual with another, these connections and much of the interaction they generate are public. Teens seek public engagement and recognition as an important part of developing from child to adult. She stresses the symbolic importance of doing something in public as opposed to in a purely private realm of activity. boyd goes on to point out, however, that when teenagers do attempt to participate in wider public life through political action, such as public protests, they are, like other minority or underrepresented groups, often dismissed as irrelevant or attacked as irresponsible. Social media offer teenagers a 'youth-centric public space' (boyd, 2014, p. 19) that may not exist elsewhere.

If society is made up of 'a whole host of publics' (boyd, 2014, p.202), then we might understand teenagers using social networks to be participating in their own 'intimate publics'. The term 'intimate public' was developed by Berlant as part of her critique of the general 'privatisation of citizenship' (Berlant, 1997, p. 3) in the United States, resulting in the lack of a genuine public sphere in contemporary society. Berlant goes on to discuss the specific exclusion of minorities from political recognition and agency in whatever might remain of a political public sphere and how, in response to this exclusion, the 'intimate public legitimates qualities, ways of being, and entire lives that have otherwise been deemed puny or discarded' (Berlant, 2008, p. 3). Berlant's particular focus is on 'women's culture' as 'the first mass cultural intimate public' (Berlant, 2008, p. viii). Her enquiry is into the way that women gain a sense of belonging and community through the consumption of literature by and for women. According to Berlant, 'intimate publics elaborate themselves around a commodity culture... organized by fantasies of transcending, dissolving or refunctioning the obstacles that shape their historical condition.' (Berlant, 2008, p. 8)

The notion of the 'intimate public' provides a fruitful perspective from which to consider Wattpad, which has gained a reputation for being the reading site of choice for 13–18-year-old-girls, many of whom discover it through reading and writing fan fiction, which makes up a large volume of content on the site. The creation of fan fiction has been recognised as a way for young women to 'narratively experiment with gender roles, primarily by casting young females as protagonists, and to participate in ongoing exchanges related to themes and concerns from their lives' (Black 2008, p. 50). Wattpad's dominant demographic also explains the predominance of teen fiction and other teen popular genres such as romance and fantasy.

Former Wattpad user, Hazal Kirci, writes that her experience of Wattpad was that it offered a safe and inspiring space for young women. Through it she was able to gain a sense of belonging, as well as be inspired to creative expression (Kirci, 2014). If intimate publics offer individuals 'a way of experiencing one's own story as part of something social' (Berlant, 1997, p.3), then the particular power of teen fiction on Wattpad, as opposed to commercially published YA literature, of which there is no shortage, is that not only does it provide stories that relate to the key issues in its readers' lives, but, like fan fiction in general, it also provides readers and writers with the chance to interact with each other as part of an ongoing exchange between peers and feel part of a community.

In her more recent discussion of intimate publics, however, Berlant (2008) states that the 'juxtapolitical' relationship of intimate publics to the political process is often problematic, since, while they offer a refuge from political injustice, oppression or lack of recognition, they may struggle to impact on broader publics that carry greater social and political legitimacy and weight.

In the case of women's literature, for example, readers often realise a sense of self and of social belonging through the conventional plot of romance, which resolves real life problems through fantasy (Berlant, 2008). While this may help women to endure real life injustices, it may not necessarily inspire women to challenge them. Even if they do, in wider society 'womens' issues' are too often treated as personal concerns rather than as matters of general public and political significance.

Although he does not himself reference either writer, Arvidsson's discussion of 'productive publics' (Arvidsson 2013, p. 381) has relevance to our consideration of the 'networked publics' identified by boyd and the 'intimate publics' discussed by Berlant, since the social and political aims and impact of particular 'publics' are central to the arguments of all three writers. Arvidsson specifically promotes the term 'public' over 'community' for the stated reason that the term 'community' within social theory involves direct interaction between members, founded upon 'actually existing social relations that really work as foundations of trust and mutual support.' (Arvidsson, 2013, p. 377) For Arvidsson, a large-scale structure of communication and experience of communality involves common interests and pursuits amongst a group of people who may contribute to a common pool of resources, yet it does not necessitate, or indeed facilitate, actual co-creation or direct interaction between all members. Such structures should not, therefore, be described as communities, but rather as publics.

There is a related point to make here, which is that members of a 'public' face outwards, towards an external object of attention, whether that be a cultural artefact, a commodity or a national government, while communities might be seen as inward facing, concerned largely with maintaining their own networks. This might explain the frequency with which the term 'community' appears in the rhetoric of politicians. Although it may represent an attempt to acknowledge and legitimise particular interest groups, it equally offers a means (intentional or otherwise) of relativizing and controlling the representation within political debate of certain collective interests, by relocating them from the realms of politics or economics and into a putatively separate social realm. This results in a failure to properly address those interests (Plant, 1990, Preston, 2005).

The use of the term 'community' may therefore enact through language the kind of bracketing off of intimate publics from the wider political sphere that concerns Berlant. It is likely, I would venture, that this tendency is also a contributing factor to Arvidsson's explicit argument in favour of the term 'public' over 'community'. Likewise, although boyd and Berlant do use the term 'community' from time to time and in particular when discussing internal relations within a particular networked or intimate public, their use of the term 'public' is bound up with their interest in the social and political influence of such communities.

Having considered how Wattpad functions as a community and as an intimate public, it therefore seems pertinent to also consider whether the activities and concerns of this community have any wider public impact.

Kirci (cited above) moved on from Wattpad to join the Social Mobility Foundation's aspiring professionals programme and to write an article in *The Guardian*. While this example of individual aspiration might fall short of the kind of collective political engagement and impact envisaged by Berlant, Kirci certainly makes an explicit and more general connection between participation in Wattpad and increased literacy and academic engagement (Kirci, 2014), as does writer Margaret Atwood, an early and avid Wattpad supporter. Atwood argues, furthermore, that Wattpad encourages both writing and reading and that literacy is vital to the future of democracy (Atwood, 2012). A further example of the way in which participation on Wattpad might provide a means for young women to exercise political agency is Emily Lindin's *The Unslut Project* (Lindin, 2013, Wattpad, 2016b). A memoir of Lindin's traumatic experience of being labelled the 'school slut' age 11, this story gained a large readership on Wattpad and was subsequently published. Lindin also went on to make a related documentary and continues to raise awareness of and campaign against the cruel and bizarre practice of 'slut shaming' through *The Unslut Project* website. Wattpad therefore clearly has the potential to provide its community, or communities, of predominantly teenage and young women with a public forum and launch pad, from which to impact on a wider public.

However, in its current phase of development, Wattpad's market potential is becoming ever more apparent. At a microeconomic level, barter and exchange of services are much in evidence on the platform. For example, some Wattpaders produce covers for writers. In return, writers may follow them, or read and comment on their story. Such exchanges are acknowledged in comments, such as the message left by a Wattpader on another Wattpader's first chapter 'Hi there! I'm here as payment for my cover… Good luck on the rest of the rewrite' ('Wilting Hope', 2015). A further form of reciprocal recognition that Wattpaders can provide is to include each others' work in a reading list. These reading lists are featured on people's profile pages and are a form of recommendation, which will drive further readers to the featured stories.

The most widespread form of direct reciprocity, however, is through users reading and voting for each others' work and following each others' profiles. This is where we see the significance of Wattpad's structure as a social network of connections, which can be leveraged by individuals to increase their status within this network. Every follow and read of every chapter of every story is logged and the total displayed publicly on the user's profile. Furthermore, Wattpad readers can also vote for each chapter of a story, signifying not only that they have read it, but that they actively liked it. This establishes a link between reader and writer since writers are notified of the identities of those who vote on their story. If the writer recognises the reader back, by following him or her, the reader is then brought to the attention of the writer's followers. Both votes and reads, are totted up and added to the writer's vital statistics, which are displayed on his or her profile.

This process of mutual self-promotion has been described as a 'Social Ponzi scheme that works because nobody gets scammed' (Romano, 2012). The vote might perhaps be identified as the unit of exchange that comes closest to a form of currency within Wattpad. One could say that readers pay writers with votes. This process does not, however, establish a market price. A story does not become more 'expensive' for a reader to read when it has more votes. Rather, it becomes an increasingly effective hub for shared value creation by both reader and writer. In this regard Wattpad functions as an attention economy. The more attention you get, the more attention you generate. Voting is not a one-way process of recognition.

Direct reciprocity, however, is not the full story. Much of the interaction that takes place on Wattpad takes the form of indirect reciprocity, a feature common to other digitally networked sites of collaborative production and consumption (Bauwens, 2005, Botsman, 2011). As Arvidsson (2013) explains, publics will tend to abide by a particular ethos, 'a set of standards and expectations that allow members of that public to make judgements as to the value of the conduct and character of other members, or other publics' (p. 379). In the case of Wattpad, Wattpaders are expected to demonstrate commitment to the activity of reading and commentary. If you do not read, vote and comment on other people's work, if you do not participate and comment in members clubs, if you do not build your network, you are unlikely to get many readers for your stories (Wattpad, 2016c, Wattpad, 2016d). Beyond straightforward tit for tat exchange of attention between individuals, Wattpaders are expected to make a more general contribution to demonstrate that they uphold Wattpad's values. In return they will render themselves a visible and valued member of the community. To be recognised as a writer, you must therefore also be recognised as a reader.

Despite the functional importance of reading on Wattpad, being legitimated as a writer is a key means of increasing one's social capital and reputation in this economy. Once value has been created and expressed in the form of reads, votes and followers, this social/reputational capital is likely to start to generate more and more capital, requiring less and less labour on the part of its owner. Reads and votes can expand exponentially into the millions and far beyond any direct relationship of reciprocity. As Arvidsson (2013) has pointed out, 'publics create new values, in the form of 'buzz', reputation and opinion' (p. 376) and 'reputation is the form that social capital takes among strangers.' (p. 380) Once a Wattpad story has gained a certain number of reads and votes and the writer has thousands of followers, he or she is no longer operating in a social network of direct reciprocity but has established a public reputation as an exceptional Wattpader, evident to Wattpad members who have never interacted with the writer or his or her work. This is likely to attract more readers and generate ever more reads and votes for the work.

There is then a further level of value that can be generated. Reputational capital amassed on Wattpad can be converted to monetary value in the form of book, film and television deals in the conventional media marketplace. Wattpad writers have had particular success in the Philippines where several books have been published based on Wattpad stories (Gardner, 2014). According to Wattpad co-founder, Allen Lau, this phenomenon can be partly attributed to the combination of a highly literate population, interested in both reading and writing, and partly to the lack of developed publishing outlets in the Philippines (Lau, 2013). These factors led to huge interest in and use of Wattpad in the Philippines and the fast emergence of Wattpad 'stars'. Films and TV series followed, including the series *Wattpad Presents*, a partnership between Wattpad and television station Kapatid TV5 (Gardner, 2014, Tomada, 2014).

British and American teen writers have also translated their popularity on Wattpad into mainstream success. These include Beth Reekles, whose story *The Kissing Booth*, was published by Random House (Kirci, 2014) and Anna Todd, whose One Direction fan fiction story, *After*, was published by Simon & Schuster and is being adapted into a film for Paramount Pictures (Hipes, 2015).

Even when Wattpad writers become Wattpad celebrities, however, they still belong to their community. Traditional conceptions of fame or becoming a 'star' might involve the idea of leaving one's roots behind. This is not the Wattpad model. As with celebrity YouTubers, fans feel a strong personal connection with these celebrities, whose continued success depends on their ability to maintain this connection with their fans (Burgess and Green, 2009). Todd is therefore developing her own app to keep in touch with her fan community and to encourage their contributions to her current work. Sam Rogoway, CEO of Victorious, the talent agency which represents Todd, makes the point that 'fans are not just consumers: they are creators in their own right, and they want to interact not just with the creators but with other fans.' (Dredge, 2015, n.p). Arvidsson (2013) identifies this type of expanded community as a 'productive consumer public' with the power to 'set the values that are attributed to consumer brands' (p. 385). Digital media celebrities function as the lynchpin of a community or network which they need to curate in line with their fans' expectations.

Meanwhile, Wattpad stars fit easily into the trend towards celebrity authors within contemporary trade publishing. In this consolidated marketplace, driven by a logic of growth, the focus is on short term high returns delivered by bestsellers (Thompson, 2012). Publishers are looking to commission and develop authors with as a 'platform' (Thompson, 2012, p. 87), i.e. a visible public presence that can attract a loyal audience that will translate into high sales figures. A further advantage is that such an audience is likely to buy not just one book, but all the author's books.

An additional reason for the increasing focus on 'platform' is that, as more and more books are produced independently (self published), without the traditional gatekeepers, reader attention is the vital currency that both traditional and independent publishers need to access and convert into monetary value. In order to achieve this conversion, they need to reward this attention with an experience of belonging and validation. Authors are therefore under pressure to engage with their audience by spending 'three or four months a year doing the literary circuit full-time' (Groskop, 2014/15, p. 9), including appearing at literary festivals, which increase in number year on year. Publishers also attempt to connect with the reading public by organizing live events, such as readings, and facilitating book groups with a range of resources (see Bloomsbury, Penguin). Since Wattpad writers bring with them large and fully engaged communities, it is not hard to understand why Wattpad writers are so appealing to publishers. While political influence might depend on a community's ability to organise itself as a public, commercial success depends more and more on converting a public into a community.

As a commercial enterprise, Wattpad's business model is, like that of many other digital social networks, to monetise its community by selling its attention, its data and also its creative services to other businesses. Wattpad's relationship with the band One Direction has been particularly fruitful in this regard. One Direction fan fiction dominates Wattpad's fan fiction pages and, prior to One Direction's US debut, their label, Sony, commissioned a Wattpad fan fiction with the same title as the debut single. This partnership raised the profile of both band and writing platform (Romano, 2012).

Wattpad has also developed relationships with established authors, including Margaret Atwood, Paulo Coelho and Dan Brown, who all have a presence on Wattpad and independent (self-published) authors also use Wattpad as an additional channel and community-building platform.

Another focus is on developing 'native marketing' campaigns for brand owners, including Unilever and Apple (Wattpad, 2016f), and Wattpad recently signed a deal with talent and literary agency UTA to represent them in developing further partnerships and licensing opportunities (Hipes, 2015). The deal with UTA consolidates and develops Wattpad's existing business strategy, which Lau has described as concentrated on two main revenue streams: content marketing and content licensing, with marketing the primary and licensing the secondary focus (Nawotka, 2015).

As I hope the above discussion makes clear, Wattpad offers a particular case study of the many ways in which, in the networked information economy (Benkler 2006), communities, markets and publics are inextricably linked together in complex networks of attention and sharing, which may be configured in various ways and for various purposes, including both interpersonal and commodity exchange. People engage in these relations and activities for a variety of overlapping aims: notably, but not exclusively, identity construction, belonging, social status and financial gain.

Some Wattpaders definitely see the platform as a stepping-stone to a traditional publishing deal or self-publishing venture. Others are less focused on professionalization of their activity and value it primarily as an outlet for creative self-expression, social interaction and validation. As well as providing a safe community, Wattpad allows users to feel that they are part of public life and contributing to a wider conversation.

Like most communities, Wattpad also facilitates barter of services amongst members. It functions as a marketplace for reciprocal exchange as well as a peer production economy based on indirect reciprocity and contribution to a shared commons (Bauwens, 2005). However Wattpad's system of votes and reads also facilitates a more capitalistic type of activity, in which it is possible and indeed desirable to accumulate reputational capital in order to gain a higher social status beyond one's immediate community of readers and writers. It is then possible for such Wattpad public celebrities to convert this reputational capital into financial gain. While Wattpad is therefore most definitely a site of economic activity, I would argue that this is not incompatible with or indeed separable from ways it might be seen to function as a community. Indeed, the continued success of Wattpad star writers is closely bound up with the continued loyalty of their fan community.

As Arvidsson (2013) points out, what is emerging here is 'a new paradigm of value that is both ethical and economic at the same time' (p. 385). Fan communities function as publics to the extent that they draw on their shared community values to exert influence on the object of attention that has originally brought them together. While this object of attention may originally have been a media text or a brand or a celebrity, as a community builds around it, the community itself, the shared values it develops and the active participation of community members become part of the object of attention and part of its economic value. It becomes impossible to separate ethical and economic value at this point. Fans are not only adding value, they are actively determining what that value is. When a publisher commissions a Wattpad writer they are not just signing up a writer or buying a commodity to distribute, they are entering into a relationship with a 'productive consumer public'.

Wattpad itself has the same considerations, now that, having established critical mass, it moves towards a great focus on monetization as the self-proclaimed 'YouTube of Stories' (Powell, 2013). It will inevitably become more commercialised. However, like YouTube, Wattpad's economic value will continue to depend on its ability to successfully maintain its function as a community/ intimate public, to satisfy the expectations of that public and further its aims. Ideally Wattpad would fulfill the function that Botsman assigns to collaborative production and consumption platforms, where 'the role of this new intermediary is therefore to create the right tools and environment for familiarity and trust to be built, a middle ground where commerce and community meet.' (Botsman, 2011 n.p)

What implications might Wattpad's business model have for traditional publishing? As discussed above, Wattpad's model of value creation is demonstrably interoperable with that of commercial publishing. Like YouTube, Tumblr and Instagram, Wattpad facilitates the feedback loop between audiences, 'prosumers' and professional producers. Traditional publishing feeds into Wattpad, just as Wattpad feeds into traditional publishing. The interests of readers and writers on Wattpad have been shaped in part by the recent explosion in YA fiction in publishing, as well as by developments in fan fiction. Wattpad readers' enthusiasm for peer-produced content therefore presents no threat to professional publishing. On the contrary, it offers publishers access to a large audience base and talent pool.

I would suggest that Wattpad also offers a potential model of how writing, reading and publishing might more generally develop as part of the networked information economy. Networked digital technologies make visible the fact that audiences not only want to own content they also want to share it with others, in order both to build relationships and to participate in collective identities. This process of sharing can involve a range of activities, including discussion, modification and co-creation of content. As these processes become more visible as part of a public conversation across digital platforms with millions of users, they attract more people to participate in them. Consequently modes of engagement that were previously considered to be the 'cult' behaviours of fans have now become more mainstream (Jenkins, 2013).

Such modes of engagement could perhaps be more fully catered for by publishers through alternative forms of content and delivery to the traditional form of the book: short form and/or serialized content, for instance, which can be easily shared and discussed; or transmedia approaches to storytelling, which encourage immersive and long term engagement with story worlds. The problem for publishers is that, to be commercially successful, such approaches might well necessitate different business models. Serialised content might better suit a subscription model, for example, while transmedia storytelling would require publishers to hold onto and exploit for themselves adaptation rights that they currently license to other media companies. As long as the book remains viable as the primary unit of value, there is no great incentive for commercial trade publishers to make such leaps into the unknown.

Nevertheless, the big publishers are cautiously exploring new approaches. Orion's recent publication *Belgravia*, written by Julian Fellowes is one such example (Martin, 2016), as is the ongoing discussion in the industry as to the pros and cons of subscription (Campbell, 2015). However, it is currently smaller publishers who are most evidently developing alternative business models that share some of the principles of collaborative production. They often focus on subscription as a revenue stream, for example, rather than on individual book sales (e.g. Salt, And Other Stories, Peirene Press, Galley Beggar Press), developing a relationship with their readers that is not one of commodity exchange so much as one of shared value creation, in which all parties are collaborators in the shared project of keeping the press running and getting the books published (see Graham, in this volume, for further discussion of this trend).

This model could of course be seen as extremely old, rather than new, since subscription to publications was prevalent in the eighteenth century. However networked digital culture makes it much easier for small publishers to connect with their readers and to maintain and strengthen the sense of community, as well as to keep their overheads low. It also facilitates an alternative collaborative approach in the form of crowdfunding, via platforms such as Kickstarter on which publishing is the third most popular category (Phillips (2016) and Patreon.

Crowd funded publishing often engages supporters not only in funding, but in creating content. Therefore, although the process may end in the stable and familiar form of a completed book, participation in the process of production itself is part of the value proposition and indeed may be of more value to participants than the final product itself. The design of this participation by the project's initiators becomes as important to the project's success as the design of the final product. In such a context, writers and publishers need to adopt a substantially different approach to production than that of conventional publishing. Not only are they curating a community in the same way as the Wattpad stars discussed above, they are designing an experience as much as a product and are very often offering readers a text that is still unfinished, open to input and potentially multifaceted.

To sum up the above discussion, we might therefore conclude that, in the current moment within publishing, we are seeing signs of a potential transformation of the sector, in line with the transformative potential of collaborative production identified by commentators such as Benkler, Botsman, Jenkins and Arvidsson.

Although mainstream publishing is moving only slowly in this direction, developments in alternative publishing contexts demonstrate ways in which it might be achieved.

The networked information economy constitutes a 'technological-economic feasibility space' (Benkler, 2006, p. 3) within which the market value of communities continues to rise, in tandem with a renewed understanding of the value of non-market activities to communities and to society in general. This is a delicate balance. While it is likely that commercial logic will eventually take mainstream publishing towards a business model of shared value creation, it is to be hoped that such developments will not crowd out alternative and smaller publishers, who have currently found a new space to operate. Rather, collaborative production has the potential to sustain alternative publishing approaches and give them a stronger market and cultural presence.

As people witness and participate in the large-scale public conversation and collaborative production enabled by digital technologies, they not only form communities of interest but also conceive of themselves as publics, who can and should exert influence. This is why Arvidsson envisages 'productive consumer publics' to have the potential to 'represent a new institutional form in which the spheres of economics, ethics and politics, tragically separated in the modernization process, come together in forms of public action' (Arvidsson, 2013, p. 35). Such public action will be necessary, since the 'spirit of capitalism' is mutable (Boltanski and Chiapello, 2005), even as its underlying logic of accumulation and reinvestment of capital remains constant. It is possible for a discourse of community to be instrumentalised and exploited within economic theory and practice in the same way as discourses around creativity (Boltanski and Chiapello, 2005, Brouillette, 2014) and well-being (Davies 2015). Meanwhile, the same imperative of growth and ROI for shareholders that drives contemporary commercial publishing frequently compels potential collaborative production entrepreneurs to 'pivot' away from a business model of shared value towards maximum value extraction, once they obtain capital investment (Rushkoff in Troncoso, 2016).

In order to establish a new moral economy to regulate these new conditions of production and exchange, 'productive consumer publics' will need to exert influence not only on businesses but on political and legal institutions to establish the kind of network and regulatory infrastructure (Benkler, 2006) in which they can function most productively.

Questions to explore beyond this chapter with regard to publishing include:

- The future role of publishers – Will the role of publisher move closer to that of community manager? How might the operations of online book distributors, such as Kobo and Amazon, and indeed platforms such as Wattpad, impact on or perhaps merge with those of publishers?
- Alternative marketplaces – Might the new space of publishing that is emerging offer alternative marketplaces for reading and writing? Might current crowdfunding platforms, for instance, evolve to provide such marketplaces, beyond what they are doing at the moment, perhaps in tandem with small, independent publishing outlets? What might be their distinctive features?
- The use-value of writing and reading – The end game for writers may not always be to publish, to achieve some kind of commercial success or public impact. How is non-market peer-to-peer writing and reading developing as a cultural activity and how might it develop in the future?

• What specific structures and approaches might support collaborative writing and reading publics in achieving the kind of social and political impact that Arvidsson envisages? The suggestions of theorists such as Hind (2010) and Couldry (2010) provide a starting point for further research.

References

Anderson, P. (2015). Digital writing: If only community weren't so communal. *The Bookseller*, 4 August. Retrieved from http://www.thebookseller.com/futurebook/if-only-community-werent-so-communal-308390.

Arvidsson, A. (2013). The potential of consumer publics. *Ephemera: Theory & Politics in Organization*, 13(2), 367–91.

Atwood, M. (2012). Why Wattpad works. *The Guardian*, 6 July . Retrieved from http://www.theguardian.com/books/2012/jul/06/margaret-atwood-wattpad-online-writing.

Balaram, B. (2016). Fair Share: Reclaiming power in the sharing economy. RSA available at https://medium.com/@thersa/fair-share-reclaiming-power-in-the-sharing-economy-499b46bd4b00#.klx0etam9.

Bauwens, M. (2005). The political economy of peer production. *CTheory*. Retrieved from http://www.ctheory.net/articles.aspx?id=499.

Benkler, Y. (2006). *The Wealth of Networks: How Social Production Transforms Markets and Freedom*. Yale University Press. Creative Commons version. Retrieved from http://cyber.law.harvard.edu/wealth_of_networks/Download_PDFs_of_the_book.

Berlant, L. (1997). *The Queen of America Goes to Washington City*. Durham, NC: Duke University Press.

____. (2008). *The Female Complaint: The Unfinished Business of Sentimentality in American Culture*. Durham, NC: Duke University Press.

Black, R. W. (2008). *Adolescents and Online Fan Fiction*. New York, NY: Peter Lang.

Bloomsbury (2016). Book groups. Retrieved from http://www.bloomsbury.com/uk/communities/book-groups.

Boltanski, L. & Chiapello, E. (2005 [1999]) (Translated by Gregory Elliott). *The New Spirit of Capitalism*. London: Verso.

Botsman, R. & Rogers, R. (2011). *What's Mine is Yours: How Collaborative Consumption is Changing the Way We Live* [Kindle Version] Retrieved from www.amazon.co.uk.

boyd, d. (2014). *It's Complicated: The Social Lives of Networked Teens*. New Haven, CT: Yale University Press.

Brouillette, S. (2014). *Literature and the Creative Economy*. Stanford, CA: Stanford University Press.

Burgess, J. and Green, J. (2009). *YouTube: Online Video and Participatory Culture*, Cambridge: Polity Press.

Campbell, L. (2015) Hachette chiefs dismiss subscription model. *The Bookseller,* 2 April. Retrieved from http://www.thebookseller.com/news/hachette-chiefs-dismiss-subscription-model.

Couldry, N. (2010). *Why Voice Matters: Culture and Politics after Neoliberalism.* London: SAGE.

Davies, W. (2015). *The Happiness Industry: How the Government and Big Business Sold us Well-Being.* London: Verso.

Dredge, S. (2015). YouTube stars Ryan Higa and the Young Turks launch 'superfan' mobile apps. *The Guardian,* 23 April. Retrieved from http://www.theguardian.com/technology/2015/apr/23/youtube-ryan-higa-the-young-turks-apps.

Gardner, A. (interviewee) (2014) How to use Wattpad as an author with Ashleigh Gardner. *The Creative Penn,* 31 January [Audio Podcast]. Retrieved from http://www.thecreativepenn.com/2014/01/31/wattpad.

Groskop, V. (2014/15). Jam Sessions. *Mslexia,* Issue 64 DEC/JAN/FEB

Hind, D. (2010). *The Return of the Public.* London: Verso.

Hipes, P. (2015). Wattpad inks deal with UTA amid 'after' success. *Deadline,* 15 October. Retrieved from http://deadline.com/2015/10/wattpad-movies-tv-hollywood-uta-1201584126.

Jenkins, H. et al. (2013). *Spreadable Media: Creating Value and Meaning in a Networked Culture.* New York: New York University Press [Kindle Version] Retrieved from amazon.co.uk.

Kirci, H (2014). The tales teens tell: What Wattpad did for girls. *The Guardian,* 16 April. Retrieved from http://www.theguardian.com/technology/2014/aug/16/teen-writing-reading-wattpad-young-adults

Lau, A (interviewee) (2013). Ancient art updated. *Beyond the Book,* 28 July [Audio Podcast]. Retrieved from http://beyondthebookcast.com/ancient-art-updated.

Lindin, E (2013) The Unslut Project: How sexual bullying ruined my childhood. *The Guardian,* 21 September. Retrieved from http://www.theguardian.com/society/2013/sep/21/unslut-project-against-sexual-bullying.

Martin, T (2016). Why Julian Fellowes's new app Belgravia won't start a revolution. *The Telegraph,* 16 April. Retrieved from http://www.telegraph.co.uk/books/what-to-read/why-julian-fellowess-new-app-belgravia-wont-start-a-revolution.

Nawotka, E (2015). Content licensing is key to Wattpad's future. *Publishing Perspectives,* 6 August. Retrieved from http://publishingperspectives.com/2015/08/content-licensing-is-key-to-wattpads-future/#.VtMTGdAjhJF.

Owens, T.J. (2014). Designing online communities: How designers, developers, community managers, and software structure discourse and knowledge production on the web. PhD Thesis. George Mason University

Penguin (2016). Book clubs. Retrieved from http://www.penguin.com/read/book-clubs/

Phillips, A. (2016) The wisdom of crowds: Crowdfunding and crowdsourcing 12 April, London Book Fair Workshop.

Plant, R. (1990) Communities v. Consumers. *The Times*, 28 August available from Lexis Nexis

Powell, C. (2013). How one direction helped make Wattpad a bestseller. *Marketing*, July 24. Retrieved from http://www.marketingmag.ca/media/how-one-direction-helped-make-wattpad-a-bestseller-84417.

Preston, P. (2005). There is no such thing as community: The idea that society comprises homogeneous groups is deluded. *The Guardian*, 18 July available from Lexis Nexis

Romano, A. (2012). Wattpad's unlikely literary revolution. *Daily Dot*, 25 July. Retrieved from http://www.dailydot.com/business/wattpad-unlikely-literary-revolution/

Thompson, J. (2012). *Merchants of Culture: The Publishing Business in the Twenty-First Century* (2nd Ed). Cambridge: Polity Press.

Tomada, N. (2014). Wattpad stories come alive on TV5. *The Philippine Star*, 22 September. Retrieved from www.philstar.com/entertainment/2014/09/22/1371641/wattpad-stories-come-alive-tv5.

Troncoso, S. (2016). Douglas Rushkoff's vision for a new, better world. P2P Foundation, 15 March. Retrieved from https://blog.p2pfoundation.net/douglas-rushkoffs-vision-new-better-world/2016/03/15.

Unslut Project, The. Retrieved from http://www.unslutproject.com.

Wattpad (2016a). About Wattpad. Retrieved from https://www.wattpad.com/press.

____. (2016b). The Unslut Project: How a private diary became a social movement. Retrieved from http://blog.wattpad.com/2016/02/26/the-unslut-project-how-a-private-diary-became-a-social-movement.

____. (2016c). How do I promote my story? Retrieved from https://support.wattpad.com/hc/en-us/articles/201415550-How-do-I-Promote-my-Story-

____. (2016d). How Wattpad Works. Retrieved from https://www.wattpad.com/168209788-how-wattpad-works-how-to-wattpad.

____. (2016e). Partnerships. Retrieved from http://blog.wattpad.com/category/partnerships.

____. (2016f). Brand stories. Retrieved from http://business.wattpad.com.

Wilting Hope. (2015). School spirit. Chapter 1. The summer is breaking up with me [Comment]. *Wattpad*, 22 July. Retrieved from https://www.wattpad.com/79301784-school-spirit-book-1-1-the-summer-is-breaking-up/page/4.

CHAPTER FIVE

The Cultural Economy of Auteurship in Independent Publishing: The Symbolic Success of the Photobook *Ponte City*

James Graham
Middlesex University

Introduction

As far as book publicity events go, it was somewhat out of the ordinary. Alongside subscribers to And Other Stories, a UK-based independent publisher specializing in translations of non-English literary fiction into English, an academic network interested in the work of South African writer and editor Ivan Vladislavić had been invited to copy-edit a section of his 1999 novel *The Restless Supermarket* and submit it to the author himself to be judged. The winner of the '*Restless* Derby'[1] would be announced at a book reading at Sussex University as part of a publicity tour promoting the novel's UK publication in the summer of 2014. As a member of said network, and at that time working on a project that happened to explore Vladislavić's influence as an editor, I was thrilled at the prospect of him casting his expert eye on my own editorial craft. I dutifully submitted my effort and booked a ticket for the event.

How to cite this book chapter:
Graham, J. 2017. The Cultural Economy of Auteurship in Independent Publishing: The Symbolic Success of the Photobook *Ponte City*. In: Graham, J. and Gandini, A. (eds.). *Collaborative Production in the Creative Industries*. Pp. 69–85. London: University of Westminster Press. DOI: https://doi.org/10.16997/book4.e. License: CC-BY-NC-ND 4.0

Sadly I didn't win the '*Restless* Derby' (I'll be the first to admit I still have plenty to learn as an editor). But along with everyone else who attended the event, including Vladislavić as far as I could tell, I enjoyed it immensely. Not only were we able to live out the kind of metatextual joke that hallmarks Vladislavić's fiction, we also got to hear him talk candidly about the making of the novel. This revealed a great deal about the impact the transformation of Johannesburg in the 1990s (the central subject of the book) had on his own career as an editor and writer. More significantly for what follows, however, he also spoke about his role in the making of *Ponte City*: a photobook by Mikhael Subotzky and Patrick Waterhouse published in 2014 that takes as its subject Johannesburg's most iconic residential building. But he didn't just refer to this book – which ostensibly had nothing to do with the publication or publisher of *The Restless Supermarket* – in passing. Rather, the *Ponte City* book ended up taking centre stage as Vladislavić took great delight in unboxing its various component parts (see fig. 5.1) and then reassembling them, by way of explaining his integral role as what he termed it's 'creative editor' (Penfold, 2014; 'The Restless Derby', 2014). He explained how his work had involved sifting through the huge archive of material Subotzky and Waterhouse collated in their six-year documentary project, identifying thematic assemblages of materials (not just the photographs but a cornucopia of 'found' material discarded by the towers' residents over the years, ranging from the love letters of migrant workers to

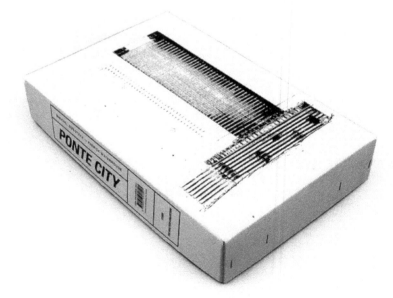

Figure 5.1: *Ponte City*, Steidl.

Figure 5.2: *Ponte City* 'unboxed'. The assemblage consists of a box file that contains within it: a 'traditional' photobook comprising of Subotsky's and Waterhouse's photographs and seventeen pamphlets written by a range of authors and illustrated with images of the photographs and found materials.

adverts for the apartment block), before writing three and commissioning (and of course editing) a further 14 short responses to accompany the main photobook section of the book (see fig. 5.3). He summarised his role as editor of *Ponte City* as 'conceptualizing and commissioning' the book, and he was clearly very proud of the result.[2] He was careful not to go as far as claiming co-authorship when he was asked about the extent of his creative input, but on a number of occasions he did refer to it as one of 'his' books. In addition to claiming a degree of creative ownership then, he also noted his pleasure in those aspects of the book's production with which he had not been directly involved, for instance in finding that the pamphlets he edited were designed and produced in such a way that they might be incorporated in the main photobook as interchangeable captions (see fig. 5.4).[3]

An event designed to cultivate an international consumer public (albeit a very modest one) around the UK publication of a celebrated South African author's 15-year-old novel turned into something quite different: a platform that promoted that and another book, authored by other people and produced by a different publisher. As much as Vladislavić was happy to talk about *The Restless Supermarket* and play along with the 'Restless Derby', he was evidently highly invested in this other book and keen to introduce it to 'his' public – something that the And Other Stories founder Stefan Tobler was more than happy to facilitate, as it was he who had brought the book to the event.

In February 2015, three months before *Ponte City* went on display at the Photographers Gallery in London alongside the other works shortlisted for the 2015 Deutsche Börse Photography Prize, the most prestigious of its kind in Europe, Vladislavić was awarded a $150,000 Windham-Campbell Prize from

Figure 5.3: 'Ponte City' installation at The Photographers Gallery London, April 2015.

Figure 5.4: *Ponte City* – 'by' Ivan Vladislavić (Author) and Ramon Pez (Author). Screenshot taken 21 August 2015.

Yale University for his fiction, specifically to provide the autonomy necessary to pursue his writing unburdened of financial constraints. In May 2015, Subotzky and Waterhouse were announced as winners of the Deutsche Börse, elevating them to the global pantheon of contemporary visual artists. Within months of being recognised by a similarly global prize that would free him from the editorial work that had subsidised his writing career to that point, an art work Vladislavić had contributed to as a 'creative editor' was similarly recognised and its own authors set on a related path to artistic autonomy.

Without going as so far as to suggest a direct causal relationship between these separate symbolic successes, my argument in this chapter is that their correlation tells us a great deal about the increasingly vital role – both practical and promotional – played by the *auteur* figure in neoliberal economies of collaborative production. In the discussion that follows I use the examples of Vladislavić's UK publisher, And Other Stories, and the publisher of *Ponte City*, doyen of independent photobook publishing Gerhard Steidl, to examine the collaborative production practices in independent book publishing in a 'post-digital age' – a term used by Alessandro Ludovico (2012) to account for contexts in which print is being revitalised rather than replaced. These examples illustrate how niche sectors of the publishing industry project collaborative production as the kind of 'art world' Howard Becker (1982) famously outlined: where 'the artist thus works in the centre of a network of cooperating people, all of whose work is essential to the final outcome' (p. 25). As I show in this chapter, however, this convivial – as opposed to Bourdieu's (1993) competitive – model of cultural production remains largely in thrall to a cultural economy dominated by the symbolic and economic capital invested in creative individuals (the author-brand, but increasingly also the *auteur*-brand), rather than the 'ethical value' (Arvidsson, 2013) generated among the networks through which the artwork is produced.

Digital convergence and collaboration in independent publishing: And Other Stories

The impact of what some commentators term 'digital disruption' (McQuivey, 2013, 2015) on the publishing industry is most visible in the convergence of previously discrete creative activities in the mainstream of this industry. For almost two decades the business of publishing has been creeping ever closer to the edge of a tectonic rift. On one side of this rift the work of the traditional publisher remains essentially unchanged: the making and taking of books to market. However, increasingly this means the creation, promotion and dissemination of books in dynamic digital formats, but also the licensing of content for adaptation in other media (Murray, 2012). Yet even as digital production becomes normalised loud voices continue to argue that demand for the physical book, and the valuable synaesthetic culture it embodies, remains strong and indeed underpins rather than is superseded by wholesale digitization. 'Books persist', as Rebecca Walkowitz (2016) recently put it. The return to profitability of the UK bookstore chain Waterstones in 2015 provides some evidence for the claims long-made by managing director James Daunt that, after the initial '—

disruption', there 'would be a natural point of equilibrium with digital reading – that it would overshoot, then come back and settle down.' For Daunt, the future of the physical book and its traditional formats is rosy: 'books that you want to treasure, look after and sit on your bookshelf – the physical book is a better thing. You are left with a memory; you've got something that has an enduring value.' (quoted in Ruddick, 2015).

On the brave new world the other side of the rift, however, the cultural and economic role of books and the mediatory function of the publisher have evolved decisively. To survive, let alone flourish in a marketplace dominated by mega-tech businesses such as Google, Apple and Amazon on the one hand, and threatened with usurpation from below by the 'disruptive innovation' of long tail economics (Christensen, 1997) on the other, the publisher must now seek to remain profitable through the curation as opposed merely to the production of content. A prominent advocate for this shift is the digital publisher Michael Bhaskar, his argument encapsulated in the transition from the title of his 2013 book *The Content Machine: Towards a Theory of Publishing from the Printing Press to the Digital Network* to his recently published *Curation: The Power of Selection in a World of Excess* (2016). Hal Robinson (2012) has similarly argued that far from being the harbinger of doom, digital in fact heralds a renaissance in publishing – not just a rebirth, rather a full blown reprise of the specifically collaborative creativity that defined the epochal shift of the Renaissance period. For the 'publishing ecosystem' to thrive in the digital age, publishers need to concentrate on 'using converging media, encouraging consumers to communicate, listening to consumers and cultivating the content they're interested in, and coordinating creative collaboration among all involved.'(p. 8) Drawing on Robinson's discussion, Stefen Tobler (2013), founder of And Other Stories and UK publisher for Ivan Vladislavić's fiction, has suggested that independent publishing houses are particularly well positioned to take advantage of each of these aspects of digitization.

Tobler (2013) describes the genesis of And Other Stories as a social enterprise: a not-for-profit publishing venture that looked to capitalise on the passionate investment of publishing professionals as well as readers in the field of international literary translations in order to cultivate a new subscription-based publishing model – and in so doing to 'curate' this neglected niche. Crucial to the sustainability of this model, according to Tobler (2013), has been finding 'a system of working that is genuinely open and collaborative.'(p. 9) He uses Robinson's description of an emergent 'digital publishing model' to describe how this works in practice, whereby "'... each content focused community, each Content Vertical, has the potential to establish its own brand in the eyes of the community it serves'" (Robinson, 2012, p. 13, cited in Tobler, 2013, p. 9). Tobler's observations from the helm of And Other Stories would seem to bear out the hypotheses offered by Bhaskar and Robinson. However, he also caveats his discussion with the observation that *offline* as opposed to *digital* networking has proven to be the key to effective collaboration in this context:

'[T]he discussion is freer, more honest, and deeper. Just because digital helps to organise people together does not mean it improves everything' (p. 9). And despite achieving significant symbolic successes in the first year of operation,[4] Tobler is candid about the risky commercial viability of such a specialist social enterprise within the larger ecosystem: 'while the new digital world opens up much trumpeted possibilities for small independents, capital is still required to take full advantage of those possibilities.' (10) He is referring to financial capital here, but in reflecting on how the 'content focused community' behind And Other Stories initially came together, it is evident that the viability of the enterprise hinged on their ability to leverage the aggregated social and cultural capitals produced through their creative collaboration, their 'labours of love', as he puts it:

> Translators, editors, designers, and other publishing folk could meet up to share their great unpublished foreign books, and talk about the best ways to publish them here. Everyone would be able to get on with their task from their own computer/home/heated public library. And there would be plenty of opportunities to be involved: accounting, reading, editing, translating, selling and marketing, fundraising, advising on business or on the editorial committee, party-throwing, web or book design, etc. (Tobler, 2009, p. 25, cited in Tobler, 2013, p. 8).

The nature and outcomes of the collaborative production Tobler describes in these short articles align closely with what Adam Arvidsson (2013) calls 'collaborative publics', the organisational form par excellence of neoliberal cultural economy:

> As ways of coordinating production, publics are different from markets and bureaucracies in that they allow for a wider range of concerns to serve as motivations. Knowledge workers are motivated by the prospect of economic gain, but also, as we move up the value chain, by possibilities for self-realisation, for having a meaningful impact, and for garnering peer recognition. (p. xi)

Such publics offer great potential for rebuilding and potentially also redistributing 'ethical value', in Arvidsson's discussion, and this is clearly the aspiration of Tobler and all those mutually invested in sustaining the success of And Other Stories. Authors who would otherwise not be known outside of their native language are introduced to international markets. The artistic value of translation as an integral creative input is recognised and promoted. This added value is returned to translators through increased legitimacy and fairer payment, and to the rest of the community in the self-realisation actuated through their contribution to the symbolic success of the collaborative enterprise – whether that is as a book designer doing work on the cheap (or for nothing), or a subscriber who gets to read their nominated author in English and see them potentially catapulted from peripheral obscurity to international recognition.

And Other Stories offers an instructive case study of the opportunities but also challenges presented to independent publishers by the collaborative cultures that attend digital convergence. In her discussion of this subject, Frania Hall (2014) explains that efforts to bridge the rift between the publisher as 'content machine' and as 'curator' requires acknowledgement of the nature and extent of existing collaboration among the creative disciplines that now converge in publishing. Hall notes that '[c]ollaborative activity has been part and parcel of publishing throughout its history and essential to innovation whether one is developing new products or finding new ways to market, preparing major new digital initiatives or developing new operations' (p. 22). But this new and dynamic environment means that:

> rather than collaborating with one main type of creative producer—the author—or with other suppliers from within the publishing industry space, like printers and software developers, publishers are now more often collaborating cross-creative sector, and doing so in new ways. The way that projects are financed, the number of players involved, the market places being considered, and the issues around ownership of intellectual property are becoming more complex in some of these new collaborations. The expected outcomes are also sometimes different; success and failure may be measured differently and collaborations may well be primarily exploratory rather than transactional. (p. 22)

Sarah Brouillette and Christopher Doody (2015) offer a more critical appraisal of this phenomenon. Publishing is no longer simply about book making or even the production of 'literature' as such. Rather, '[m]ost major publishers exist within enormous media conglomerates eager to see the literary endlessly repurposed.'(p. 99) In such a scenario the production – or rather, the relentless reproduction of the 'literary' in transmedia formats, most notably in the form of sprawling TV, film and video game franchises with their attendant merchandising and prosumer paratexts – requires unprecedented cooperation among a multitude of actors. Yet the collective nature of the creative labour responsible for creating the content is doubly occluded. First, through the marketing discourse of an industry that remains commercially wedded to the romantic notion of the author as solitary creative genius – or indeed as the author-brand, in the neoliberal manifestation of this trope. Second, by the mega-tech corporations who not only seek to exploit the value spread through collaborative publics, but who from their very outset have, as Arvidsson (2013) describes, constituted themselves around the accumulation of what he terms 'ethical capital' (p. 99).

In recent years numerous studies have critiqued the effect such dynamics have on the nature and experience of work across disciplines in the creative industries. These typically focus on the exploitation and self-exploitation involved in 'passionate work' (Arvidsson et al., 2010) and consider the ways and extent to which creative economy discourses normalise the exploitation of workers in a promotional culture that understands creative labour as a socially necessary mode of self-articulation, rather than solidarity (McGuigan 2014, Banks, Gill and Taylor 2014). These critiques have tended to focus on craft and screen-based media industries (e.g. Curtin's and Sanson's broadly-titled *Precarious Creative: Global Media, Local Labor* (2016) is almost exclusively concerned with television and cinema). One typically finds references to 'mass publishing' included in summary discussions (e.g. McKinlay and Smith, 2009, p. 11), but with the exception of Hesmondhalgh's and Baker's case study of work in the magazine industry (2009) the varied forms of cultural work and creative labour involved in publishing – especially as other creative disciplines increasingly converge in publishing – have received scant attention.

Tobler's (2013) précis of the activities and tasks required for a publishing startup – 'accounting, reading, editing, translating, selling and marketing, fundraising, advising on business or on the editorial committee, party-throwing, web or book design' (p. 8) – presents a scenario where book publication is made possible by a range of ancillary actors and activities not dissimilar to the 'collective activity' of what Howard Becker (1982) terms an 'art world'. 'Works of art, from this point of view,' writes Becker, 'are not the products of individual makers, "artists" who possess a rare and special gift. They are, rather, the joint products of all the people who cooperate via an art world's characteristic conventions to bring works like that in to existence.'(p. 35) Art worlds – not artists – produce art works. Just as importantly, they also confer aesthetic value. This is a defining characteristic of the collaborative labour harnessed through the collective activity of the art world: 'the interaction of all the involved parties produces a shared sense of the worth of what they collectively produce.'(p. 39) Yet despite all the while acknowledging that this art world is cleaved by an 'extensive division of labour' (p. 13), Becker chooses to overlook what happens when this collectively produced aesthetic value, much like the similarly hypostatized 'ethical value' intrinsic to collaborative publics in Arvidsson's argument (Zwick, 2015. p. 401), is transmuted into exchange value by cultural economies dominated by competition among artist- (or in this case, author- and auteur-) brands. Needless to say, as the literature on cultural work and creative labour invariably attests, the symbolic and economic rewards of this competition are unequally distributed across this division.

Gregory Sholette (2003) provides an important corrective to Becker's depoliticised account of art worlds. He describes the creative labour that undergirds the art world as being structurally – which is to say, necessarily – occluded. What Becker terms 'support activities' (p. 5) and 'support personnel' (p. 17), Sholette figures as 'creative dark matter': a multitude which 'makes up the bulk of the artistic activity produced in our post-industrial society ... [but which] ... is invisible primarily to those who lay claim to the management and interpretation of culture – the critics, art historians, collectors, dealers, curators and arts administrators.'(p. 4) However for Sholette there exists immanent liberatory potential within this dark matter, or 'shadow creativity' as he also refers to it, which he traces in examples of amateur and specifically *social* art practice that 'displays a degree of autonomy from the critical and economic structures of the art world' (p. 6).

The examples of networked, collaborative production in independent book and magazine production that Alessandro Ludovico discusses in *Post-Digital Print* (2012) share the same semi-autonomy, and to an extent also the immanent liberatory potential of Sholette's 'dark matter'. For Ludovico, cultural production that is socialized through the networks characteristic of independent publishing enables critique and resistance: 'artists use networks as a platform for critical reflection and intervention within the global distribution structure (thus playing a major role in re-conceptualising it).' (p. 11) These networked practices are at the same time also instrumental for independent publishing as the specifically *social* enterprise Tobler describes, which by leveraging social and cultural capital inevitably sees a trade off between critical autonomy and the imperatives of the market:

> "networking" also becomes synonymous with the "sharing" of cultural products – underexposed or otherwise invisible materials, whether printed or digital. Here, the individual reputation of each (known and shared) cultural product becomes a key factor in the success of a new business model established by the network. (p. 11)

As independent publishers respond to digital transformations by looking to incorporate and capitalise on this model of networked collaborative production, and even as they engage with participatory culture and acknowledge that the 'ethical value' of their literary products is co-produced among collaborative publics, what Alessandro Gandini (2016) terms 'reputational capital' – and so inevitably in this case the mark of the author-brand – retains a privileged position in the publishing ecosystem (Phillips 2014, p. 20).

Just as the title of John B. Thompson's study of the publishing industry, *Merchants of Culture* (2010), anticipates Brouillette's and Doody's discussion of contemporary publishing and the market imperative for adaptation, whereby the very notion of the literary has itself become a cultural industry, his exhaustive enquiry into the mechanics of how this plays out as publishers struggle against the forces of disintermediation points to the increasingly important *promotional* function played by the author-figure. In order to accumulate sufficient cultural capital to be consecrated as such, this figure must possess the strikingly paradoxical 'star' quality Joe Moran (2000) identifies in his discussion of North American authors in the late twentieth-century. For Moran, literary celebrities cannot simply be reduced to their exchange value – they are complex cultural signifiers who are repositories for all kinds of meanings, the most significant of which is perhaps the nostalgia for some kind of transcendent, anti-economic, creative element in a secular, debased, commercialized culture. (p. 9)

Only once they are elevated to this pedestal of supposed autonomy can the author become what Thompson terms the 'platform' – through which the gamut of their cultural and social capital might be commodified:

Essentially, platform is the position from which an author speaks – a combination of their credentials, visibility and promotability, especially through the media. It is those traits and accomplishments of the author that establish a pre-existing audience for their work, and that a publisher can leverage in the attempt to find a market for their book. (p. 86)

In what Thompson terms as 'a new economy of favours' (p.155), smaller, niche publishers look to carve a space in this new environment by leveraging their author-brand platforms as well as the social and cultural capital embedded in the products they promote. This is precisely what I witnessed at the 'Restless Derby' event in 2014. The most plausible reason for why Stefan Tobler (and also Vladislavić himself, for that matter) was happy for Vladislavić to promote *Ponte City* would be precisely because it leveraged Vladislavić's value as the kind of a cross-promotional 'platform' Thompson describes. It associated And Other Stories with the accumulated cultural capital of Vladislavić's career as a writer *and* as an influential editor who plays an instrumental role in both the realisation and consecration of artworks across a number of fields. Put a little less mechanistically, the event showed how the author was in fact an *auteur*.

Collaborative networks, auteur authorship: *Ponte City*

Vladislavić described *Ponte City* as one of 'his' books. Intriguingly, amazon.co.uk would seem to agree. Amazon's UK website lists the book as being 'by' – and so one might be led to believe, *authored by* – Ivan Vladislavić. But then, it also credits authorship to the book's designer, Ramon Pez, and is indexed to both of their Amazon UK author pages (see fig. 5.4). On Amazon's US site, by contrast, the authorship is credited to Subotzky and Waterhouse with no mention at all of Vladislavić or Pez. In yet another credit iteration, the book is catalogued in the British Library with the following description: 'Title: Ponte City : Mikhael Subotzky, Patrick Waterhouse /edited by Ivan Vladislavić; [book] designed by Ramon Pez ; the Walther Collection.' These crediting discrepancies may be attributed to different cataloguing methods or simply mistakes in the metadata supplied by the publisher. But that the book's editor and designer are credited so prominently in the metadata, and that *everyone* who had a hand in its making is given a 'production' credit in the book,[5] is a testament to how, in independent publishing generally and photobook publishing in particular, the typically hidden labour of what Becker might have termed 'support personnel' and Sholette calls 'shadow creativity' is increasingly acknowledged. And yet the copyright holder for the book is neither the prize-winning photographers nor the prize-winning editor, nor (one would imagine) the soon-to-be-awarded designer, but instead: Steidl Publishers.[6]

To those in this particular niche cultural industry the symbolic success of *Ponte City* no doubt confirms the powerful consecratory role of its pre-eminent publisher, Gerhard Steidl,[7] a self-proclaimed craftsmen devoted to the artistic success of his clients. Steidl began work as a designer and publisher in 1967 and learnt screen printing from no less than Andy Warhol, publishing the first book under his own imprint in 1972 (Steidl, 2014). In their history of the artist's book, Janneke Adema and Gary Hall (2013) argue that the medium of the book proved instrumental in the politicization of artistic practice in the 1960s and 70s counterculture, a context crucial for understanding Steidl's practices and ethos. The artist's book was democratic in the sense of being more widely available and accessible than traditional artistic outputs, but also radical in terms of offering an alternative exhibition space that fostered experimentation and artistic autonomy. As Steidl himself notes time and again in interviews, 'Books are commodities but can also be works of art if well made'. (Scheufelen, nd) Celebrated for its potential to dissolve distinctions between high and low culture, the artist's book was at the vanguard of what Adema and Hall, following Johanna Drucker (1995), term the 'democratic multiple': it's affordances are democratic, anti-institutional, but also reflexive: 'the book offered artists a space in which they were able to experiment with the materiality of the medium itself and with the practices that comprised it, and thus ultimately with the question of what constituted art and an art object.' (Adema and Hall, 2013, pp. 142–3) Steidl likewise insists the book is an inherently democratic medium and should not be produced in limited runs, but also that the books he makes are not 'industrial objects'. Under his exacting auteur-like command of the book-making process, the concept of the book is realized through the same assemblage of skills, materials and production technology 'as fine art printers use for limited edition prints' (Steidl, 2014). Steidl's seemingly contradictory belief in the nature of the book as democratic art object (in principle widely available yet designed as if for a field of restricted production) encapsulates the wider tensions observable in independent publishing.

The prominence given to the production network in the credits of *Ponte City* provides an example of how the independent publishing sector attempts to resist the (self-)exploitation of creative labour observable across the creative industries more generally (which, as discussed, increasingly converge in publishing). Very rarely are such books made with commercial success in mind. For those involved in their production – from the artists who provide the primary content to the craft professionals who play their part in assembling the book, aided and abetted by the intermediaries whose work it is to connect, cultivate and consecrate – the co-operative activity involved in realizing the artwork *as a published book* is integral to its aesthetic value. The high production values typical of this publishing format do not merely add an appealing lustre to what is an already rarefied art object (or tactility, or scent, though these are essential synaesthetic ingredients according to Steidl (Scheufelen nd)). Rather, they are intrinsic to the creation and circulation of value in a cultural economy that is structurally reliant on the collaborative productive input of a wide range of agents, intermediaries and institutions, and yet is dominated by the symbolic power of the auteur-figure as a cross-promotional platform.

Conclusion

The example of the social enterprise publisher And Other Stories – committed to the curation of translated literary fiction that might otherwise never come to the attention of English speakers – suggests that the auteur-figure serves a vital purpose. Coalescing in this figure is the aggregate cultural and social capital – the platform – the independent publisher needs to cultivate the kind of productive consumer public, and indeed benefit from the nascent 'ethical economy', that Adam Arvidsson (2013) proposes. The success of Ivan Vladislavić in the case of *Ponte City*, as an auteur as opposed to 'just' an editor or even an author in the traditional sense, provides grounds for optimism. Having gained financial autonomy through a prize that consecrated him as an author in his own right, he continues to edit and invest in the work of others through his editorial craft and participation in joint projects made possible through the collaborative cultures and network practices of independent publishing. As an *auteur* he continues to provide a platform through which others might share in his success.

Steidl's practice of providing full production credits for his books similarly projects independent publishing as the kind of cooperative art world Howard Becker described. But Tobler's cautionary note concerning the necessity for a bare minimum of financial capital for the sustainability of And Other Stories, and Steidl's relationship with patrons ranging from Karl Largerfeld to the investment banker-turned private art collecter Artur Walther, remind us that this nascent 'ethical economy' is structurally imbricated in a neoliberal cultural economy where the symbolic and the economic dividends of ethical and aesthetic investments are typically both privatized and financialised.

It is in the making and promotion of photobooks such as *Ponte City* that we find perhaps the greatest concentration of intersecting modes of collaborative production across the creative industries: the 'post-digital' network practices of independent book and magazine publishing; the 'collaborative culture' but also the 'economy of favours' operative among smaller publishers in the publishing ecosystem; the aesthetic valorization intrinsic to the collective activity of an art world; and the reputational or ethical economy that emerges when this collective activity is expanded to incorporate a productive consumer public. Yet at the same time this case study also reveals the continued structural role played by the art world's 'shadow creativity' – the division of labour that is occluded precisely so the auteur figure can provide a coherent promotional platform to leverage the aggregate social and cultural capital embedded in the artwork.

Notes

1 The joke here being that fans would carry out the same project that animates the novel's anti-hero, retired editor Aubrey Terle – what he calls 'The Proofreaders Derby' (Reid, 2014).

2 This was not a one off. Before coming to the UK, Vladislavić gave an interview for the South African *Leadership* magazine where he includes *Ponte City* among the books he has helped 'conceptualise and commission' (Penfold 2014).

3 This conceit amplifies the design rationale provided in the introduction to the photobook, illustrating how over its 30-year history the building has served as a monumental screen on to which has been projected some of the city's most pervasive and powerful social myths; but also how it might be encountered otherwise – as a frame for the realization of dreams and desires of those who have actually lived in it, as well as the fears and anxiety of those who have not. Similar to the *Restless Supermarket* in some ways, *Ponte City* doesn't just document the geographical and social changes in Johannesburg from the twilight of apartheid to the present moment, it deconstructs the mythic layers of meaning the building has accrued by asking readers to engage in the writerly act of reconstructing the social history it embodies.

4 'Our first four authors were published in late 2011. From those four authors, Villalobos's *Down the Rabbit Hole* was the first translation ever to be shortlisted for the Guardian First Book Award and his 2013 *Quesadillas* was a winner of an English PEN Writers in Translation Award, while Deborah Levy's *Swimming Home* made the Man Booker Prize shortlist in 2012, and her 2013 story collection *Black Vodka* was shortlisted for the Frank O'Connor International Short Story Award.' (Tobler, 2013, p. 8).

5 At least, one presumes the following credits, appearing on the final page of the photobook, are exhaustive:

Editing: Ivan Vladislavić
Book Design: Ramon Pez

Research: Nadiva Schraibman
Interview transcription: Minky Schlesinger
Scans: Tjorven Bruyneel/Tony Meintjes
Separations: Steidl's digital darkroom
Production and printing: Steidl, Gottingen
Additional Production: Chantelle Booysen/Serame Metsing
Caitlin Pieters/Rebecca Simpson
(*Ponte City* 2014, p. xx)

6   In the main photobook section of the book and the 17 accompanying pamphlets the same copyright details are provided:

© 2014 Mikhael Subotsky and Patrick Waterhouse for images
© 2014 individual authors for texts
© 2014 original copyright holders for archival material
© 2014 Steidl Publishers for this edition

7   As well as the investment banker-turned art patron Artur Walther, who also receives credit for co-producing the book with Steidl – which no doubt means he underwrote what would have been extremely high production costs. Walther is reputed to have assembled the largest collection of African photography in the world (Doran 2015) and in 2011 nominated Subotzky and Waterhouse for the Rencontres d'Arles Discovery Award – which they duly won – for *Ponte City*. Although the book had not been published and the project itself not yet completed according to the timeframe given in the photobook introduction, 'Ponte City' was first installed at The Walther Collection in 2011 as part of the 'Appropriated Landscapes' exhibition curated by Corinne Disrennes (2011).

References

Adema, J. and Hall, G. (2013) The Political Nature of the Book: On Artists' Books and Radical Open Access (co-authored with Janneke Adema), New Formations, Number 78, Summer.

Arvidsson, A. (2013). *The Ethical Economy: Rebuilding Value After the Crisis*. Columbia, OH: Columbia University Press.

Arvidsson, A., Serpica, N., Malossi, G. (2010). Passionate work? Labour conditions in the Milan fashion industry. *Journal for Cultural Research*, 14(3), 259–309.

Banks, M., Gill, R. and Taylor, S. (2014). *Theorizing Cultural Work*. London: Routledge.

Becker, H. (1982). *Art Worlds*. Berkeley, CA: University of California Press.

Bourdieu, P., & Johnson, R. (1993). *The Field of Cultural Production: Essays on Art and Literature*. Columbia, OH: Columbia University Press.

Bhaskar, M. (2016). *Curation: The Power of Selection in a World of Excess*. — London: Little, Brown

_____. (2013). *The Content Machine: Towards a Theory of Publishing from The Printing Press to the Digital Network*. New York: Anthem Press..

Brouillette, S. and Doody, C. (2015). The literary as a cultural industry. In Kate Oakley and Justin O'Conner (Eds.), *The Routledge Companion to the Cultural Industries*. London: Routledge.

Christensen, C. M. (1997) *The Innovator's Dilemma: When New Technologies Cause Great Firms to Fail*. Boston, Mass: Harvard Business School Press.

Curtin, M. and Sanson, K. (2016). *Precarious Creativity: Global Media, Local Labor*. Oakland, CA: University of California Press.

Disrennes, C. (2011). Appropriated landscapes. The Walther Collection, Neu-Ulm. Exhibition.

Doran, A. (2015). Photographic Memory: Artur Walther has built what may be the world's largest and most important private collection of African photography'. Online, 11 June. Retrieved from http://www.artnews.com/2015/11/06/photographic-memory-artur-walther-has-what-may-be-the-worlds-largest-and-most-important-private-collection-of-african-photography-2.

Drucker, J. (1995) *The Century of Artists' Books*. New York, NY: Granary Books.

Gandini, A. (2016). *The Reputation Economy: Understanding Knowledge Work in Digital Society*. Palgrave Macmillan: London.

Hall, F. (2014). Digital convergence and collaborative cultures: Publishing in the context of the wider creative industries. *Logo, vol. 25 (4): 20-31*. DOI: 10.1163/1878-4712-11112055

Hesmondhalgh, D. and Baker, S. (2009). "A very complicated version of freedom": Conditions and experiences of creative labour in three cultural industries. *Poetics* 38, 4–20. DOI: 10.1016/j.poetic.2009.10.001

Ludovico, A. (2012). *Post-Digital Print: The Mutation of Publishing since 1894*. Santa Monica, CA: Ram Publications.

McGuigan, J. (2014). The neoliberal self. *Journal of Current Cultural Research*, 6: 1, 223–40.

McKinlay, A., & Smith, C. (eds). (2009). *Creative Labour: Working in the Creative Industries*. Basingstoke: Palgrave Macmillan.

McQuivey, J. (2015). Publishing leaders happily disrupt themselves to avoid being disrupted. In Jeremy Greenfield (Ed.) *Finding the Future of Digital Publishing*. F+W Media Inc. Digital Book World..

_____. (2013). *Digital Disruption: Unleashing the Next Wave of Innovation*. Amazon Publishing.

Moran, J. (2000). *Star Authors: Literary Celebrity in America*. London: Pluto Press.

Murray, S. (2012). *The Adaptation Industry: The Cultural Economy of Contemporary Literary Adaptation*. New York and London: Routledge.

Nash, R. (2013). What is the business of literature? *Virginia Quarterly Review*, 89: 2. Retrieved from http://www.vqronline.org/articles/what-business-literature.

Penfold, G. (2014). 'Ivan Vladislavić: the most famous unknown', *Leadership*, 1 July. Retrieved from http://www.leadershiponline.co.za/articles/ivan-Vladislavić-11579.html.

Phillips, A. (2014) *Turning the Page: The Evolution of the Book*. Abingdon: Routledge.

Photographers Gallery, The (2015). 'About the Photography Prize'. *Photographers Gallery*, 10 April. Retrieved from http://thephotographersgallery.org.uk/3180/About-The-Photography-Prize/890

Reid, K. (2014 June 3). Register for the 2014 Derby – from 'The Restless Supermarket' by Ivan Vladislavić. Retrieved from: https://africainwords.com/2014/06/03/call-for-entries-the-2014-restless-derby-of-the-restless-supermarket-by-ivan-Vladislavić-fame/

"The Restless Derby." Promotional event to support the UK publication of *The Restless Supermarket* and *Double Negative* (And Other Stories), with Ivan Vladislavić in conversation with Katie Reid, held at the University of Sussex. 24 June 2014.

Robinson, H. (2012.) Digital publishing: Does it herald a renaissance for the industry?, *Logos: Journal of the World Publishing Community*, 23: 4, 7–20.

Ruddick, G. (2015). Waterstones prepares for new chapter as bookshop chain returns to profitability. *Guardian*, 20 November. Retrieved from http://www.theguardian.com/business/2015/nov/20/waterstones-profit-books-amazon.

Scheufelen, (nd). The scent of books: interview with Gerhard Steidl. *Scheufelen.com*. Retrieved from http://www.scheufelen.com/en/phoenix-ausgabe-0212/the-scent-of-books-interview-with-gerhard-steidl.html

Sholette, G. (2003). Dark matter: activist art and the counter-public sphere. Retrieved from http://www.gregorysholette.com/wp-content/uploads/2011/04/05_darkmattertwo1.pdf.

Steidl, G (2014). Gerhard Steidl: "I Turn Everything Upside Down" *The Talks*. 7 May. Retrieved from http://the-talks.com/interview/gerhard-steidl.

Tobler, S. (2013). And Other Stories: literary publishing as a social enterprise. *Logos: Journal of the World Publishing Community*, 24: 4, 7–11.

____. (2009). Supply + Demand + Magic. *In Other Words*, 33, 24–7.

Walkowitz. R. L. (2016). The persistence of books. *World Literature Today*. May. Retrieved from http://www.worldliteraturetoday.org/2016/may/persistence-books-rebecca-l-walkowitz.

Zwick, D. (2013). Utopias of ethical economy: A response to Adam Arvidsson. *Ephemera: Theory and Politics in Organization*, 13: 2, 393–405.

CHAPTER SIX

From the Workshop of J. J. Abrams: Bad Robot, Networked Collaboration, and Promotional Authorship

Leora Hadas

University of Nottingham

Whether 'New golden age' (Leopold, 2013) or 'Peak TV' (Paskin, 2015) – whatever glowing accolades cultural commentators now choose to use, all describe television in the United States as going from strength to strength. For a sustained number of years now, critics and popular opinion alike has celebrated a qualitative transformation in the output of an industry that has struggled for years to shed the image of a 'vast wasteland' (Minow, 1961). In critical and academic circles alike, credit for these exciting developments and the transformation of US television has tended to focus on a specific feature of the contemporary industry: the figure of the showrunner, television's new *auteur* (Martin, 2013).

The emergence of the showrunner-as-auteur has provided US television with a crucial source of cultural legitimacy, one traceable back to Bourdieu's concept of the '"charisma" ideology' (1980, p. 262) at work in judgements of artistic value. Shyon Baumann (2007) has analysed how film found legitimation as

---

How to cite this book chapter:

Hadas, L. 2017. From the Workshop of J. J. Abrams: Bad Robot, Networked Collaboration, and Promotional Authorship. In: Graham, J. and Gandini, A. (eds.). *Collaborative Production in the Creative Industries*. Pp. 87–103. London: University of Westminster Press. DOI: https://doi.org/10.16997/book4.f. License: CC-BY-NC-ND 4.0

an art form in the 1960s through the celebration of autonomous film artists. The showrunner fills for television the same function of elevating 'an artist of unique vision whose experiences and personality are expressed through story-telling craft, and whose presence in cultural discourses functions to produce authority for the forms with which he is identified' (Newman & Levine, 2012, p. 38). Described as '[a] curious hybrid of starry-eyed artists and tough-as-nails operational managers' (Collins, 2007), the showrunner takes the positions of both 'creative' and 'suit', acting as both the creative leader of a show – head writer, manager of the writers' room, ultimately responsible for plot and character decisions – and its executive producer, thus also being its representative and advocate with the network. The show is therefore presented as the expression of one person's singular, authentic vision, an exciting development from popular perception of television as entertainment by factory and formula, which have hounded the medium in the past (Mittell, 2015, p. 95).

As John Thornton Caldwell (2008) has argued in his tellingly named Industrial Auteur model, the creation of a television show is inevitably a complex collaborative endeavour, characterised by a multiplicity of voices. Auteurist discourse, however – to return to Bourdieu's observations – obscures the logic of production in the process of legitimation. Since the early 2000s, HBO has won fame, respect, and crucially also ratings by advertising the creative freedom it afforded early showrunners such as David Simon and Alan Ball, in comparison with broadcast television's unfortunate reputation for executive meddling (Feuer, 2007). The showrunner-auteur thus emerged as 'a branding strategy for upscale television as it contrasts the authored series against an undifferentiated mass' (Newman and Levine, 2012, p. 42). Nowadays, however, prominently visible showrunners are everywhere, on cable channels, broadcast networks, and netlets alike, in all cases serving in a similar auteurist capacity.

This has provided TV with its own 'commerce of auteurism', to paraphrase Timothy Corrigan (1991), in which author figures are deployed as a promotional device. In contrast with the traditional anonymity of TV creators (Pearson, 2011), today many showrunners are celebrities for whom the function of being the public face of their show is a crucial third hat alongside their roles as writer-producer. Increased visibility and ability to interact with viewers, for example through social and digital media, contribute to the association between *visionary* and *vision*. In this way they create a focal point for audience engagement, which can sometimes travel beyond the one show, as for example in the fans that have followed creator Joss Whedon from *Buffy the Vampire Slayer* (WB/UPN, 1997–2003) to *Firefly* (Fox, 2002). Similarly, shows marketed as the brainchildren of such creators advertise their names as a stamp of approval and quality, in fact a brand name (Mittell, 2015, p. 97). The showrunner figure thus stands at the core of contemporary American television's use of promotional authorship – the practice of applying author figures and authorship discourses for the branding, distinction, and marketing of content. Newman and Levine argue that in order to moonlight as auteur, it is usually necessary for the showrunner to also be the creator of the show (2012, p. 39).

Increasingly, however, it seems that the showrunner-auteur pedestal is being shaken by structural and economic forces within the industry which render the model of creator-showrunner driving a single passion project increasingly unviable. On May 2014, following the announcement of greenlit new shows at Fox and NBC, *Deadline* reported that more than half of those shows were still without showrunners, and that networks were 'scrambling' to find showrunners for new series and often encountering difficulties in finding people with the appropriate background and experience (Andreeva, 2014). As original content online becomes more prevalent via services such as Amazon and Netflix, television networks attempt to keep up by turning to event programming and to short-form content that reject the seasons system and long-term seriality. Both these formats, with their appeal to respectability and the ideals of quality television, call for powerful showrunners and push the demand ever upward. Yet despite the Writers' Guild of America West running a showrunner training programme since 2005, showrunner supply continues to fall short. The sheer complexity and amount of responsibilities and functions involved in the role – 'creative', 'suit', 'PR agent', and 'auteur' in one – mean that even decorated veterans of the industry are not necessarily qualified.

The industry abhors a vacuum, and in recent years American television production frequently sees new variations on the relationship between visionary and vision: shows swapping out showrunners, 'hired-gun' showrunners working on shows where they are not the original creator, and even shows marketed via the promotional authorship of a figure who is neither creator nor showrunner. However, auteurist ideas are powerful and entrenched, especially as they provide a counterweight to the traditional accusation, from Minow to Mittell, of television's creative poverty. Hence, as new models are deployed, they must grapple with the need to apply the auteurist discourse of singularity, creative control, authenticity, and vision to industrial realities of collaboration and complex work.

This chapter focuses on a particularly successful instance of such grappling, in which the practices of collaboration are brought back under the promotional aegis of auteurism through the application of what may be termed a master studio or workshop model of promotional authorship. As my case study I use one of contemporary American media's greatest author-brand names: J. J. Abrams, multihyphenate writer-director-producer of film and television, visionary leader of the tightly knit creative cabal that has emerged from his production company, Bad Robot.

'When They Say It's a J. J. Thing, That's Cool with Me': Collaboration and subsumption

J. J. Abrams has a long-standing reputation for repeatedly working with the same individuals both above and below the line. His collaborative practices date back to the transition from his first television series, *Felicity* (WB, 1998–2002), to his second, *Alias* (ABC, 2001–6), where he had brought with him actress Jennifer Garner and director Jack Bender. It was with his breakout hit *Lost* (ABC, 2004–10), however, that the trickle became a torrent. No less than six above the line crewmembers carried over from *Felicity* and *Alias* – Bender, producer Bryan Burk, writers Drew Goddard, Jeff Pinkner, and the writing partners Edward Kitsis and Adam Horowitz. Some seventeen *Lost* cast and crew members have gone on to collaborate with Abrams again, as have *Felicity* and *Alias* alumni that had no part in *Lost*, and others from Abrams' cinematic directorial debut *Mission: Impossible III*. Still others, such as *Fringe* (Fox, 2008–13) and *Almost Human* (Fox, 2013–14) showrunner J. H. Wyman, were picked up even later but have remained in the fold. The complicated task of mapping Abrams' collaborators results in 25 names that to date have moved in and out of his orbit, and the number grows when considering people who have collaborated with him and then gone on to work with his other collaborators in an ever-expanding game of six degrees of separation. While studies of media labour often emphasize the crucial importance of networking in Hollywood (see for example Hesmondhalgh and Baker, 2010), the repeated connections and overt identification of Abrams' collaborators with his brand ensures the 'cabal' stands out.

It is the nature of the collaborations, however, that distinguishes this clique from the practices and networks of other creators. The secret to Abrams' empire is the quintessential function of the author name as brand name, which allows a networked group of collaborators to present the image of a unified creative vision, and enjoy the legitimacy conferred through auteurist discourse. To speak of J. J. Abrams is to speak of his production company Bad Robot, which has delivered no less than 11 television series (plus three failed pilots, and three unaired pilots in the pipeline) to various networks between 2001–16, as well as producing 12 films. Abrams is credited as executive producer on each and every one of those projects, but it is hard to say how much direct involvement he has had in most of them. He has written a mere four of Bad Robot's films (*Joy Ride* (Dahl, 2001), *Super 8*, and writing credits as part of a team on *MI:3* and *Star Wars: The Force Awakens*) and directed five (*MI:3* and *Super 8* once more, as well as the two *Star Trek* films and *SW:TFA*). On television his record is even spottier. He is credited as co-creator, writer, and director on his first two series, *Felicity* and *Alias*, and as co-creator of *Lost*, for which he co-wrote and directed the pilot. However, following this and the unaired pilot *The Catch*, he holds only executive producer credit on the vast majority of Bad Robot's projects – he is credited only as co-creator of *Undercovers* (NBC, 2010) and *Fringe*, to which he has contributed nine scripts in total, and no directorial involvement. The people claiming showrunner credit for Bad Robot's myriad shows are all Abrams' frequent and numerous collaborators: Damon Lindelof (*Lost*), Pinkner and Wyman (*Fringe*), Jonathan Nolan and Greg Plageman (*Person of Interest*, CBS, 2011–), Elizabeth Sarnoff and then Jennifer Johnson (*Alcatraz*, Fox, 2012), Wyman again on *Almost Human* and a succession of showrunners in the brief four-month life of *Believe* (NBC, 2013–14). *Revolution* (NBC, 2012–14) went one step further and employed a showrunner with his own significant claim to fame in the person of Eric Kripke, creator of the long-lived *Supernatural* (The WB/CW, 2005–).

It is in the promotion of Bad Robot shows, however, that all collaborating participants are rendered invisible, or at best are diminished. A look at the promotion of the studio's many shows reveals how, without fail, the focus is on Abrams, with even the name Bad Robot itself making very few appearances. The trend begins with *Lost*, where the season one DVD trailer announces the show to be 'from J. J. Abrams, the creator of *Alias*'. *Fringe* shows a mixture, advertised as 'from J. J. Abrams and the writers of *Transformers* Roberto Orci and Alex Kurtzman' in one trailer, and 'from J. J. Abrams creator of *Lost* and *Alias*' in another (Abrams' actual position as *Lost* co-creator is given a promotion). An NBC behind the scenes feature/trailer on *Undercovers* 'sum[s] up Wednesdays [when the show is due to air] in two words […] "J. J." – neglecting even the director's surname, on the assumption that the audience will know who 'J. J.' is – and the show's other promos all mention Abrams and omit co-creator Josh Reims. Trailers for *Person of Interest* deign to mention creator Jonathan Nolan as the screenwriter of *The Dark Knight*. However, their overall tone is better exemplified by the promo starring the cast of *The Big Bang Theory* (CBS, 2007–), which glosses over Nolan's involvement before excitedly namedropping half a dozen past Abrams projects. The *Alcatraz* trailers mention 'executive producer J. J. Abrams' and the nameless 'producers of *Lost*', while that of *Revolution* mentions pilot episode director Jon Favreau besides Abrams but leaves out Kripke. An especially telling absence is that of the one collaborator who has, in fact, been present for all of Abrams' projects: Bryan Burk, Bad Robot's co-founder and executive vice president. Burk's complete invisibility, in spite of the fact that he shares executive producer credit with Abrams on all Bad Robot shows, serves to drive home the fact that the careful construction of promotional discourse is intrinsic to the auterism of Bad Robot shows.

Subsumption is a key part of auteurist discourse, which relies on an immediate, intimate connection between auteur and artwork: it is perfectly run-of-the-mill for the author's name to stand in for the dozens or hundreds of people working on a movie set. Yet here, uniquely, one creator's name brings together a constellation of projects that have no connection *beyond the presence of that name*. This is even a degree removed from the 'authorship by management' that Mittell refers to as typical of the showrunner's work, which 'filter[s] the contributions of performers, designers, editors, and network executives, but the responsibility for the end product rests with the showrunner' (2015, p. 91). Abrams himself admits that he is hands-off with the work of other creators under the Bad Robot banner, saying 'When we hear a pitch we like and develop a show […] we don't get involved with people who need to be babysat.' (Molloy, 2013) In the end, however, it is his signature that is touted in the promotion of the project and connects it to the exalted family of other projects that bear the same signature as their authenticating mark and proof of lineage. His name, as a selling point and a promise, obscures the involvement of other creators and creates the illusion of a genius that is a bottomless creative font. Being tied directly to various projects allows him to legitimise them all as works of equal standing, regardless of his differing level of involvement. As Wyman himself puts it, 'just from the sale aspect, he's such a force to be reckoned with [...] when they say it's a J. J. thing, that's cool with me' (ibid).

Yet Abrams must also be cautious with his brand name, as we learn from the trailer of the Bad Robot produced *Morning Glory* (Michel, 2010), from which Abrams' name is conspicuously absent. *Morning Glory*, a comedy with neither fantasy elements nor any central mystery, was advertised as 'from the screenwriter of *The Devil Wears Prada*' and 'the director of *Notting Hill*', both left nameless, so that neither director Roger Michel nor Abrams get direct credit. It seems that Abrams' producer credit had no place in promoting a movie so removed from his usual fare, identifying the limit point of the brand name. The projects that are brought together under Abrams' aegis do all have something more in common: a broad generic definition as telefantasy and, as I discuss further, an emphasis on a storytelling and pop cultural sensibility. Functioning as a brand name, Abrams' name must guarantee a certain known set of qualities. Without doing so, it is displaced and meaningless.

'The J. J. Abrams Business'

Abrams' involvement as producer supersedes the more standard ascriptions of authorship in both film and television, where it is normally the director and showrunner respectively who are understood to have the most creative control. The promotion of Bad Robot shows complicates the centrality of the showrunner-auteur to the post-network era as discussed for example by Emily Nussbaum (2009). Even the 2013 edition of *The Hollywood Reporter*'s top showrunners list refers to Jonathan Nolan and Greg Plageman (*Person of Interest*) and Eric Kripke (*Revolution*) as 'Team J. J. Abrams', complete with Abrams's photo (THR Staff, 2013). This shift in focus suggests that, while there is indeed greater visibility of television creators and an increasingly prevalent idea of creative leadership in television, the question of who takes credit for this leadership is still being contested.

Series where the promotional authorship function of the showrunner is overtaken by the brand name of a producer are uncommon but not unknown. Television is following in the footsteps of film in this regard, where directors-turned-producers from Spielberg to Tarantino, as well as superstar producers such as Jerry Bruckheimer, have a long history of 'presenting' a film. *The Hollywood Reporter*'s 2013 list featured two more 'teams' following the similar logic of an executive producer and studio head overseeing a number of shows each run by its own creative team of current and former collaborators. 'Team Chuck

Lorre' in the comedy category is composed of Don Reo and Jim Patterson on *Two and a Half Men* (CBS, 2003–15), Steve Molaro on *The Big Bang Theory*, Al Higgins on *Mike & Molly* (CBS, 2010–) and Eddie Gorodetsky on *Mom* (CBS, 2013-). 'Team Greg Berlanti' in drama includes Andrew Kreisberg and Marc Guggenheim on *Arrow* (The CW, 2012–) and Phil Klemmer on *The Tomorrow People* (The CW, 2013–14).

In both cases, the situation differs somewhat from Abrams', as evidenced by the lesser presence granted to either men in the official promotion of their associated shows: while popular in the press, neither get name credit and are only mentioned in terms of previous successes in trailers. Use of their names is inextricable from an association with a particular network, as well as conditional upon other factors. Lorre, an active television producer since the early 1990s, rightly belongs to an earlier generation of producers and has had a significantly longer time to build up his presence in the industry, while Berlanti is tied to the 'Arrowverse', The CW's shared televised universe based on DC Comics properties. Nonetheless, the decision by *The Hollywood Reporter* to present them in similar templates suggests the emergence of a new paradigm.

The thinking here is no longer in terms of the single show, its production and creative leadership, but in terms of ownership of 'a whole block of programming', as the list says. The role of showrunner is not necessarily reduced in responsibility, as shows still have to be run on a day to day basis, yet the emphasis in promotional discourse – on brand name and creative visionary – shifts to the head of the production studio, or the central node of the collaborative network. In the case of Abrams, this shift is tied in with the search for larger and more expansive franchises and for brands that operate across media. Here is a form of authorship suitable to an industry that thinks in terms of conglomeration, horizontal integration, and large-scale exploitation of assets. The commercial imperative for broadly transferrable IP, across projects and platforms, is already understood as standard media industry practice, for example with Marvel Studios announcing itself as being 'not in the movie business, we're in the "Iron Man" business right now' (Boucher, 2008). Here, similarly, NBC can announce itself to be 'in the J. J. Abrams business' (Rose, 2011), with the author name acting as an exploitable, transferrable brand.

The showrunner's position of absolute creative authority, in this scenario, takes on the cast of a property manager. This is not however to reduce the showrunner position to merely executing another's vision, which would undermine the auteurist discourse on which its promotional function is based. *The Hollywood Reporter* frames Nolan, Plageman, and Kripke as his 'primetime partners', which in turn plays a key part in their ability to arrive and stay on air. The relationship between the creative leadership of a show, and the brand power that it relies upon in its relationship with both industry and audiences, grows more complex. However, unlike the normal tension evident between 'creatives' and 'suits', this relationship between showrunner and brand-name producer is not characterised by an oppositional dichotomy between art and commerce, authenticity and executive meddling. If anything, the power of Abrams' bankable name and the Bad Robot affiliation create a buffer between the showrunners on individual shows and their network overseers. Despite differences of rank, Abrams and 'his' showrunners portray themselves very much as *collaborators*, making extensive use of a language of meeting of minds and similarity of interests, as well as stressing cooperation as a creative ethos. As *Variety* describes it in a 2009 article about Abrams' 'fanboy family':

> Abrams, Kurtzman, Orci, Lindelof and Burk spent many hours together hashing out the basic story for the *Star Trek* reboot – knowing what a tricky assignment they had on their hands – while Kurtzman and Orci would bring the group pages to review as they progressed on the screenplay. [...] Says Orci: "The best idea wins. Collaboration wins. It's not about individual achievement when we get together." (Littleton, 2009)

The article, a lengthy feature on Abrams and co., provides an overview and a discursive framework of creative relationships not only within Bad Robot, but throughout the network of media creators that '[speak] Abrams' language, a dialect of *Star Wars*, comicbooks, Steven Spielberg's canon, *The Twilight Zone*, *Super Mario Brothers*, Stephen King and other common influences and obsessions'. This list of influences suggests the qualities of Abrams' author brand – science fiction and fantasy, adventure, geekdom, and a kind of pop culture nostalgia – which he himself has articulated on multiple occasions, for example his 2007 TED talk (TED2007, 2008) . All of these are now described as essential parts of his collaborators' identities, as much as they are part of his. *Variety* continues to stress the cohesion of the group:

> Out of such shared visions, the Abrams footprint has expanded from TV to film, with his productions proving to be a wellspring of writers, directors and producers who have become major biz players in their own right. He's been a magnet for like-minded creatives who share his professional DNA [...] While Abrams' alumni now have no shortage of opportunities separately, they remain a tightly knit creative cabal that continues to work frequently with one another. [...] "What's made us all come together in a way is that we recognize each other as long-lost brothers", Kurtzman says of his and Orci's strong connection with Abrams and Lindelof. "We were influenced by the same things growing up. [...] We come to story from a similar place." (Littleton, 2009)

The emphasis on authentic personal and creative connection serves to defuse issues of power and characterise all involved in the role of 'creatives', regardless of the nature of their involvement with individual projects. It functions well to erase, or at least obscure, questions of individual self-expression by rendering all participants as sharing a mind-set, a set of interests and obsessions that replenishes the creative font. Though the family 'fans out', their shared core values make them able custodians of each other's ideas. Part of Abrams' reputed talent, and as such his brand, becomes the ability to choose his collaborators, verify, and ultimately vouch for their suitability to the creative network. His role includes the maintenance of a coherent vision and image for the whole family, something that can be seen in the language of training often used to describe his collaborative relationships. The *Variety* feature used the term 'Abrams alumni' and references the 'lessons learned' on his shows by creators who have since ventured out on their own. In the network of mostly-equals that results, Abrams is able to function as a central node. He need not be personally involved in the collaboration at all. As Edward Kitsis says:

> We've become great friends with a lot of people who've worked on other J. J. projects [...] Even if you've never worked with them, you can call them up and say, "Can I get your opinion on something?" (Littleton, 2009)

It almost goes unsaid that there results a distinct creative identity for Bad Robot, a house style of sorts that informs audience expectations and understanding. It is likely no coincidence that the most successful Bad Robot shows seem to share the 'mystery box' style of storytelling that Abrams emphasizes in his TED talk as key to his work. All share a reliance on a central mystery and a multi-layered, hyper-complex narrative full of leads, clues, and red herrings. *Fringe, Person of Interest*, and *Revolution,* the three Bad Robot shows that have so far enjoyed the longest runs, all followed this formula, with similar characteristics in their premise of cutting edge technology gone awry and modern fears of science, surveillance, and technological dependence. Abrams applies this logic in his attempt to justify the failure of *Undercovers*, telling *Seriable*:

> The conceit of the show was to do a much more frivolous, fun show, but ultimately, I think it was just too frivolous and too simple, and we didn't go deep enough. We were really desperately trying to stay away from mythology and complexity and intensity and too much serious, dark storytelling and, ultimately, that's not necessarily what I do best. I think audiences felt that it was a little bit lacking. (Roco, 2011)

Abrams' explanation hinges on the idea that the studio had strayed outside its comfort zone, and that the audience was naturally not receptive to a Bad Robot show that was 'desperately trying' to eschew the Bad Robot brand qualities of complexity and mythology. There are a number of other aspects to the network's creative identity, which Abrams and others have outlined clearly: high concept science fiction and fantasy, a mixture of action and emotion, a drawing on pop cultural resources and particularly early blockbuster films. Yet the central element that dates back most famously to *Lost* – but was already present in *Alias* – is the convoluted mystery and mythology. It is notable as such that this of all elements is the one most personally associated with Abrams himself. The mystery box as a metaphor for storytelling is the closest thing to Abrams' personal signature, and serves as the guiding vision by merit of which he claims ultimate creative ownership of, and presence in all (successful) Bad Robot productions. Wherever there is a narrative mystery box, Abrams is present, regardless of whether his title is in the credits.[1]

This combination of a unified, auteurist creative identity on the one hand, yet a dispersed network rather than a corresponding absolute hierarchy on the other, distinguishes Bad Robot from the similar model of corporate authorship found in film production studios of brand-name directors, such as Steven Spielberg's Amblin Entertainment or Francis Ford Coppola's American Zoetrope. Coppola and Spielberg have been known to append their names as promotional devices to films either produced or released by their companies. Both have also produced the films of other brand-name directors: for example, Coppola with Bill Condon with *Kinsey* (2004) and Tim Burton with *Sleepy Hollow* (1999), and Spielberg with Joel and Ethan Coen's *True Grit* (2010) and of course Abrams himself with *Super 8*. What no studio in this model has done is create a cohesive network of *repeated* collaborations, which is then capable of being branded throughout by its association with its central node. While Spielberg and Amblin did, for example, work with Clint Eastwood on four of his films, it would be hard to argue for Eastwood being a part of a Spielberg-centric network – and harder to think of the two as sharing a creative signature.[2] Nor have any of the directors mentioned above been known to 'delegate' in the manner of Abrams, who for example was billed as the original creator of *Lost*, directed its pilot episode but then subsequently passed showrunning duties on to Damon Lindelof and Cartlon Cuse. Therein lies the critical differences between the author-company brand and Bad Robot's network-company brand.

Models of corporate authorship have, indeed, been explored before in both the film and television industries, in a number of studies that have sought to challenge auteurism as a discourse. Considering film, Thomas Schatz (1998) has written of 'The Genius of the System' of early Hollywood, while Jerome Christensen (2011) has argued for film as a 'corporate art', drawing attention to the studio brand. Similarly in television, *The Mary Tyler Moore Show* has been considered as primarily a studio product (Feuer et. al., 1984). It is, however, on the promotional side that Abrams and Bad Robot show the unique model of a continued appeal to auteurism, embodied in the studio head, combined with the use of a stable of individual talents working on individual, unconnected projects. A more useful model to compare with Abrams' 'fanboy family' may be found not in the companies of either classical Hollywood moguls or New Hollywood auteurs, but much further back in the past, with different brand name creators altogether.

Models old and new: The Renaissance workshop and the production studio

It is useful not only to consider Abrams and Bad Robot within the framework of the future of the media industries, but also to historicize this unique emergent model in relation to older models of creativity. As mentioned, the studios of brand-name Hollywood directors offer only a limited comparison for understanding the operation of such networked promotional authorship. Instead, we might look at another kind of studio model, which has the added distinction of having emerged around the same time that the concept of individual creative genius, and its accompanying charisma ideology, was budding in the West. This is the Renaissance *bottega:* the master's studio or workshop. Modern workshop models, such as those of Andy Warhol's Factory or the William Morris Company, offer more recent takes on the same concept. Yet looking at the *bottega* in its original historical context allows the analysis to provide perspective on the interaction between he emergence of modern authorship discourses, and the shape and functionality of collaborative production.

Much of the scholarship of Renaissance fine art focused on exalting the work of solitary masters: such 'Renaissance Men' as Da Vinci, Raphael and Michelangelo who provide the model for the genius artist. We know, however, that actual working practices in the Renaissance were in fact much more collaborative and even corporate, making extensive use of hands other than the master's own. According to historian Peter Burke, when paintings produced in the workshop were signed, 'the function of the signature was probably to guarantee the product rather than to express the pride of an individual creator' (Burke, 1994, p. 3).

Standard practice in Italian Renaissance art saw the master painter oversee a workshop, populated by apprentices, assistants, and specialized workers of varying ranks. Though apprentices were educated in those workshops, their role was considerably more important and involved than merely adding in flourishes or backgrounds. Rather, they were frequently responsible for the execution of central figures and scenic compositions (Maginnis, 1995). Apprentices and assistants were required to practice the master's brush so that 'the apprentice's idiom would become indistinguishable from his teacher's' (Cole, 1995, p. 89), in order to allow for a seamless product to emerge from a process that was essentially corporate. The junior artists within a workshop were not employed solely in working on the master's commissions, but were able and even encouraged to take on commissions of their own. As Anabel Thomas writes:

> It was normal workshop practice for assistants to accept orders independently. [...] Established masters might be recruited as assistants to a separate major project, the management of which might be in the hands of another workshop. [...] Workshop assistants, for their part, could and did secure commissions in their own right, in other words as "masters" (Thomas, 1995, p. 2).

While some apprentices 'graduated' from their master's workshop and opened shops of their own, others might remain under the workshop's aegis for years as workers both independent and corporate. Artists running large workshops with a number of such workers at their disposal might take large-scale commissions where they would direct and supervise the work rather than carrying it out themselves (Burke, 1994). Graduates who have gone independent might return to workshops in which they have trained, and collaborate with their former master or, indeed, work under him on individual projects. References to old workshop associations can be seen to appear in contractual agreements (Thomas, 1995): patrons might ask an artist who has worked in a certain shop to paint in the style of his former master, or indeed even copy his work – sometimes in collaboration with that same master (Cole, 1995).

This independence had its limits, however, as the workforce of a shop was encouraged to maintain a consistent 'house style', often through reproduction of previous merchandise. Burke (1994: 3) continues to note that 'it was the *bottega* rather than the individual which had a style'. Thomas (1995) adds, 'Renaissance workshop apprentices were trained to work towards a consistency of style rather than to place their own particular mark on those parts of the shop's merchandise with which they were involved.' (p. 213) The workshop thus had a creative signature – in effect, its brand. This derived from the style of the master, which the apprentices had trained to copy, and increasingly became tied to his signature. In the mid-sixteenth century, Titian, who was in high demand among continental nobility, was sanctioning use of his signature on pieces produced by his workshop in order to authenticate them (Cole, 1995).

The image of Bad Robot as a Renaissance studio is easy to conjure up, and elucidates the advantages that the model provides for different agents within it. Abrams acts as the master, setting the tone, creating the composition, and authenticating with his signature, his name metonymic to the studio. Finished works are, to take a common style of reference to Renaissance paintings, 'from the workshop of J. J. Abrams'. However execution is often in the hands of his apprentices and assistants, each of whom may act as the master in their own right on certain commissions. All are propped up by the reputation of the studio, and work within its house style, creating works that are consistent regardless of whose hand has produced which of their parts or even their entirety. Apprentices who branch out into studios of their own, such as Roberto Orci and Alex Kurtzman with K/O Paper Products, remain associated with the master's studio and often collaborate with or employ other apprentices. Orci and Kurtzman do this for example on *Sleepy Hollow*, employing actors John Noble (*Fringe*) and John Cho (the *Star Trek* film) and producer Ken Olin (*Alias*).

While attempts have been made to emulate the Renaissance workshop in the modern production of fine art, there is nothing to indicate that the similarity is conscious on Abrams' part. More likely, the model has returned as conditions demanded it. Hence, noting the resemblance allows us to consider key aspects of commonality between the contemporary US television industry and the fine art 'industry' of sixteenth-century Italy, particularly around the dynamics of cultural legitimation and the creation of new cultural producers as legitimate artists. This, in turn, allows insight on the market and labour conditions that shape authorship discourses around individuality and collaboration. One such condition may be an emerging need for an apprenticeship system for the education of showrunners. The range of skills required from a showrunner is wide, at times contradictory, and frequently more than the sum of its parts – which is to say, more than a mere extension of production and writing. Perfectly competent producers, writers, or managers of a writers' room may still prove unable to fill the position; the only real training for showrunnership, it seems, is in actually running a show. Failure rate in the television industry is extremely high; most new pilots never make it to series, so that the industry offers much fewer opportunities to gain showrunner experience than it opens demand for people who possess it.

As the discursive and promotional centrality of the showrunner outpaces the supply of capable individuals, there is a vital need for some system to both increase opportunities available and to mitigate the risk of failure. I mention above how former Bad Robot employees cite the pedagogical aspects of studio life, the lessons learned under Abrams the master. As part of the studio, producers and writers are able to amass experience on different projects, and finally to take their own commissions – create and run their own shows – with the backing of that studio as a safety net of sorts. Within the studio structure, in which best practices are already entrenched and experienced support available, an aspiring showrunner can work as executive producer on a number of projects before taking such front of house responsibility. Indeed this has been the pattern with a number of Bad Robot showrunners such as J. H. Wyman and of course Orci and Kurtzman.

The association with the studio brand also works to ease a burden that is unique to the showrunner role and causes particular difficulties – the need to manage a new visibility of what has in the past been a behind the scenes job. Showrunners in contemporary television must be not only competent writers and producers, but also competent celebrities, handling press and audience attention and acting as the face of their shows (Cuse, 2012). It has by now become not only common but expected of showrunners to engage with their audience via promotional devices such as podcasts and behind the scenes features, and through social media, with all the PR pressure and dangers involved (Newman and Levine, 2012; see also McNutt, 2016). The attachment to the established name of the studio's master reduces this pressure to perform and allows a showrunner the possibility of success without creating and maintaining an individual brand. This is yet another means for the reduction of risk in the unstable and project-based work environment of the industry. Working within a studio allows one person's name and reputation to secure the position of many. According to Anabel Thomas (1995, p. 2), the key ability of the Renaissance master was 'to sustain a workshop organization economically by generating a viable income through securing and dispatching business'. *Variety*'s description of networks clamouring to join the 'Abrams business' gives a vivid image of how the master's ability to generate business for their studio works in contemporary television.

It is equally worth considering the studio brand in light of the development of the Renaissance workshops' house styles. In both cases, the maintenance of a coherent style led by the master allows for that master's reputation to continue working in its brand capacity, as a guarantor of quality and assurance to the customer of what they would be getting. As Mittell notes, 'identifying the creators of a new series can serve [...] functions of creating common audiences and branding' (2015, p. 97), and fans will frequently follow the auteur between shows. Yet in both cases it also operates to allow the work of many to pass for the work of one. Abrams on his own is no more able to run all of Bad Robot's shows than Titian was able to personally paint all his commissions. Just as the maintenance of a workshop allowed the nobility of Europe to declare their mutual status by possessing paintings by Titian, so the Bad Robot model allows the Abrams brand to be dispersed while maintaining its power, allowing different networks the prestige of owning Abrams shows. The gathering of a group of creators united by a proven stylistic signature, legitimised by the master's actual signature – even if merely in the form of a name on the credits list– is very convenient for patrons as well, allowing them to get more mileage out of the brand and cheat the auteurist demand for 'one man alone'. This offers another way to ease if not solve the problem of the showrunner shortage, and is especially useful as increasingly, in Denise Mann's words, showrunning is 'not TV, it's brand management' (2009, p. 97).

Sixteenth-century Italy is where the roots of the concept of the genius artist lie. Although it would only come into its modern form with nineteenth-century Romanticism, interest in and reification of the 'master' appears already in Giorgio Vasari's canonical *Lives of the Most Excellent Painters, Sculptors, and Architects,* published 1550. Yet as the above example of Titian shows, the interest in the artist's signature also led to more demand for said signature than the artist himself could satisfy, inviting the answer of the workshop model. US television is now in a position curiously similar to Renaissance Italy, with focus turning to its own masters to validate it as an art form. It stands to reason then that a studio model has re-emerged, to allow those masters to sate the demands of the market for their authorised work.

The master workshop model of promotional authorship, much like any model in an industry facing as constant and rapid change as the television industry, must be seen in context as emergent and competing rather than established. In 2015, while J. J. Abrams was breaking cinematic records with *Star Wars: The Force Awakens*, Bad Robot had disappeared from the *Hollywood Reporter* list of 50 Power Showrunners. Yet at the same time, showrunners signed on to more than one or even two shows have become increasingly visible, making up a full fifth of the list (O'Connell and Hunt, 2015). Some, such as Abrams collaborator Carlton Cuse, and Greg Berlanti in a return appearance, seem to be following in the footsteps of the model. Others represent competing possibilities, inviting further research into the transmutations of promotional authorship in television under the pressure exercised by the introduction of auteurism. Bad Robot's success with the master workshop model shows that while the discourse at the heart of auteurism is consistent, traceable back through cinema to nineteenth-century Romantic authorship, its expressions are flexible and its uses manifold. We are likely to see it continue to evolve.

Notes

[1] If one were unkind, one might point out that it is quite convenient for Abrams that his role only calls for him to place the closed mystery box. The opening of said box, which Abrams himself confesses is inevitably disappointing, is left to individual showrunners to take either the credit or the fall for – and it is often a fall. It was Damon Lindelof and Carlton Cuse who bore the brunt of the audience's frustration following the *Lost* finale. Being very kind myself, I leave such speculation to the footnotes.

[2] There may be more room for comparison with Zoetrope producing Sofia Coppola's films, yet of course the family connection muddies the water considerably.

References

Andreeva, N. (2014). Showrunners wanted: Networks grapple with lack of experienced writing producers. *Deadline*, 7 May Retrieved from http://www.deadline.com/2014/05/showrunners-wanted-networks-grapple-with-lack-of-experienced-writing-producers/

Baumann, S. (2007). *Hollywood Highbrow: From Entertainment to Art*. Princeton, NJ: Princeton University Press.

Bennett, T. (2014). *Showrunners: The Art of Running a TV show*. London: Titan Books.

Boucher, G. (2008). Marvel is on a mission. *Los Angeles Times*, (9 March. Retrieved from http://www.latimes.com/entertainment/la-ca-marvel9mar09,1,2967693.story.

Bourdieu, P. (1980). The production of belief: Contribution to an economy of symbolic goods (R. Nice, Trans.). *Media, Culture and Society*, 2, 261–93.

Burke, P. (1994). The Italian artist and his roles. In Peter Burke (Ed.), E. Bianchini and C. Dorey (Trans.) *History of Italian Art, Volume One*. Cambridge: Polity Press.

Caldwell, J. T. (2008). *Production Culture: Industrial Reflexivity and Critical Practice in Film and Television.* Durham, NC: Duke University Press.

Christensen, J. (2011) *America's Corporate Art: The Studio Authorship of Hollywood Motion Pictures.* Stanford, CA: Stanford University Press.

Cole, B. (1995) Titian and the idea of originality. In A. Ladis and C. Wood (Eds.) *The Craft of Art: Originality and Industry in the Italian Renaissance and Baroque Workshop* (pp. 86–112) Athens: University of Georgia Press, 1995.

Collins, S. (2007). Who really runs things. *Los Angeles Times,* 23 November. Retrieved from http://articles.latimes.com/2007/nov/23/entertainment/et-channel23.

Corrigan, T. (1991) The Commerce of Auteurism. In *A Cinema Without Walls: Movies and Culture after Vietnam* (pp. 101–36.) New Brunswick, NJ: Rutgers University Press, 1991.

Cuse, C. (2012). *Lost's* Carlton Cuse relives dealing with the modern celebrity of the TV showrunner. *Vulture,* 19 October. Retrieved from: http://www.vulture.com/2012/10/carlton-cuse-lost-showrunner-celebrity.html.

Feuer, J. (2007). HBO and the Concept of Quality TV. In J. McCabe and K. (Eds.) *Quality TV: Contemporary American Television and Beyond* (pp. 145–57). London: IB Tauris.

Feuer, J., Kerr, P., & Vahimagi, T. (Eds.) (1984). *MTM: "Quality television".* London: BFI Publishing.

Hesmondhalgh, D. & Baker, S. (2011). *Creative Labour: Media Work in Three Cultural Industries.* Abingdon and New York: Routledge.

Hibberd, J. (2013). "Almost Human": J.J. Abrams answers 8 burning questions. *Entertainment Weekly,* 15 November. Retrieved from http://insidetv.ew.com/2013/11/15/j-j-abrams-almost-human-interview.

Leopold, T. (2013). The new, new TV golden age. *CNN Entertainment,* 6 May. Retrieved from http://edition.cnn.com/2013/05/06/showbiz/golden-age-of-tv/

Littleton, C. (2009). Fanboy family fans out. *Variety,* 461, 1–2, 19 October

Maginnis, H. B. J. (1995). The Craftsman's Genius: Painters, Patrons and Drawings in Trecento Siena. In A. Ladis and C. Wood (Eds.) *The Craft of Art: Originality and industry in the Italian Renaissance and Baroque Workshop* (pp. 25–47). Athens: University of Georgia Press.

Mann, D. (2009). It's Not TV, It's Brand Management TV: The Collective Author(s) of the *Lost* franchise. In V. Meyer, M. J. Banks and J. T. Caldwell (Eds.), *Production Studies: Cultural Studies of Media Industries* (pp. 97–114). New York: Routledge.

Martin, B. (2013) *Difficult Men: Behind the Scenes of a Creative Revolution: From the* Sopranos *and* The Wire *to* Mad Men *and* Breaking Bad. New York: Penguin Press.

McNutt, M. (2016). When fan engagement goes wrong. *A.V. Club,* 4 April. Retrieved from http://www.avclub.com/article/when-fan-engagement-goes-wrong-234346.

Minow N. N. (1961). *Television and the Public Interest*. Address to the National Association of Broadcasters, 9 May Washington, DC.

Mittell, J. (2015). *Complex TV: The Poetics of Contemporary Television Storytelling*. New York: New York University Press.

Molloy, T. (2013). How much does J.J. Abrams do on a J.J. Abrams show? *The Wrap*, 14 November. Retrieved from http://www.thewrap.com/j-j-abrams-tv-shows-almost-human-how-involved-star-wars/.

Newman, M. Z. and Levine, E. (2012). *Legitimating Television: Media Convergence and Cultural Status*. New York: Routledge.

Nussbaum, E. (2009). When TV became art. *New York Magazine*, 4 December. Retrieved from http://nymag.com/arts/all/aughts/62513/.

O'Connell M. and Hunt, S. W. (2015 October 14). The most powerful showrunners 2015. *The Hollywood Reporter*. Retrieved from http://www.hollywoodreporter.com/lists/top-showrunners-powerful-executive-producers-831725/item/jack-amiel-michael-begler-greg-831742.

Paskin, W. (2015). What does "peak TV" *really* mean? *Slate*, 23 December. Retrieved from http://www.slate.com/articles/arts/tv_club/features/2015/best_tv_of_2015_slate_s_tv_club_discusses/what_does_peak_tv_really_mean.html.

Pearson, R. (2011) Cult Television as Digital Television's Cutting Edge. In J. Bennett and N. Strange (Eds.), *Television as Digital Media* (pp. 105–31) Durham, NC: Duke University Press, 2011.

Roco (2011). J.J. Abrams explains why "Mythology-lite" Undercovers failed. *Seriable*, 16 January. Retrieved from http://seriable.com/jj-abrams-explains-why-mythology-lite-undercovers-failed/#ixzz3HomPht1R.

Rose, Lacy (2011 September 25). J.J. Abrams, "Supernatural" creator sell thriller to NBC. *The Hollywood Reporter*. Retrieved from http://www.hollywoodreporter.com/news/jj-abrams-supernatural-creator-sell-239996.

Schatz, T. (1988). *The Genius of the System: Hollywood Flmmaking in the Studio Era*. New York, NY: Pantheon Books.

TED2007. (2008 January). *J. J. Abrams: The mystery box*. Retrieved from http://www.ted.com/talks/j_j_abrams_mystery_box.html.

THR Staff (2013 16 October). The Hollywood Reporter names the 50 power showrunners of 2013. *The Hollywood Reporter*. Retrieved from http://www.hollywoodreporter.com/lists/hollywood-reporter-names-50-power-648546.

Thomas, A. (1995). *The Painter's Practice in Renaissance Tuscany*. Cambridge: Cambridge University Press.

CHAPTER SEVEN

Elegies to Cinematography: The Digital Workflow, Digital Naturalism and Recent Best Cinematography Oscars

Jamie Clarke

Southampton Solent University

Introduction

In 2013, the magazine Blouinartinfo.com interviewed Christopher Doyle, the firebrand cinematographer renowned for his lusciously visualised collaborations with Wong Kar Wai. Asked about the recent award of the best cinematography Oscar to Claudio Miranda's work on *Life of Pi* (2012), Doyle's response indicates that the idea of collegiate collaboration within the cinematographic community might have been overstated. Here is Doyle:

> Okay. I'm trying to work out how to say this most politely ... I'm sure he's a wonderful guy ... but since 97 per cent of the film is not under his control, what the fuck are you talking about cinematography ... I think it's a fucking insult to cinematography ... The award is given to the technicians ... it's not to the cinematographer ... If it were me ...

How to cite this book chapter:

Clarke, J. 2017. Elegies to Cinematography: The Digital Workflow, Digital Naturalism and Recent Best Cinematography Oscars. In: Graham, J. and Gandini, A. (eds.). *Collaborative Production in the Creative Industries.* Pp. 105–123. London: University of Westminster Press. DOI: https://doi.org/10.16997/book4.g. License: CC-BY-NC-ND 4.0

I wouldn't even turn up. Because sorry, cinematography? Really? (Cited in Gaskin, 2013)

Irrespective of the technicolor language, Doyle's position appeals to a traditional and romantic view of cinematography. This position views the look of film as conceived in the exclusive monogamy the cinematographer has historically enjoyed on-set with the director during principal photography. Alternatively, the digital workflow in special effects-heavy, 3D extravaganzas such as *Life of Pi* has caused the director's allegiances to wander to the back-end of the production process where no-collar digital hipsters finalise the look of the film at their workstations. Championed elsewhere, by the likes of Richard Florida (2012), as constituting a new creative class characterised by tolerance, talent and technology, Angela McRobbie points to the paradoxes of this 'hipster economy' (McRobbie, 2016, p. 50). For McRobbie, this model is nothing less than a wholesale attempt to rewire the priorities of a new generation of workers. Following the fieldwork of Andrew Ross's *No-Collar: The Humane Workplace and its Hidden Costs* (2004) that investigated the workers at the digital media company Razorfish in New York, McRobbie's argues that surface style is a palliative for the precarious, informal and casualised working conditions that characterise the sector. Correspondingly, whilst Doyle bewailed the promiscuous origins of *Life of Pi*, digital effects workers themselves were also unhappy with the new ménage à trois between themselves, the cinematographer and the director. As the *ancien régime* was bunkered inside the Dolby Theatre, outside, representatives of Rhythm and Hues (the team responsible for the visual effects on *Life of Pi*) threatened to storm the citadel protesting Hollywood's 'race to the bottom' following the announcement ten days earlier that their company were laying off over 200 workers (see Curtin & Vanderhoef, 2015, pp. 219–220).

These events hence provide a *mise en scène* of the struggle for supremacy over the filmic look since the ascent of the digital workflow that displaced the cinematographer's status whilst failing to safeguard that of the insurgents. The 2013 ceremony was merely the crescendo of this particular hoo-ha whereby the best cinematography Oscar had previously been awarded to a series of CGI-intensive spectacles, with authority over the look increasingly scattered across the workflow and outsourced overseas. The controversy began in 2009 with the Academy's recognition of Mauro Fiore's work on *Avatar* (2009), a film with extensive pre-visualisation having taken place before Fiore's arrival to the team in New Zealand, and with much of the cartoony aesthetic having been accomplished in Los Angeles by Twentieth Century Fox's in-house digital design team, Lightstorm. Since *Avatar*, the Oscar has subsequently been awarded to similarly effects-freighted work: Wally Pfister's work on *Inception* (2010); Robert Richardson's on *Hugo* (2011); Claudio Miranda's on *Life of Pi* and Emmanuel Lubezki's on *Gravity* (2013). The look of digital film, so the argument runs, is now illegitimately conceived long after image capture and the departure of the cinematographer in the dark corners of the visual effects department.

Technological change is here leveraged as a profit-seeking and costs-reducing mechanism that challenges established hierarchies, redefines job descriptions and may well be contributing to the end of what was once called the cinematographer, perceived now as an expensive luxury in this new globally mobile and digitally supple production culture.

This chapter investigates these developments. I begin with a review of the recent critical attention allocated to the cinematographer. From here, the essay introduces the main features of the digital workflow that I read principally through the optics of production studies as advocated by the work of John Caldwell. The article culminates with an analysis of the candidates for the best cinematography Oscar in 2015. As indicated in this introduction, I view the Oscar ceremony as a site where such labour positions are packaged for public reception, contested and fought out.

Collaborative partnerships

One irony in these developments is that the role of the cinematographer has only recently begun to seriously receive critical attention. Richard Misek provides the following classical definition of cinematography as presented by The American Society of Cinematographers (ASC):

> The ASC's view of film production can be summarized as follows: a film's director has a mental image (a "vision") of how the script will appear on screen; the DoP [or cinematographer] realizes this "vision" by registering moving images with a "look" that corresponds to, or improves on, what the director imagined (Misek, 2010, p. 405)

This understanding sees the workflow as originating with the director's seedling vision. The labour involved in giving birth to this vision however requires the cinematographer who acts as an essential handmaiden positioning the collaborative act as a consummation uniting the two roles in keeping with the ASC's motto: 'Loyalty, Progress, Art' (cited in Keating, 2010, p. 16). The ASC motto hence carefully positions seniority-based hierarchy and linear workflow as the foundational rock on which art is built. In the literature emerging since 2010, the cinematographer remains loyal and deferential however 'collaboration' has emerged as a watchword that suggests a more equal role with the director. Symptomatic of this trend is Christopher Beach's *A Hidden History of Film Style: Cinematographers, Directors and the Collaborative Process* (2015). Beach's volume is structured around a series of case studies whereby frequent director-cinematographer collaborations are documented from D.W. Griffith and G.W. 'Billy' Bitzer to Oliver Stone and Robert Richardson. If the case studies serve to highlight classic director auteurs on the one hand, then the ambition of the book on the other is to widen the attribution of credit beyond a solitary visionary genius and towards the collaborative photochemistry within partnerships seen to midwife the look. Ultimately however, Beach's radicalism proves to be rather more modest and can be reductively summarised as the assumption that behind every good director is (or at least was) a good cinematographer. As such Beach's position seems anxious to ring-fence the director-cinematographer axis, something that more 'meta' approaches to auteur studies have been anxious to deconstruct (See here Gerstner and Staiger, 2003 and Wexman, 2003). Arguably this discourse on director – cinematographer collaboration seems elegiac in its soft-focus longing for a less turbulent, analogue era where everyone supposedly knew their place and when directors were simply directors and cinematographers were simply cinematographers.

What is perhaps new in the reheating of this auteur debate is the attempt to nudge the cinematographer into the light. It is perhaps no coincidence that a commonplace in the revisionism is the relationship between Orson Welles and his cinematographer on *Citizen Kane* (1941), Gregg Tolland. Tolland's work features extensively in the work of Patrick Keating (see Keating, 2010, pp. 231–7), is afforded a chapter in the work of Beach (see Beach, 2015, pp. 55–85) and preoccupies an article by Philip Cowan (2012). Cowan, for instance, follows the 'whodunit' narrative of auteurism by attributing *Kane*'s deep focus and staging-in-depth innovations to the experienced Tolland rather than his brief encounter with the ingénue, 26-year-old radio impresario (see Cowan, 2012, pp. 77–8). No doubt the frequency of references to *Kane* is strategic given its centrality in the annals of film reception, but it is then perhaps reception that is key to understanding auteur criticism more generally. Tim Corrigan (1990) similarly draws attention to how auteur discourse is not so much a phenomenon of production as reception. For Corrigan, auteurism consolidates meaning for audiences and provides a shorthand for quality that can subsequently be leveraged in marketing. That the discourse of auteurism seems shot through with the chivalric language of romance, conquests and elegiac longing for origin myths is perhaps because it is always already packaged as a publicity narrative geared toward reception. Disregarding the accuracy of Cowan's thesis (and it is certainly convincing as a piece of historical revisionism) what interests this discussion is precisely why this flurry of attention surrounding the cinematographer should appear now.

I want to view 'collaboration' as an unstable term that acknowledges the potential for disruption over the control of the filmic look whilst attempting to defuse this instability. Precisely because they are today only one part in a more cluttered digital workflow, the cinematographer requires intensified external affirmation to consolidate their now precarious position and moreover is prepared to stimulate this affirmation via a series of discursive tactics. The sudden intensification of references to the cinematographer as collaborator *sine qua non* is a symptom of this stabilisation strategy. The case studies discussed above are therefore, I argue, as much about the contemporary status of the cinematographer as they are about the historical and romantic figure of the cinematographer that they invoke. It is arguably no coincidence therefore that two of the critics spearheading the critical attention to cinematography, Keating and Cowan, are themselves practicing cinematographers. Ultimately, the digital landscape of globally networked production, elsewhere celebrated for increasing democratic access to the production workflow, is the self-same trigger for increasing competition over who authors the look of the film.

Producing the 'Cinematographer'

The controversy surrounding the attribution of credit is, of course, not merely aesthetic but also materialist. As John Caldwell illustrates in his path-breaking work on production cultures, such controversies are perhaps best understood in terms of prestige and particularly job security and remuneration (see Caldwell, 2008, 2013, 2014). The positioning of the cinematographer as central collaborator can be viewed as the discursive product of stakeholders who themselves helped to produce a romantic idea of 'cinematography'. Critical here was the anxiety to move away from a mechanical gear-grinding view of practice to something more akin to a labour of love. This understanding is consistent with Keating's historical account that, beyond a merely formal poetic approach, wraps style within an institutional and discursive mainframe. Keating thus investigates the role played by the ASC and its journal *American Cinematographer* in crafting an 'idealised' view of the cinematographer for reception (Keating, 2010, p. 17). Chartered in 1919, the ASC and its trade journal *American Cinematographer* (first published in 1920) lobbied for the elevation of cinematography to the status where the energies circulating on set were condensed into a particular figure who might merit recognition by a further valorisation mechanism: the Oscar ceremony. According to Keating, the ASC initially promoted an assertively aesthetic style during the silent period and especially between 1922 and 1927, with cinematography then 'designed to be noticed' (Keating, 2010, p. 28). Precisely because the cinematographer did not yet exist as such, assertive style was leveraged to generate attention. As Keating demonstrates, the ASC deliberately redefined the role away from a functionary following orders, towards that of an aesthete who was an arguably an equal collaborator with the director. As Keating summarises:

> The cinematographer had acquired a new public identity. He had come to be perceived as a person with good taste [and] emotional sensitivity ... the ASC crafted a compelling narrative about the development of a new kind of art – and a new kind of artist. No longer a laborer turning a crank, the cinematographer was a skilled professional making a valuable contribution to the cinema – a contribution that could best be described as aesthetic (Keating, 2010, pp. 15–16)

The key phrase here is 'come to be perceived as a person'. Once the look of film was allocated an aesthetic sensibility, the popular understanding of art required that an individual should be seen as author of this look. Counter-intuitively, it is not so much artists that produce great works but rather great works that produce artists. Downstream, this ability to 'to be perceived as a person' organises industrial contractual relationships. The films industry's division of labour is administered by the separation of workers as below-the-line (BTL) and above-the-line (ATL). This system has historically seen ATL roles within the production process individually rewarded via handsome residuals rather than the comparatively minor collective residuals (such as pension and health care entitlements) received by BTL interchangeable con-tributors (see Stahl, 2009, pp. 54–68). The closure of the silent period saw the elevation of the cinematographer from the anonymity of the crew's BTL ranks into an individual person who was eligible for ATL benefits. It is not coincidental this period sees the first Oscar awarded to individual cinema-tographers, with the first statuette awarded in 1927–8. Viewed through this wider-angle lens, the surge in academic discourse testifying to the signifi-cance of individual cinematographer's contributions seems less a sign that the cinematographer's time has finally come. Instead, the sudden heat surround-ing 'painters with light' can be interpreted as a response to the increasing destabilisation wrought by the digital workflow and the subsequent inten-sification of the personal branding strategies of cinematographers and their entourages.

The digital workflow

Clearly, these materialist concerns are the forcefield that structures the sup-posedly more rarefied and refined discourse of cinematographer as the dis-interested auteur documented above. The romantic view of the cinematogra-pher's craft as happily collaborative is synchronous with a specific technological moment that has now perhaps passed. This discursive formation lasted from the silent period to the rise of digital and as Richard Misek states stems from, 'the limitations of photochemical postproduction technology' (Misek, 2010, p. 405). Nevertheless, the cinematographer would largely oversee these limita-tions. As discussed by Stephen Prince, during the photochemical period, the look would be controlled organically on-set via production design, the selection of a particular stock with inherent image characteristics, through the manip-ulation of natural or artificial light sources and in-camera through exposure adjustments (see Prince, 2004, p. 26). In postproduction, colour timing tactics (such as flashing, pushing, bleach bypass and cross-processing the negative) could make adjustments to contrast and colour but such processes were lim-ited to the entire image, again, following the cinematographer's instructions in the laboratory. Colour timing was hence capable of only primary correction (where the entire image is altered) because attempts to change exposure would inevitably effect colour and vice versa. As Misek concludes, 'the "look"' of a photochemical film is indeed primarily dependent on choices made when filming' (Misek, 2010, p. 405). This situation is now a thing of the past as digital grading allows for secondary colour and contrast correction via the application of, for instance, masks enabling specific parts and specific qualities of the image to be warped. Commentators point here to *O Brother, Where Art Thou?* (2000), photographed by Roger Deakins for the Coen brothers, as a landmark film – the first to be scanned and digitised in its entirety (see Prince, 2004, p. 28). Secondary digital grading here allowed the postproduction team to isolate and de-saturate the lush-green footage captured during the Mississippi Summer to evoke the Dustbowl 1930s photorealism of the Farm Security Administration. This process cracked open the filmic look, allowing local chroma and luma alteration by insurgent contributors with alternative, now digital, skillsets. The possibility to effectively re-shoot the film in postproduction meant that the role of the cinematographer was also redrawn. As Caldwell points out of these developments:

> Distinctions have been leveled, workflow is no longer linear and lock-step (with discrete, successive stages), and artistic responsibility has been re-delegated and dispersed across the porous boundaries that once defined the production and postproduction process. (Caldwell, 2008, pp. 183–4)

As such, Caldwell provides a labour-inflected twist to these technological developments investigating the fallout on craft relationships scrambled by the digital workflow. New roles have hence flooded into this process, including the digital colorist, the digital intermediate technician, and the visual effects supervisor. The transition to digital bloats a now distended and non-linear workflow, intensifies competition and undoubtedly downgrades the hard won status of the cinematographer. As Caldwell states:

> The best way to study BTL authorship is not to look for some essential BTL authorial trait or profile but to look at each production as a dynamic process involving tensions and struggles between "strategic" ATL "control schemes" and "tactical" BTL "counter-measures" (Caldwell, 2013, p. 361)

The ultimate implication is that collegiate discourses of who is the principle collaborator occlude a battle for survival whereby industry craft-workers operate as entrepreneurs deploying an arsenal of promotional technologies of the self to consolidate their role within the new production ecology. It is in this context that I understand the 2015 nominees for the best cinematography Oscar.

The 2015 Oscars

The Academy of Motion Pictures Arts and Sciences was chartered on 4 May 1927 and, according to John Atkinson's history of the Oscars, was 'something between a union and a marketing organisation' (Atkinson, 2001, p. 8). Since its inception in 1929, the Academy's Oscar ceremony has therefore operated not merely to, in the Academy's works, 'honor outstanding achievement' but as a shop window for industry practices and workflows. The impact of an Oscar victory are difficult to calibrate due to the number of variables involved, however the successful can expect to enjoy a surge in box office receipts following nomination and a further kick following an individual win. For instance, Danny Boyle's *Slumdog Millionaire* (2009) earned 30 per cent of its take following its nomination and a further 30 per cent following its victory in the best picture category (see Buckley, 2014). The voting system for individual categories is byzantine (operating according to a variation on the single transferable vote model) but significantly academy members eligible to vote in any given category are, according to Gehrlein and Kehr, 'associated with the specialization of the category' (Gehrlein and Kher, 2004, p. 227). Hence the shortlist for any category designates a form of peer recognition whilst simultaneously providing a mechanism whereby a particular craft is able to manage an ideal self-representation for public reception. The publicity extends beyond the high-profile acting categories and also affects the crew. As Peter Bart, editor of *Variety*, indicates, 'Without question, the Oscar has a great effect on behind-the-scenes people ... if for no other reason that they come into the spotlight for the first time in their careers' (cited in Goodale, 2004).

The nominees for the best cinematography Oscar in 2015 were Dick Pope for his work on *Mr. Turner*; Robert Yeoman for lensing *The Grand Budapest Hotel*; Lukasz Zal and Ryszard Penczewski's work on the Polish film *Ida*; 12-time nominee and digital pioneer Roger Deakins' work on *Unbroken*; and the eventual winner Emmanuel Lubezki for *Birdman or (The Unexpected Virtue of Ignorance)*. The nominees indicate that the transition to digital was all but complete in that for the first time in the history of the award, 4 of the 5 nominees were shot digitally with only Yeoman shooting on 35mm film. Perhaps because of this trend toward a total digital workflow, I read the cinematography nominees as advancing a neo-traditional discourse and as such an example of Caldwell's ATL rear-guard control schemes. The films shortlisted for the 2015 ceremony seemed to privilege an almost auto-referential approach with stakeholders eligible to vote in the cinematography category celebrating films that showcased classical techniques and that were in some way about a particular understanding of filmmaking itself. The nominated films all thematise appropriate aesthetic conduct, featuring characters that modestly craft a self-consciously pictorial look ostensibly over a real environment. This emphasis on artistic beauty gestures to its conditions of production, positioned in this instance as a commitment to traditional cinematographic practice over computer wizardry.

Beauty here serves to consecrate the workflows that shape its realisation. In the following I argue that these post-digital control schemes are organised around two interlocking principles: nostalgia for neo-traditional craftsmanship (that would institutionalise aesthetic sensibility within the lineage of recognised professional communities) and shooting strategies (that would emphasise physical, on-set techniques that I call 'digital naturalism').

In a review of *Mr. Turner*, Peter Bradshaw comments on the film's representation of the eponymous pre-impressionist painter: 'It doesn't show him being tormented by self-doubt ... He is prosperous, confident, self–assured ... He's an artist who is at the peak of his profession, almost like a professional man, a craftsman' (Brooks et al, 2014). Timothy Spall's J.M.W. Turner is presented as embedded in a genealogy of respectful, old-school pro-fessionalism as is implicit in the film's title. Mr. Turner is less an anguished, solitary visionary, more a jobbing artisan anchored in his household workshop and surrounded by loyal, if under-appreciated, acolytes including his father (a former barber) and his housekeeper. Painting materials too are locally sourced including pigs' heads from the town butchers and pigments such as bladders of ultramarine and bottles of poppy oil from the neighbouring colourman's empo-rium of curios. Turner is also part of a broader professional network via his membership of the Royal Academy of Arts, a circle of rivaling co-dependents who bicker affectionately about light and colour. The film thus functions as a riposte to mythopoeic accounts of creativity operating in a vacuum and instead works to locate the production of art in traditional trade methods, craft com-munities and cottage industries. These humanist communities of workers and enthusiasts are contrasted in the film with mechanical, technocratic science as represented by the encroaching steam age. The film's reproduction of Turner's *Rain, Steam and Speed: The Great Western Railway* (1844) underscores the film's elegiac tone in implying that Turner's practice, anchored in familial, local and fraternal communities, is to be superseded by technological progress. No doubt these concerns would speak to the cinematographic community whose own long-standing set of practices and communities are similarly under threat. The film therefore performs a high-wire act in balancing Turner's extreme ordi-nariness with his undoubted artistic exceptionalism; an exceptionalism whose truth, despite all the modesty, is visible on the screen in cinematographer's Dick Pope's reproduction of Turner's aesthetic.

In this regard, the film's repudiation of technology points to the second ATL control scheme visible in the nominees in how discourses that circulate around the films position creative practice. There is a nostalgic trend here too that I call 'digital naturalism'. Apparently regretting and almost apologetic for the use of digital technology, the approach emphasises on-set procedures and organic materials, and hence traditional methods. In sympathy with this posi-tion, responses to *Mr. Turner* focused on the naturalistic look of Pope's com-positions alongside the corporeality of Spall's performance. If, as Ariel Rogers has indicated, digital technology is positioned as disembodied, Turner's craft is alternatively presented as weighty and materialist (see Rogers, 2012). Creativity here is neither an intellectual idea nor a feat of technology. Instead, Turner's aesthetic is understood as a relationship to natural surroundings and hard-won through the senses. Spall's Turner grunts, spits and ejaculates his way through the film leaving a DNA signature of his body on his canvases. Concomitantly, Turner's use of naturally occurring materials and organic colour pigments implicitly afford the resulting images heft, authenticity and life. Indeed, art is seen to be co-extensive with Turner's bodily life force. The film is shot through with portents of Turner's own mortality viewed as coterminous with the passing of a way of life rooted in long-standing institutions and techniques. When a photographer who Turner visits claims, in a premonition of digital hubris, to have 'captured the rainbow', Turner responds, 'I fear I too am finished'. The implication is technology will annihilate the lovingly antiquated craft communities and embodied practices documented in the film. Similarly, *Mr. Turner* reproduces the inspiration for Turner's elegiac masterpiece *The Fighting Temeraire* (1838). When Turner encounters the warship, tugged now by a steamer, he comments, 'Going to her death I fear … We're observing the future'. The film's cinematographer Dick Pope echoes Turner in his own comments on shooting this scene. Pope reveals, 'The warship is CG, but everything else is real' (cited in Bergery, 2015, p. 68). The film can be read as an obituary to the superannuated practices of Turner and the traditional cinematographer. However, digital naturalism preserves these realistic traditions alongside judicious use of CGI, commemorating Turner's craft not only in the film's narrative but also in the look on the screen.

In *The Grand Budapest Hotel* these themes are extended in how the film remembers the hotel's concierge, Gustave. Continuing our elegiac motif, a character known only as 'The Author' reminisces about his previous visit to the hotel where he is told of its golden age under Gustave's stewardship. If the film's politics are a conservative appeal to the refined manners of yesteryear, then these qualities are actualised in the hotel's 'look', as sculpted by Gustave during its 1920s heyday. Gustave's fastidiousness constitutes a neo-traditional elegy for a lost world of precision and attention to detail, qualities seen to be under threat by the brutal philistinism of the modern age. It is not enough then that the nominated films be beautiful, they also must be shown to me made beautifully by devotees committed to beauty. If Turner is represented as the prototype 'painter with light', Gustave is the cinematographer of the Grand Budapest's look. Gustave artfully orchestrates delicate compositions from the meticulously designed chocolate box colour palette to the pleasingly balanced symmetries of the hotel's décor and table settings: a skillset that he passes on to his apprentice, Zero. Implicitly the skills are also passed onto the crew ultimately responsible for the film's look in the present. David Bordwell draws attention to formal signatures within director Wes Anderson's portfolio crafted alongside his frequent collaborator, cinematographer Robert Yeoman. These include planimetric compositions and an avoidance of deep staging that are consistent with Gustave's similar professional exactitude. Bordwell writes, 'The director's "dollhouse" shots yield cross sections … Thanks to right angles, central perspectives, and symmetrical layouts, his carpented world gains a layer of formality, almost ceremony' (Bordwell, 2015, p. 238). Just as Gustave's ceremonial aesthetic belongs to a bygone era, Bordwell stresses the carpentry work done by the film's crew, again balancing artistry and traditional craftwork in a further example of neo-traditional digital naturalism. As reiterated by Yeoman:

> Wes tried to plan out as much of the movie in advance as possible …
> We plan our shots pretty carefully during prep. Occasionally, new ideas
> come up while we're shooting, but we generally have a pretty good idea
> of what to expect for each scene (cited in Stasukevich, 2014)

An origin myth is constructed to guard against subsequent tampering that might compromise the authors' original vision in the manner that, in the film, the hotel itself has fallen into disrepair following Gustave's death and the subsequent collapse of standards amongst the hotel's retinue. The impression is that the look of the film is authored in the pre-visualisation sequences, storyboarding and the production design, vouchsafing a traditionalist emphasis that is underscored by Yeoman's use of 35mm film. As with *Mr. Turner*, pictorial prettiness is not mere ornamentation; the film's politics are instead reducible to its mise-en-scène and the collaborative circle of followers dedicated to its realisation. Both the film's crew and the hotel's staff testify to a traditionalist dedication to aesthetic principles, seniority and an established workflow. The resulting beauty justifies an otherwise conservative and arbitrary division of labour. This 'natural order of things' is further ratified in the film by Gustave's membership of the Society of the Crossed Keys that positions him as following the time-honoured rules of a profession. Riffing on the motto of that other mysterious organisation, the ASC, if authority stems from dedication to traditional practice and workflows, it is an authority that can be safeguarded by exacting principles of 'art' and 'loyalty', if not exactly 'progress'.

Themes of art and loyalty to a vanishing way of life are also prominent in Pawel Pawlikowski's *Ida* that narrates the experiences of the eponymous young novitiate in Poland in the early 1960s. Before her vows, Ida is released from the convent to meet her aunt 'Red Wanda', a public prosecutor of the Stalinist era. A mournful road movie emerges whereby Poland's wartime anti-Semitic past is excavated as the pair search for the burial site of Ida's murdered Jewish parents. In the course of their journey the pair encounter emergent pop culture via a young hitchhiking saxophonist whose group plays 1960s Polish pop and American jazz. The film thus offers Ida compromised responses to the scorched earth of central European postwar experience. Wanda's apostate commitment to socialist ideology has exhausted itself in a retreat to alcoholism, promiscuity and eventually suicide, yet the representation of liberal individualism in the figures of the musicians seems empty and directionless. The film is more ambivalent regarding Ida's Catholicism. Religion in the film is presented less as a belief system and instead as a way of life orchestrated around a set of rituals, administered by a group of adherents and anchored in a particular place. Like Turner's workshop and Gustave's hotel, the convent offers something selfless and permanent that is abstracted from the violent experience of historical change. In contrast to individual extroverted flamboyance, the convent represents a sanctum of introspection where the self commits to contemplative, communal practice. This culminates towards the end of the film where one of Ida's fellow novices takes her vows, repeating the catechism, 'I vow chastity, poverty and obedience'. If *Ida* is ultimately agnostic about institutionalised belief, like *Mr. Turner* and *The Grand Budapest Hotel*, it surrenders to the transcendent as represented in aesthetics. The truth of this alternative is self-evident in the beauty of the film's look on the screen that, as with the other nominees, threatens to overwhelm competing meanings in the film. Tellingly, many commentators regarded that the key to *Ida*'s meaning was locked in an understanding of its enigmatic look. Representative here is David Denby's review in *The New Yorker*:

> I can't recall a movie that makes such expressive use of silence and portraiture; from the beginning, I was thrown into a state of awe by the movie's fervent austerity … Sometimes the figures are positioned at the bottom of the frame, with enormous gray Polish skies above them, as if the entire burden of a cursed country weighed on its people (Denby, 2014)

Denby's response seeks symbolic closure whereby the aesthetic ultimately references Polish history, yet his language suggests a less intellectual, more experiential and transcendent response. This alternative interpretation is consistent with the positioning of Pawlikowski's work as 'poetic realism'. As described by Claire Monk, 'A "poetic" aesthetic is framed as a matter of auteurist "personal expression" and celebrated for its own sake as a desirable end in itself' (Monk, 2012, p. 486). Poetic realism locates meaning less in something as crude as history and more in artistry as a self-sacrificing testimony to itself. Perhaps of more interest than the meaning of the film's look is the very compulsion to seek meaning in this assertive beauty. *Ida*'s aesthetic freezes narrative time into a rapturous state and focuses attention on the image's opaque density; its purely formal qualities. Accounts of Lukasz Zal's shooting strategy for *Ida* are in keeping with a sympathetic model of digital naturalism that similarly attempts to stop time:

> *Ida*'s form was designed to be as unadorned as possible. Almost all the shots are locked off … There is no traditional coverage. Zal describes the approach as creating scenes with "posters" – wide, static frames that enclose the characters (Bergery, 2014, p. 57).

'Unadornded' by layers, the craft here is stripped down to its essentials and cloistered from the ravages of progress. The static, wide-angle compositions, black-and-white aesthetic, the 1:33:1 aspect ratio alongside the absence of coverage serves to pull the film's aesthetic in the direction of still photography. The cinematography hauls the craft back to its origins in 'painting with light' and underscores the film's own retreat into ancient certainties. The look of Ida is ultimately its own sanctuary, where beauty rather than Polish history manifests the film's timeless answer to modernity. As with *Mr. Turner* and *The Grand Budapest Hotel*, *Ida*'s politics are ultimately aesthetic: art is its own purpose and reward, inviting the viewer to seek refuge in its austere purity.

Birdman's protagonist is Riggan Thomson, an actor previously famous for his role in a superhero franchise who stakes his reputation on a theatrical adaptation of a Raymond Carver short story. In *Birdman*, art is again anchored in a community of (in this case cranky) professionals whose individual self-absorptions ultimately dissolve in the successful execution of a collaborative aesthetic project. Alongside Ida's convent, Turner's workshop and Gustave's hotel, the physical space of *Birdman*'s Broadway theatre is the crucible that allows the creative process to be organically realised in contrast to the implicitly CGI-showy mass culture represented by Riggan's previous career. If the antagonists of *The Grand Budapest Hotel* are those that do not respect craftsmanship, *Mr. Turner* is anxious to produce an anti-technological appeal to natural craftsmanship, and *Ida* works to craft a compositional beauty that outdistances the temporal, *Birdman* celebrates a theatrical aesthetic. The central conceit of *Birdman* is the long take that reinforces the live-action immediacy of this theatricality. The long take is also the technique in the cinematographer's arsenal apparently least affected by the transition to the digital workflow. Accounts of the rise of the Steadicam, for instance, highlight how the technology in the words of Ramaeker might, 'replace the need for cutting' (Ramaeker, 2014, p. 120). Seemingly renouncing postproduction, *Birdman*'s resulting digital naturalism testifies that events were filmed in real time by a real crew. The 'realism' of this long take is showily theatrical, however. As described by Peter Bradshaw, 'there's traditionally a fair bit of cinephile machismo involved in the continuous tracking shot … No movie flourish draws attention to itself quite as emphatically as this' (Bradshaw, 2016). Accounts stress the labour-intensive techniques deployed by cinematographer Emmanuel Lubezki in principal photography, including practical lighting and Steadicam operation. *American Cinematographer*, for instance, points to the physicality of Lubezki's camera whirling through the sinewy passages of the set built by production designer Kevin Thompson:

> The camera was in constant motion, executing dozens of 360-degree moves, with Lubezki following characters or pedaling backwards in front of them, scaling catwalks and descending to the stage (Oppenheimer, 2014, p. 57)

If *Ida*'s shooting strategy attempts to make time stand still, *Birdman*'s attempts to make it run, or, better, fly. The result is not merely consistent with the setting of theatre with actors spontaneously improvising in motion but also with digital naturalism as a strategy for consolidating the cinematographer's centrality. The long take underlines the live athleticism of Lubezki's camera as an embodied fellow actor whereby cinematography itself becomes a theatrical performance to be noticed and acclaimed.

If one platform of the neo-traditional ATL narrative is the Oscar ceremony, another is the behind-the-scenes machination of the ASC. In 2002, the ASC president Steven Poster intensified the activities of its Technology Committee with a multi-million dollar research centre devoted to postproduction workflow (See Misek, 2010, p. 407, Lucas, 2014, p. 135). The fallout was felt in 2007 when the Technology Committee established a 'colour decision list' (CDL) described by Caldwell as a way to do digital production 'the film way' (2008, p. 184). The CDL lists the metadata recorded on set meaning that any subsequent alteration can be tracked and potentially regulated. Misek summarises the compromise: 'Cinematographers control the overall colour scheme of a film; colourists have control over more precise shot-by-shot colour effects' (2010, p. 408). All the same, the fallout of these upheavals continues to be felt in the anxiety surrounding authorship of the digital look. Alongside the ATL control schemes documented above are lower profile BTL counter-measures including leaks from digital production houses revealing their input into the final aesthetic of nominated films including Rhythm and Hues work on *Life Of Pi* (see p. 106, *Life After Pi*, 2014), the intensive grading of LOOK Effects on *The Grand Budapest Hotel* (see Wilson, 2014) and Rodeo FX team's work on stitching together the illusion of continuity in *Birdman* (see Fotheringham, 2015). It is perhaps not coincidental therefore that a final trope of the current discourse surrounding the digital look attempts to foreground management and supervision to discipline the workflow (see Lucas, 2014, p. 155). If my emphasis has been on a conservative account of the 'art' of the cinematographer as 'loyalty' to traditional communities, the films nominated in the 2015 awards are keen to also stress the cinematographer's management of the workflow's entire crew extending now into new arenas of digital postproduction and effectively acknowledging the compromise negotiated by the ASC. The nominee where the question of management of the digital team is perhaps most prominent is Roger Deakins' cinematography on the otherwise critically savaged *Unbroken*. I want to speculate that the unity of Deakins' management of the workflow is, in part, shored up by disavowing the input of a substitute newcomer who was still less part of the team than the digital effects workers. Accounts of Deakins's contribution stress his own seniority in comparison with the film's inexperienced director, Angelina Jolie. Jolie's celebrity, her association with CGI through appearances in *Lara Croft: Tomb Raider* (2001) and *Beowulf* (2007) and her femininity cast her not as an active rival, but as a passive screen onto which are projected narratives of masculine control. As Guy Lodge writes:

> If any film-maker were to give Zamperini's a chance, it's not the green, humourless Jolie, who has a clear gift for choosing collaborators – cinematographer Roger Deakins, the usually electric Jack O'Connell – but can't marshall them for saccharine, amber-coloured coffee (Lodge, 2015)

The male crew is measured and venerated against the backdrop of Jolie's managerial incompetence. Into the vacuum steps the cinematographer-as-manager. Behind the scenes publicity shots positioned the young Jolie alongside Deakins as did *American Cinematographer* that stated, 'Standing by her side was Roger Deakins, ASC, BCS, whose presence undoubtedly inspired confidence' (Oppenheimer, 2015, p. 41). Deakins is represented as authoritative, professionally accredited and marshaling his team with aesthetic grace and managerial skill. It is apparent then that accounts were keen to exonerate Deakins from the film's problems and instead situate him as a reassuringly patrician figure who implicitly rescued Jolie from her own fledgling status by orchestrating his male team. As Deakins states, 'Our Australian crew was top-class: Shaun, Toby, AJ … Brian Cox. They were all terrific – as were my regulars, Andy, Bruce and Josh' (cited in Oppenheimer, 2015, p. 53). The collaborative process now extends beyond principal photography and into the similarly masculine arena of postproduction. Deakins's regulars here include digital imaging technician Josh Gollish and digital colourist Mitch Paulson, now also within the fold of Deakins' management. As Deakins continues, 'We actually had quite a lot to do … because of the number of visual – effects shots' (cited in Oppenheimer, 2015, p. 53). Ultimately, the discourse around the film asserts the cinematographer's authority over previously warring factions within the workflow with the director herself relegated to the margins. The newfound harmony under Deakins' management is, in part, a function of the 'green', 'saccharine' and female Jolie's expulsion that tightens the remaining circle of experience, aesthetic refinement and masculinity.

Postscript: The cinematographer as revenant

The Oscar ceremony of 2016 took place at the Dolby Theatre on 28 February. Whilst controversy swirled around the hashtag #OscarsSoWhite, Emmanuel Lubezki would return to win his third consecutive best cinematography Oscar for a further collaboration with director Alejandro G. Iñárritu. *The Revenant* (2015) recounts the 'harrowing survival story' of Hugh Glass who awakens in a shallow grave following a ferocious attack from a CGI rendered grizzly bear and pursues the party of former colleagues that betrayed him. In a review for *Vanity Fair*, Richard Lawson describes the film as 'über-masculine' and a form of 'macho vérité'. His review concludes:

> Much hay will be made about *The Revenant's* white-knuckle gruesome-ness, and I suspect many viewers will take pleasure in feeling ragged but a little tougher for having sat through this slow, torturous adventure. Which, I think, is the intended effect. (Imagine how tough everyone feels for making it.) (Lawson, 2015)

The Revenant follows the 2015 nominees in its symmetry between Glass's own engagement with the elements of the frontier and the crew's own digital naturalism experienced during the shoot in Canada. Michael Goldman's account in *American Cinematographer* also positions the film's internal narrative as an allegory for the filmmaking process stating 'the entire crew performed "as true filmmakers" — a hearty band of collaborators on their own adventure, mirroring the saga they were putting onscreen'. (Goldman, 2016, p. 28) His account is anxious to stress the direct, unmediated naturalism of the shoot that, whilst shot digitally on the Arri Alexa and Alexa Xt, exclusively used natural lighting, was shot in chronological order and, like DiCaprio's resourceful protagonist, had to deal with primal, elemental forces such as lenses contracting due to sudden drops in temperature. Lubezki himself speaks of the process:

> We discovered that when you are exposed to the weather and these conditions every day, you have to adapt. I had to shoot the movie chronologically, because that is how it is written — it starts in autumn and moves into winter. And the character goes through a very real physical experience of being in the middle of nowhere for months. So we couldn't do it on a set, under normal Hollywood rules, and bring in snow and put in bluescreens. I wanted to absolutely kill any artifice. In keeping with that truth, we had to go through a true natural process (cited in Goldman, 2016, p. 38)

This unmediated naturalism would extend to the crew enlisting the Canadian authorities to trigger an actual avalanche using a helicopter that dropped explo-sive charges in coordination with Glass's reaction on the foreground as he real-ises the extent of his betrayal. The narrative hence recounts the importance of loyalty between hyper-competitive communities within brutal conditions apparently, at least, similar to the crew's experience described by Lubezki as 'the roughest and hardest thing I have ever done in my life' (cited in Goldman, 2016, p. 37). Goldman's account hence acknowledges the input of the apparently all-male crew consisting of production designer Jack Fisk, gaffer

Martin Keough, digital imaging technician Arthur To, camera operator Scott
Sakamoto and supervising finishing artist Steve Scott – described by Lubezki
as 'my right hands' (cited in Goldman, 2016, p. 38). In short, *The Revenant*
would recapitulate the major themes of the 2015 nominees including the ideology that a return to muscular methods in natural conditions can reinvig-
orate an aesthetic alongside the significance of loyalty and hierarchy within
neo-traditional, homo-social working communities. As argued above, these
Oscar nominees for best cinematography demonstrate an anxiety on behalf of
the cinematography community to stress that the cinematographer is himself
a revenant, and that despite attempts to kill him off he remains the key collaborator in the production of the film's look in the digital age. As such, the
nominations can be read following Caldwell as an example of an ATL control
scheme designed to reassert a neo-traditional workflow and division of labour
that polices established professional and sometimes gender hierarchies. The
films and the trade publicity circulating around their release work in tandem
to recentralise the cinematographer as the dominant figure in the conception,
management and execution of the look.

References

Atkinson, J. (2001). *The Oscars: The Pocket Essentials*. Harpenden: Pocket
    Essentials.
Beach, C. (2015). *A Hidden History of Film Style: Cinematographers, Directors
    and the Collaborative Process*, Oakland, CA: University of California Press.
Bergery, B. (2014). Divine purpose. *American Cinematographer* 95 (5): 54–64.
____. (2015). Eloquence through art. *American Cinematographer* 96 (1): 66–75.
Bordwell, D. (2015). Wes Anderson takes the 4:3 challenge. In Seitz, M. (Ed.).
    The Wes Anderson Collection: The Grand Budapest Hotel. New York, NY:
    Abrams pp. 235–51.
Bradshaw, P. (2016). Victoria Review – gripping one-take thriller on the
    streets of Berlin. *Guardian*. Retrieved from http://www.theguardian.com/
    film/2016/mar/31/victoria-review-one-take-berlin-schipper-heist-thriller.
Brooks X. et al (2014). The Guardian Film Show: Mr Turner, Nightcrawler, The
    Overnighters and Horns – video reviews. *Guardian*. Retrieved from http://
    www.theguardian.com/film/video/2014/oct/31/mr-turner-nightcrawler-
    the-overnighters-horns-video-reviews.
Buckley, C. A statue more than worth its weight in gold: Measuring the effects
    of Oscar nods and wins. Newyorktimes.com, 3 December. Retrieved from
    https://www.nytimes.com/2014/12/04/movies/awardsseason/measuring-
    the-effects-of-oscar-nods-and-wins.html?_r=0
Caldwell, J. (2008). *Production Culture: Industrial Reflexivity and Critical
    Practice in Film and Television*, Durham, NC: Duke University Press.

____. (2013). Authorship below-the-Line. In J. Gray and D. Johnson (Eds) *A Companion to Media Authorship*, Somerset, NJ: John Wiley and Sons, pp. 349–69.

____. (2014). Para-industry, shadow academy, *Cultural Studies*, 28 (4): 720–40.

Coleman, L. (ed.) (2016). *Transnational Cinematography Studies*, Lanham, MD: Lexington Books.

Corrigan, T. (1990). The commerce of auteurism: A voice without authority. *New German Critique*, 1 (49): 43–57.

Cowan, P. (2012). Underexposed: The neglected art of the cinematographer. *Journal of Media Practice*, 13 (1): 75–96

Curtin, M. & Vanderhoef, J. (2015). A vanishing piece of the Pi: The globalization of visual effects labor. *Television and New Media*, 16 (3): 219–39.

Denby, D. (2014). "Ida": A Film Masterpiece. *New Yorker*. Retrieved from http://www.newyorker.com/culture/culture-desk/ida-a-film-masterpiece.

Fotheringham, S. (2015). The use of VFX to stitch Birdman together. *BTLNews*. Retrieved from http://www.btlnews.com/awards/the-use-of-vfx-to-stitch-birdman-together.

Florida, Richard. (2012). *The Rise of the Creative Class: Revisited, Revised and Expanded*, New York: Basic Books.

Gaskin, S. (2013). Christopher Doyle interview part 2: "Life of Pi" Oscar is an insult to cinematography. Retrieved from http://sea.blouinartinfo.com/news/story/874483/christopher-doyle-interview-part-2-life-of-pi-oscar-is-an.

Gehrlein, W. and Kher, H. (2004). Decision rules for the Academy Awards versus those for elections. *Interfaces* 34 (3): 226–34.

Gerstner, D. and Staiger, J. (Ed.) (2003). *Authorship and Film*, London and New York: Routledge.

Goldman, M. (2016). Left for dead. *American Cinematographer*, 97 (1): 36–53

Goodale, G. (2004). Oscar winners reflect on getting gold. *The Christian Science Monitor* Retrieved from http://www.csmonitor.com/2004/0227/p11s02-almo.html.

Keating, P. (2010). *Hollywood Lighting from the Silent Era to Film Noir*, New York, NY: Columbia University Press.

Lawson, R. (2015). The Revenant is a harrowing survival story that strains for meaning. *Vanity Fair*. Retrieved from http://www.vanityfair.com/hollywood/2015/12/the-revenant-review-leonardo-dicaprio.

Lodge, G. (2015). DVDs and downloads: Birdman, Unbroken, The Last Five Years and more. *Guardian*. Retrieved from http://www.theguardian.com/film/2015/may/03/birdman-unbroken-the-last-five-years-dvd-review-guy-lodge.

Lucas, C. (2014). The Modern Entertainment Marketplace, 2000-present. In P. Keating (Ed.) *Cinematography (Behind the Silver Screen)*, New Brunswick, NJ: Rutgers University Press, pp. 132–57.

McRobbie, A (2016). *Be Creative: Making a Living in the New Culture Industries*, London and Malden, MA: Polity Press.

Misek, R. (2010). The 'look' and how to keep it: Cinematography, postproduction and digital colour. *Screen*, 15 (4): 404–9.

Monk, C. (2012) 'If you can't make a good political film, don't': Pawel Pawlikowski's resistant poetic realism. *Journal of British Cinema and Television*, 9 (3), pp. 480-501

Oppenheimer, J. (2014). Backstage drama. *American Cinematographer*, 95 (12): 54–67.

___. (2015). Ultimate survivor. *American Cinematographer*, 96 (1): 40–53.

Prince, S. (2004). The emergence of filmic artifacts: Cinema and cinematography in the digital era. *Film Quarterly*, 57 (3): 24–33.

Ramaeker, P. (2014). The New Hollywood: 1981-1999. In P. Keating (ed.) *Cinematography (Behind the Silver Screen)*, New Brunswick, NJ: Rutgers University Press, pp. 106–31.

Rogers, A. (2012). "You Don't So Much Watch It As Download It": Conceptualizations of digital spectatorship. *Film History*, 24: 221–34.

Ross, A. (2004). *No–Collar: The Humane Workplace and its Hidden Costs*, Philadelphia, PA: Basic Books.

Stahl, M. (2009). Privilege and distinction in production worlds: Copyright, collective bargaining and working conditions in media making. In Mayer, V., Banks, M. Caldwell, J. (Eds) *Production Studies: Cultural Studies of Media Industries*, New York: Routledge, pp. 132–57.

Stasukevich, I. (2014). 5 star service. *American Cinematographer*, 95 (3): 30–41.

Wexman, V. (ed.) (2003). *Film and Authorship*. New Brunswick, NJ: Rutgers University Press.

Wilson, T. (2014). A distinctive look for 'The Grand Budapest Hotel'. Retrieved from https://library.creativecow.net/wilson_tim/VFX_The-Grand-Budapest-Hotel/1.

CHAPTER EIGHT

Improbable Curators: Analysing Nostalgia, Authorship and Audience on Tumblr Microblogs

Dinu Gabriel Munteanu
Bournemouth University

Introduction

Launched in 2007 and hosting around 280 million blogs as of February 2016, Tumblr[1] is one of the most popular yet under-researched microblogging platforms currently in existence. Having established itself as a premier venue of online popular and youth culture (Dewey, 2015), the service provides an idiosyncratic synesthetic space wherein countless visual and stylistic statements are shared daily, ranging from digital images to literary excerpts, journal entries to animations. The absence of subordinating vertical structures (there exists no real 'mainstream' vs. 'underground' dynamic here), the possibility of interpreting the blogs both as niche and micro youth media (see Thornton, 1995, pp. 137-151) and the socially interactive element of these unregulated exchanges all reflects a parallel world rich in psycho-social connotations that remains largely uncharted by social scientists.

How to cite this book chapter:
Munteanu, D. G. 2017. Improbable Curators: Analysing Nostalgia, Authorship and
    Audience on Tumblr Microblogs. In: Graham, J. and Gandini, A. (eds.). *Collabo-
    rative Production in the Creative Industries*. Pp. 125–156. London: University of
    Westminster Press. DOI: https://doi.org/10.16997/book4.h. License: CC-BY-NC-
    ND 4.0

This chapter draws on a project that investigated these novel circulatory dynamics over a period of three years by employing digital ethnographic and semiotic analyses. By becoming highly selective content curators, these users develop independent, privately informed yet interpersonally mediated, digitally synesthetic narratives. The Tumblr infrastructure provided a system of content distribution and collaborative design that not only destabilises the three conventional 'sites' of an image ('production', 'image', 'audience') (cf. Rose, 2007, pp. 14–27), but also raises interesting questions with regard to individual agency and the 'naturalisation' of creative practices online.

What type of vicarious 'curatorial' visions are being articulated here, what psychological and cultural functions might they serve and in what ways do these phenomena interact with mainstream material realities? How does Tumblr's potential as a platform for anonymous, flexible and easily accessible aesthetic expression, stylistic experimentation and emotional catharsis compare with other social media offerings, and what might we learn from it in terms of encouraging reflexivity and meaningful social communication online? Finally, how do these loosely-woven user communities compare to cultural and creative practises employed in contemporary museography and collaborative or activist online productions more broadly?

I will begin with a brief description of the Tumblr platform itself, followed by a number of relevant semiotic and ethnographic examples extracted from the fieldwork for this project. These inform a more theoretical discussion in the latter part of the chapter, where I consider to what extent Tumblr might model the ideal 'curatorial' platform for emergent modes of collaborative production, as discussed by Jean-Paul Martinon in his book *The Curatorial: A Philosophy of Curating* (2013). I also use Tumblr-related observations to address issues related to contemporary museography and artistic knowledge transmission more broadly, referring in this process to the work of authors such as Malraux (1978) and Rancière (2009). I conclude by suggesting that there exists considerable potential for Tumblr communities to function as independent sites of knowledge (re)production, acting as non-commercial user archives, or reflexive and dialogical repositories of individually-filtered cultural content. My analysis thereby also attempts to offer a more positive, conciliatory perspective on the debates within new and social media, which tend to oscillate between optimism and pessimism (e.g., Fuchs, 2015; Gauntlett, 2015; Turow, 2012; Jakobsson & Stiernstedt, 2010; see also Hesmondhalgh, 2013, chapter 9).

Tumblr: History and corporate topography

Although considered a social networking or social media tool, the microblogging service Tumblr retains a number of unique characteristics, both in terms of interface design and functionality, as well as corporate philosophy. It is, for example, more complex and more eclectic than Pinterest, with which it shares only superficially similar 'curatorial' mechanics, in the sense that both services provide the tools to create collections of digital material. The latter, however, has over time become associated with a relatively sectarian community fuelled by a largely female demographic focused on creating massive archives of recipes, wedding gift ideas, crafts and the like (see Friz & Gehl, 2015), while Tumblr continues to harbour a much more culturally heterogeneous user-base and content pool. In this sense, statistical data and industry commentaries (Tan, 2013; Dewey, 2015; Reeve, 2016) suggest that Tumblr has already surpassed Facebook as one of the most popular digital social network for teenagers (aged between 13 and 25). As Tech-Crunch's Adam Rifkin noted, the service can perhaps even be understood as a sort of 'Facebook 2.0': 'Facebook has become a real-life social network infested with parents, co-workers, ex-friends, and people you barely know, [while] Tumblr has become the place where young people express themselves and their ACTUAL INTERESTS with their ACTUAL FRIENDS' (Rifkin, 2013, p. 2, original emphasis).

Founded in February 2007, by November 2012 Tumblr had 'shouldered its way into the top ten online destinations, edging out Microsoft's Bing and drawing nearly 170 million visitors to its galaxy of user-created pages [...]. Tumblr's tens of millions of registered users create[d] 120,000 new blogs every day, for a total of 86 million and counting, which drive some 18 billion page views per month' (Bercovici, 2013, p. 1). Even before that, in September 2011, its funding rounds 'valued Tumblr at $800 million, making [David] Karp's [the then 26-year-old Tumblr CEO's] 25%-plus stake worth more than $200 million. Then its traffic doubled' (ibid, p.1). And then, of course, in June 2013, Tumblr was acquired for a little over one billion dollars by the legendary (ex) Googler Marissa Mayer, acting as Yahoo!'s new CEO. This move, meant to extend Yahoo!'s reach with a younger and more mobile demographic, immediately sparked concerns throughout the Tumblr 'vernacular', with corporate- and advertising-related anxieties soaring and industry commentators watching the developments closely (Walker, 2012). The deal struck between Mayer and an apparently uncompromising Karp hinged on the promise that the service would stay independent, and that no changes at CEO level would happen. In other words, Yahoo! accepted the challenge of acquiring Tumblr 'without ruining it' (Brustein, 2013). This is all extremely significant, all the more so because Karp's condescension towards conventional advertising is well known and has persisted even as his platform continues to face difficulties in turning a profit and sustaining its growth (see Walker, 2012; Edwards, 2013; Kim, 2016). As Elspeth Reeve (2016) notes, this tension is unlikely to be resolved in the near future:

> In 2010, its founder, David Karp, said, "We're pretty opposed to advertising. It really turns our stomachs." Then in 2011: "Making money off of Tumblr would be incredibly easy" — he'd throw up an AdSense ad on every user's dashboard and make the site "wildly profitable". In April 2012 sponsored content began appearing in users' streams. Tumblr was, at that time, still a unicorn; the possibility of making money was just

as powerful an asset as the actual making of it. In 2013, Yahoo bought
Tumblr for $1 billion and began a new ad rollout, but after a year, Karp's
wild profitability still hadn't materialized. A former Tumblr executive
told *The New York Times* that Tumblr's anonymity was a hurdle: "Real-
world identities are valuable to advertisers. Tumblr doesn't have that".
(para. 43)

What renders Tumblr relatively unprofitable at a corporate level, however,
is precisely what makes it extremely appealing to its users, who continue
to benefit from an extremely streamlined sign-up process and intuitive pri-
vacy controls that allow for complete anonymity, while encouraging effective inter-blog communication. Its potential for virality is further enhanced
through the minimalistic yet effective use of 'reblogs' and 'likes', while users
continue to have complete aesthetic and functional control over the look of
their microblog(s). All of these things create an overall non-commercial, even
alternative feel to the entire platform, generating a radically emotive value to
it that David Karp clearly understands and cultivates: 'to me, Tumblr is very
much about creative expression [...] limitless creative expression, your page
can look any way you want, you can tear out the Tumblr branding if you want
and create something that just looks totally unique on the Web' (Karp, 2011,
cited in Dixon, 2011, 4:10). This relatively utopian state of affairs — where
profitability is placed second to user interface and design — is arguably due
to its CEO's uncompromising principles (his disdain for standard advertising
and popularity indexes is notorious— 'they're gross'), making Karp one of the
most contrarian internet entrepreneurs of the century ('Tumblr *is* David' - see
Walker, 2012, para. 3).[2]
    Until July 2016, when Yahoo! itself was acquired by the US telecommunica-
tions giant Verizon, no structural changes had been made to how the platform
functioned, and no advertising had been forced inside the actual space of users'
tumblrs. The odd Samsung commercial popping up behind the scenes, so to
say, in users' *dashboards* (see below), with its little dollar sign hanging almost
ironically in a corner, was the most visible effort being made, something the
community appeared to tolerate. Unfortunately, it is no coincidence that on 26
July 2016, the same day that Verizon confirmed the $4.8 billion Yahoo! acquisi-
tion, Tumblr discreetly announced that it would start serving ads directly on
users' microblogs, on slide-out sections on the web, and on its mobile apps and
web (see Perez, 2016). This announcement, in essence a development that Karp
had opposed for years, was 'softened', indeed almost pivoted on the promise
that the income will be shared with bloggers ('getting you paid for your work' –
Karp, 2016, para. 4). Also, users were given the ability to simply turn off the
on-blog advertising feature, which itself was activated only on blogs using the
service's default Optica theme (in effect 'protecting' the milions of users who
had in one way or another customized their tumblr). As of December 2016,
many questions still remain unanswered, including how the ad revenue sharing system will work; Verizon itself failed to even mention Tumblr in its press

release, though it did say Yahoo!'s services and brands will continue to operate separately. As one commentator suggested, the new investor may indeed lack a real idea what to do with Tumblr (see Walters, 2016). Despite all of this, Karp's vision still appears deeply influential, with official Tumblr ad-related messages remaining simple and to the point, indeed at times touched by a provocatively apologetical tone: 'a post-consumerist society built on an economy of surplus instead of scarcity would enable Yahoo! and Tumblr to procure both labor and materials at zero marginal cost. Just something to think about' ('Tumblr Ads and You', Tumblr.com, para. 15).

The young nostalgics: Introducing a Tumblr capsule

Within the deeply eclectic Tumblr universe, the 'young nostalgics' are remarkably well encapsulated. 'Young nostalgics' is the term I use to describe a relatively elastic, and somewhat elusive, community. The microblogs

Figure 8.1: Screenshot of author's tumblr dashboard. Embedded (reblogged) image source: https://www.flickr.com/photos/belladayys/9144559116/

belonging to this community, essentially digital scrapbooks, are loosely integrated within a larger architecture of digital visuality and affect. They are often pervaded by an oneiric air of ambiguity, of interpenetrated psycho-symbolic accents — stressing the feminine here, the mystical there, the childish or the tragic a few images lower. However, despite the differences in general mood (some blogs are softer, with a light and innocent air — the cases of Luna and Lara — while others are a little darker, stressing the magical or the mysterious elements of nostalgia — Charlotte — with others falling somewhere in between — M. & W; see below), all of the analysed tumblrs share, in varying but distinct proportions, a combination of aesthetic and affective themes that make them recognizable as belonging to the same community.

The first 'nostalgic' microblog that I encountered, M.'s *La Douleur Exquise*, was discovered accidentally in the autumn of 2010. I did not realize, at that time, that tens of thousands of people followed it regularly, nor did I anticipate that it would become, together with a number of similar blogs, the focus of my research. As I imagine many of M.'s followers did, I browsed through its content simply because I found the website's aesthetic consistency alluring and wistful mood fascinating. Following a 'snow-ball' sampling (i.e., a non-probability sampling technique where an original subject's context, in this case 20-year-old M.'s tumblr, redirected me, either through a direct recommendation, or through various 'chain links', to additional sources), I identified, successfully contacted and interviewed the following tumblr owners (beginning with M.):

- M., Tbilisi, Georgia (blog description – 'Miss Wallflower'/*La Douleur Exquise*; ~ 86,000 followers, as of April 2012); native Georgian; born in 1991; started microblogging in May 2009; will be referred to as: **Wallflower** / **M.** (archived screenshot below, retrieved 7 March 2012).

  "I'm a very nostalgic person in general. And I tend to daydream a lot, and daydream about the past, and older times, and yes, of course, [my tumblr] it's very nostalgic. The mood is nostalgic" (Wallflower).

- C., the Netherlands (blog description - *Cygnes de la Nuit*; ~1,500 followers, as of June 2013); originally from Syria; born in 1995; started microblogging in November 2011; will be referred to as **Luna** (archived screenshot below, retrieved 9 June 2013).

  "I certainly think my tumblr draws inspiration from the past, in almost every single way. Almost all the pictures from my blog are somehow related to the past. (building from the past, vintage clothing, screencaps from old movies and a lot of pictures from Lana Del Rey, who's a huge inspiration to me and who always looks very vintage" (Luna).

Figure 8.2: Screenshot of Wallflower's blog (with blogger's permission).

- M.T., USA (blog description, *Whimsical Nostalgia*; ~4,527 followers, as of November 2012); originally from the US; born in 1992; blogging 'on and off for a few years', but only 'recently got into it when my friend introduced me to tumblr in my freshmen year of college in 2011'; will be referred to as **Charlotte** (archived screenshot below, retrieved 9 June 2013).

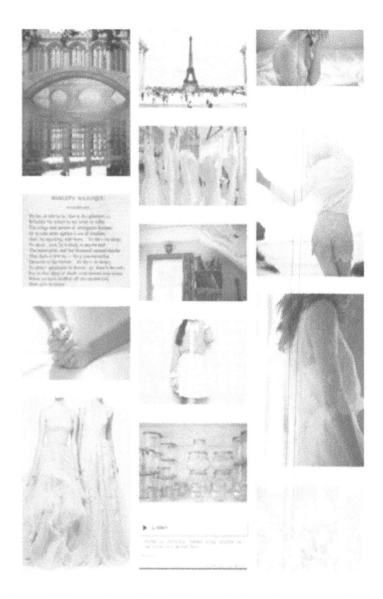

Figure 8.3: Screenshot of Luna's blog (with blogger's permission), low contrast original.

"Eclectic. Pensive. Ethernal. [...] I have always been in love with odd or whimsical things or things that evoke strong emotions. I was in love with period films at the time when creating the blog so I was very much

Figure 8.4: Screenshot of Charlotte's blog (with blogger's permission).

into Victorian art, literature, and architecture (like Charlotte Bronte or Jane Austen). [The title] kind of just came to me after that because I wanted something that captured the essence of my blog in short, precise, 'elegant' words that were not too complicated but were just as beautiful in text as they were to hear just like the literature that I was so in love with" (Charlotte) .

- **W.**, France/USA (blog description, *Memories Unmade*; unknown number of followers; screenshot attached below, retrieved 3 March 2012; started microblogging in early 2011; will be referred to as **W.**); W.'s case is interesting. Although she declined to later participate in a full interview, her prolific and often idiosyncratic commentaries allowed me to position myself more judiciously towards the other participants. Although W. was antagonized by what she perceived as my (excessively) academic attempts to 'conceptualise' the uniquely affective material collected by her (*'You're asking me to conceptualize my images ... which is something I hate'*), her suggestions and contestations have proved to be of considerable, possibly indispensable (reflexive) value to my study.

- K., USA (blog description, *Queen of the Waters*; 755 followers, as of December 2012); has been blogging 'for over three years now, perhaps even longer! I'm afraid I've lost track of time much too easily'; originally from the US; born in 1993; will be referred to as **Lara** (screenshot attached below, June 2013).

" I certainly believe my blog draws a lot of its inspiration from the past, starting with my childhood. I've always been fascinated with not only

Figure 8.5: Screenshot of W.'s blog (with blogger's permission).

fairy-tales, but the whole aspect of 'other worlds' – a world full of fantasy. [...]
They all play a part reflecting my world and thus, revealing my blog" (Lara).

These final five participants have been selected after filtering through considerably more invitations and (often lack of) replies. It still remains relatively difficult to approach a blogger on Tumblr; not only are contact details hard to identify, but some users simply disable or hide the already frugal 'ask' option from their blog. Interacting with the community as an academic (outsider) makes the task all the more challenging. Overall, I was quite fortunate to establish a positive rapport with these young participants, whose case studies have shed light unto what is a rich, though often 'self-guarded' nostalgic community.[3] In terms of the selection procedure for the analysed visual material, this was informed by a combination of random number extraction, participatory observations and individual inter-blog examples and comparisons. Ethnographic data was gathered between 2010–13 through the use of synchronous and non-synchronous interviews (e-mail and real time chat services), as well as from an extended real life encounter with Wallflower in Tbilisi, which alone has yielded 53 pages of transcribed text (approx. 19,000 words). A Foucaultian (1979) – Barthesian (1991) interpretative discourse analysis, combined with photographic semiology and compositional interpretation (see Rose, 2007, chapter 4; West, 2000), have provided the necessary qualitative methodological framework with which to approach the material. Particular attention was given to the empirical sources themselves, especially because the bloggers' idiosyncratic narratives are often of a deeply (inter)personal nature. Their complicated forays into history, art, emotion, biography, and self-reflection create intricate, ambiguous mythologies.

Figure 8.6: Screenshot of Lara's microblog (with blogger's permission), original low contrast.

As I will explain below, often Barthes' semiotic/theoretical work appeared limited, insufficient or excessively politicized, restricting the understanding of my participants' complex relationships in regard to authorship, individuality, community, aesthetics, memory and imagination. Nevertheless, I agree with his founding idea that 'myth' can, indeed, often be a 'type of speech' (Barthes, 1991, p. 109). More so, as the human potential for suggestion is infinite, everything can be(come) a myth (*idem*); pictures in particular 'are more imperative than writing […], [as they] become a kind of writing as soon as they are meaningful: like writing, they call for a lexis' (*ibidem*, p. 111). That is to say, they become 'language', 'discourse', 'speech', thus entering the analytical province of semiology. Equally, of course, they enter the anthropological realm of culture, which itself, as Geertz suggested, 'is essentially a semiotic one. Believing, with Max Weber, that man is an animal suspended in webs of significance he himself has spun, I take culture to be those webs, and the analysis of it to be therefore not an experimental science in search of law but an interpretive one in search of meaning' (Geertz, 1973, p. 5, emphasis added). I therefore approached the microblogs as open-ended, non-linear discursive entities, dialectically engaged within the social, aesthetic and stylistic realms of contemporary, as well as integrated in broader historical and cultural dynamics.

In terms of participant demographics, it is also worth noting that, although they come from different areas of the globe and share different cultural heritages (Wallflower and her friends are ethnic Georgians living in Tbilisi; Lara is North American; Luna is originally Syrian but lives in Holland; W. is from France, with US links; Charlotte has French, Spanish, Italian and Guamanian blood and lives in the US; many other tumblrs include individuals from Brazil, Russia, Italy or Greece), they all speak English and feel utterly at home on the Internet. In this sense, the act of organising and analysing these blogs revealed a cellular dispersion of the young nostalgic community throughout the larger Tumblr infrastructure. Indeed, the type of affective, mainly visual semiotics, relying on the symbols, themes and codes that I describe and contextualize in the following section, can be found in a growing number of tumblrs, either discovered by me, or explicitly mentioned by my participants. As of mid-2013, some of these bloggers include: autumnalreading, dearthimble, alice-eve-lithium, timetravelingscamp, paminamozartienne, debourbon, crownthewitchking, tangledboughs, beautifullyeternal, and many more (users such as Charlotte also have blogrolls where they promote hundreds of similar tumblrs). Often I found it impressive how much time, work and web design expertise (many tumblrs feature discreet soundtracks, video effects, various navigational 'blurs', etc.) these young people invest in their websites — all the more so because they seem to exist in a strange Tumblr bubble far outside the 'Tumblr meme' world, which is to say completely devoid of the usual deluge of cat humour, celebrity quotes or Internet-dividing debates on the exact colour of a dress (e.g., McCoy, 2015; Dewey, 2015; see also Goriunova, 2012).

The issue of exactly how this community's semiotic content is being circulated, however, poses a number of distinct challenges. For the same things that prevent advertisers and marketers from adequately penetrating the platform also make it hard to keep track of where everything goes and where everything comes from — as I will attempt to explain below.

Overlapping 'production', 'image' and 'audience'

Although the exploration of the following ideas could inform several studies and is perhaps one of the Gordian knots of 'digital culture' debates, I wish to underline here the simple fact that visual microbloggers do to the analysis of photography what no other phenomenon seems to have done before. In certain ways, they converge the three main sites of the Image — production, image itself, and audience (see Rose, 2007, pp. 14–27). One can hardly ignore, or indeed understate the importance of the multiple roles that these subjects inevitably assume in the act of designing cultural products such as their microblogs.

First of all, the image's actual source, its literal production site, is often so obfuscated by the intricate immensity of the Internet, that it becomes virtually impossible to retrieve. Some of my participants occasionally link back to an 'original', though typically that too is a re-presentation; in some cases, not even this weak act of ghost referencing happens. Its 'author' (see Barthes, 1977; Foucault, 1979) becomes, in a way, the blogger her or his self. If we then consider the (micro)blogger as an agent, an architect who uses the data for her or his own aesthetic-affective purposes, it can be argued that the totality of these images becomes — or allows for — an altogether different, but nonetheless new, or 'original', site of (re)production. We are then left with the image itself and with what John Fiske considered the most important dimension, that of the audience, where senses become pliable, renegotiable — in a way, where senses are (re)created: '[the audience] is the final site at which the meanings and effects of an image are made, for you are an audience of that photograph and, like all audiences, you bring to it your own ways of seeing and other kinds of knowledges' (quoted in Rose, 2007, p. 22). Similarly, the work of Jenkins (2013) takes the point further, documenting fans' 'transformative and expansive influence on culture … [their] working through central concerns around creativity, collaboration, community, and copyright' (p. xxxvi).

Then again, the senses have already been (re)created, for in that crucial moment when the blogger hijacks, or 'poaches' (Jenkins, 2013), or 'construes' (Firat & Dholakia, 2016) the photograph from somewhere else, she is herself, for a few seconds, the audience. Also important — particularly in the case of Wallflower's immensely popular blog, from which some of my other participants indicated they acquired many images — is the more conventional understanding of the 'audience', reflected by the thousands of people actively following a tumblr. Often these 'receivers' are 'authors' in their own right, having tumblrs of their own where they reblog much of the content they follow, thus creating a collaborative wave of continuous, and often somewhat similar content. Here is, for example, one of my own photographs circulating throughout the young nostalgics' tumblrsphere. In this case, my spontaneous 'artwork' was a celebration of fairytales (themselves an important, Romantically-informed theme running throughout the community). The image was created by me as a sort of good will gesture and included in one of my first messages to Marie.

Seeing that Wallflower's blog is very popular, the image has over the course of several days been reblogged by over a hundred of her followers (thus marking the beginning and the end of my 15-minute Tumblr fame), as some of the examples below can attest (see figures 8.8–8.9).

Figure 8.7: Reblogged photograph (copyright granted by author: D. G. Munteanu).

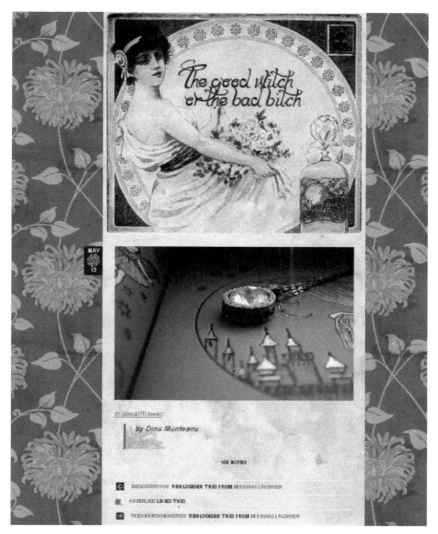

Figure 8.8: Reblogged photograph (copyright granted by author: D. G. Munteanu).

In this case, Wallflower mentioned my name, and some of her followers decided to keep the copyright reference, as the image was reproduced across many other microblogs. However, this is far from being the rule. Although some of my participants are increasingly aware of this 'attribution' dilemma,[4] much of the material circulating on tumblrs is 'free floating', devoid of direct references and therefore living parallel lives, with no direct authorial connections to

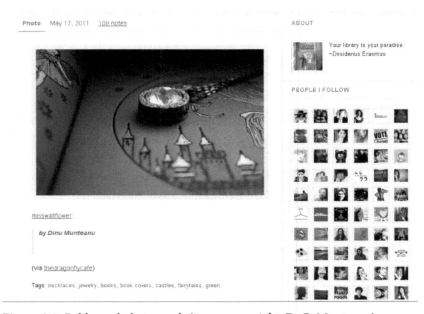

Figure 8.9: Reblogged photograph (image copyright: D. G. Munteanu).

safeguard their origin (for a philosophical exploration of the dilemmas associated with such 'remixing' environments, see, for example, Gunkle, 2016).

These last two sites of (re)production, imagery and audience, point us in two main directions before collapsing back on themselves: one is the semiological constituency of the image, the other is the bloggers' agency, their projective intentionality. Put simply: their individual reworking of said image(s). These nuances do not escape Marie's own assessment of authorship and meaning:

> Yes, [the photograph] [it] takes a life of its own. It's interesting, and it ... loses its meaning and it gains another meaning. Because everyone who posts and reblogs, they gave, for example I posted a photo of a sad girl, but I didn't see it in a sad way, I saw it differently, but someone reblogged and wrote underneath "I miss you" or something like that […] and it takes another, different [meaning].

Nostalgia and Tumblr space: Some examples

In essence, the microblogs I analyse are scrapbooks. They are public, interactive and integrated within a larger framework of visuality and affect. Their content is eclectic, almost never of an explicitly biographical colouring, and draws inspiration from many centuries of history without however losing the aesthetic, stylistic and, perhaps even more importantly, emotional and symbolic coherence that makes them instantly recognizable as 'young (tumblr) nostalgics'.

My participants are well aware of these dynamics, and they explicitly acknowledge that they navigate through difficult historiographic waters; in fact, they reflect upon their strokes with particular clarity: 'The Classical Antiquity, La belle époque, the roaring twenties, the fifties and the late sixties (Woodstock festival)' (Luna); '60s, this moment the 60s, [the] 19th century ... also, yes, my favourite periods, 19th, 18th century and the 60s' (Wallflower); 'the Victorian era, but I have also been interested in the 1920-1960's because I have also loved the music and dance styles from this time period as well as the dress' (Charlotte); 'the 40's, 70's, Regency, Georgian, and Victorian era' (Lara).

It is important to note here that the young nostalgics' intoxication with 'pastness' is to a large extent governed by a sense of psycho-historiographical control: they do not want it back, their intention is not what Svetlana Boym would call 'restorative', but rather it might be best characterised as 'reflective' (Boym, 2001, p. xviii). Beyond the transhistorical/ahistorical nature of how this 'pastness' is envisioned (encapsulating many epochs and times, with no clear focus on one or another), this desire to re-present the past is rooted in the faculty of imagination and so reliant on metaphor and allusion, rather than on any type of temporally grounded, sequentially arranged 'genealogy' of memory. In this respect the bloggers' creative practices throw into question the old adages about nostalgia's social 'pathology' – its 'simulational' cultural sterility, reactionary bourgeois symptomatology, 'abdication of memory', etc. (see Jameson, 1991; Baudrillard, 1981; Stewart, 1993, p. ix; Lasch, 1991, p. 83).

On the contrary, as I will argue below, the nostalgics' semiotic play and stylistic improvisations put significant stress on what Andrew Wernick rather pessimistically insisted is the hegemonic institutional transformation of all 'promotionally' circulating objects ('commodity-signs', be they images or messages) (see Wernick, 1991, pp. 15-16). In this sense, despite the fact that some of the material on these tumblrs is most certainly embedded, at least at its point of origin, in deeply commercial spheres (artefacts pertaining to the movie, fashion and beauty industries are conjoined here with artistic, activist and fandom-related material), it will become apparent from my respondents' input that they are well aware of these tensions, and that they approach them with an almost subversive reflexivity, arguably investing their blogging efforts with 'a posture, a matter of perception, the result of a conversation that allows the development of a mechanics of resistance to the present … [a] permanent quest for an inner balance […] always an in-between' (Valentin, cited in Boundas, 2006, p. 22).

For example, despite, or alongside a certain oneiric escapism permeating the community, the bloggers also exhibit an almost taken-for-granted awareness that the 'objective' past is not at all the focus of their psycho-aesthetic interests. These young bloggers seem 'not directed towards the past […], but rather *sideways*. The nostalgic feels stifled within the conventional confines of time and space' (Boym, 2001, xiv, emphasis added). When asked how they 'feel about *the* past', observations related to bigotry, sexism or hygiene are constantly and robustly invoked, and the ease with which these are delineated from the sense of self-cultivated, eclectically interiorized 'pastness' that defines these blogs further attests to their introspectively reflexive nature. In other words, we deal here not with a regressively temporal desire per se, but rather with intrinsic tendencies towards reverie, centered on the 'algia, the longing itself' (Boym, 2011, p. xviii). Similar points are invoked by Silke Arnold-de-Simine (2013) in her defence of a more equivocal, empathy- and reflexivity-centred approach to the topic of memory mediation in museums:

> But what happens when nostalgia is no longer seen as a means to an end, a symptom pointing towards a problem that can be solved, but if the person who is nostalgic indulges in the melancholic awareness that the past cannot be regained? What is longed for is not only unattainable because it is lost but because it is absent in a much more emphatic manner. In this case the yearning becomes an end in itself: one cannot recover something one never had and will never have but is possible to long for it […], a melancholia for an absence that often cannot be specified or clearly articulated but that is nevertheless acutely felt. (p. 59)

In fact, Tumblr in particular reflects this notion of non-temporal 'space' well. Note, for example, the environment's quintessentially visual nature. Even the textual material, from various literary quotes to other text-dependent journal entries, are often presented by my participants in the form of photographs, collages or screenshots, seamlessly integrated in the imagistic flux of one blog or another, and thus transcending their one-dimensional, conventional representation of simple, monochromatic rows of text (this is something that in my view no other platform, from Instagram to Pinterest, has managed to do so well) (see Figures 8.10–8.12., below).

In this sense, Tumblr's ability to create spatial collages replete with cinematic, visual and musical cues, takes full advantage of powerful affective characteristics often associated with:

> Cinema — like the cemetery — […] a space that is home to residual body images. Film and the cemetery share this special, corporeal

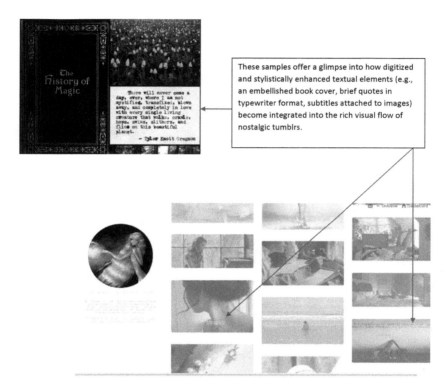

These samples offer a glimpse into how digitized and stylistically enhanced textual elements (e.g., an embellished book cover, brief quotes in typewriter format, subtitles attached to images) become integrated into the rich visual flow of nostalgic tumblrs.

Figure 8.10: (Screenshot of Charlotte's tumblr) & **8.11** (Screenshot of Lara's tumblr) (annotated).

geography. [...] As a machine of death, film technology engages in a time play with spatial movements. Capable of not only multiplying time and space but of extending time with prolonged mechanical movement, as well as freezing frames [...], the language of film inhibits a boundless desire to capture life [...], to overcome the finiteness of death. Preserving the moment in time and space, film travels the geography of death and immortality. (Bruno, 2002, p. 147)

Yet Tumblr seems to go a step further, eschewing any potential for directorial 'auteurism', as the material circulated here takes on a completely different life, or rather *comes* alive through subtle innuendoes and *mise en scènes* that only the bloggers themselves understand, control, and share. Indeed, their engagements with these mosaical signifiers are built on a collaborative ethos possessive of depth and sincerity, not unlike the 'labour of love' invested by fans in certain celebrity-dedicated websites (see Cook, 2012). Sometimes, these interiorized hedonic impulses combine biography with cognitive-imagistic

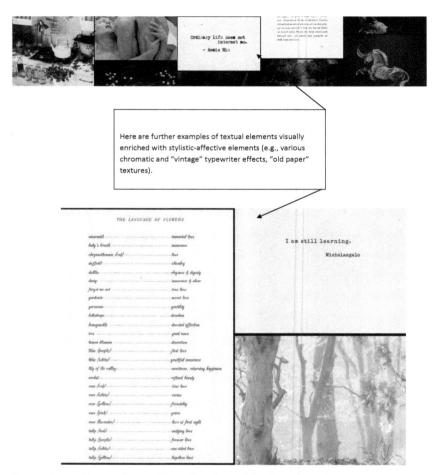

Figure 8.12: (Screenshots of Charlotte's tumblr) (annotated).

projections, and an unattributed blurred image of a girl running through rain in a suburban garden becomes an explicit 'enjoyment of summer, laughing, dancing' (Luna), just as an image of an old, unidentified musical score reminds Luna that 'I've never played an instrument, but one day I will'. Likewise, similar images apparently extracted from vintage movie stills 'remind me of the bliss of summer. The warmth of the sun against skin and the gentle breeze rustling the grass and tree's leaves' (Lara). This imaginative synaesthesia and anticipatory attention to 'lived' or reminiscent detail continues with 'a sweet aroma of flowers and the buzzing of bees' (Lara, on an image of a rose garden at dusk), a 'Castle in the Clouds' (Lara, on what appears to be a cropped version of an anonymous cloud) or with a 'cool touch of the window, fingers pressed against it while another's figure walks away' (Lara, on yet another graceful visual slide of a woman's hand pressed against a window). For W., an unknown balcony becomes simply a 'Wednesday morning in Lyon', just as a Victorian mansion overcome by ivy signifies 'another place where you want to be and to paint all the life it would have given you'; the same W., who possesses a poetic kind of brevity, described another unattributable architectural snapshot as 'Heathcliff's thrown away toys', capturing the inaccessible sort of sadness radiating from a washed out image of a gigantic building of apparently Tsarist descent.

Along similar lines, the recurrence of 'Parisian' details or miniatures (vintage fragrance vials, postcards, the Tower on the Champ de Mars, etc.) blends here not only with the eclectic connotations discussed above, but also with the sort of escapist/affective whimsicality that even the unforgiving Roland Barthes seems to feel ambivalent about when he empathetically acknowledges, perhaps in a secret reverie of his own, its blending of mythology with personal contemplation (note the allusion to childhood): 'the Tower can live on itself: one can dream there, eat there, observe there, understand there, marvel there, shop there; as on an ocean liner (another mythic object that sets children dreaming), one can feel oneself cut off from the world and yet the owner of the world' (Barthes, 1997, p. 17). Indeed, the young nostalgics, and Luna in particular, use the Tower as an instrument of imaginative projection, just as they all do with representations of French patisseries and macarons (themselves notable tumblr leitmotifs), i.e. to 'participate in a dream of which it is (and this is its originality) much more the crystallizer than the true object' (Barthes, 1997, p. 7).

The way in which these dream-like reveries intersect biography and introspection, as well as how they can blend with social commentary is a key finding from this project. In a way picking up from where Barthes (1991) left off, these examples show how, far from being 'victims' of an extraneous mythology, individuals can to a large extent control their own 'mythologies', building layer upon layer of individualized connotations, and finding pleasure in this very process.[5] As Lara put it: 'I wish I could tell the younger generations [note that Lara was born in 1993] that the things that make them expressive and unique is [sic] not a flaw at all, but makes them *beautiful*. That they don't have to look like an air-brushed model on a magazine or those in Hollywood to feel like they're worth it'. Charlotte made a similar point but also demonstrated a level of reflexivity typical of my respondents: 'I feel like men and women alike have lost the values that previous generations had, almost like a more modern day chivalrous code. [...] We need to find alternatives, and we definitely need to start caring less about materialistic things'.

Ultimately, in such cases, these reveries can safely be referred to as a form of 'nostalgia'. However understood in psycho-historical terms, following the emotion's Romantic acculturation from psychiatry into literature and the cultural vernacular (Dodman, 2011, pp. 280-325; see also Fritzsche, 2004, passim), these nostalgic expressions articulate cultural-affective potentialities, manifestations and codes, rather than ideology or political position-taking. Indeed, 'where the negative sense of nostalgia prevails, there is a tendency to neglect the reciprocal relationship between audience and media [in this case, between the blogger and an already ambiguous flow of visual data] in generating the conditions for making sense and meaning' (Pickering & Keightley, 2006, p. 930). In fact, the most prevalent keywords in my case studies — 'dreamlike', 'soft', 'tender', 'expressive', 'imaginative', 'eclectic', 'pensive', 'ethereal', 'lightweight', 'deep emotions', 'sadness', 'happiness', 'love' — seem to confirm psychologists' recent findings that nostalgia retains positive, curative and adaptive characteristics for individuals living in contemporary societies (Wildschut et al., 2010; Hepper et al., 2012; Routledge et al., 2013; Cheung et al., 2013; see also Wilson, 2005; Davis, 1979, pp. 106–7).

Tumblr, curation and optimism

With regard to the 'curatorial' mechanics that enable all of these dynamics, I want to outline here the fact that on the face of it these allow for an almost complete circumvention of the conventional trappings of capitalist production and consumption, although this scenario is, of course, only made possible by the fact that Yahoo! (and now Verizon) continue to subsidize Tumblr's servers. Which is to say that, although many of these images are extracted from commercial venues (fragrance advertising, fashion marketing, and so on), the commercial element per se emerges from the exchange deeply deteriorated. In this sense, I agree with Henry Jenkins' position, articulated in his commentary on Michel de Certeau's suggestion that readers' activities are harder to document than theorise, that a modern audience's productivity and transformative influence on culture 'can be glimpsed only through local details rather than measured in its entirety' (Jenkins, 2013, p. 3).

Take, for example, the case (out of many more) of the image below, silently 'borrowed' by the bloggers from what I discovered, with difficulty and only by using Google Image's tracing algorithms, to be a quintessentially neoliberal icon of mass-production within the convenience-food industry, a Betty Crocker (General Mills) official website.

In the context of how this image is reproduced through these tumblrs, those 'little pink cupcakes with edible pearls on top' are hardly attributable to any Betty Crocker brand machination. Rather, they facilitate the simple making of a psycho-aesthetic point, acting as soft punctuation marks in the overall nostalgic mythology bonding the blogs together (in this case, the point is centered around the bloggers' culinary/Proustian/hedonic invocations of childhood memories or scents, e.g. Wallflower's stories of her grandmother's baking). It is equally true that General Mills participates in, or rather reflects, unwittingly and unprofitably, this process. The company tries, as it were, to make the same point, or rather to monetize the same fantasy or aesthetic impulse (by producing the image in the first place). That its attempt to use the image to sell (on the

Figure 8.13: 'Pink Champagne Cupcakes', Betty Crocker Recipes (Official Website); original source (via Google Images): http://goo.gl/FqT8V6

dull remoteness of the company's website) their 'Betty Crocker® SuperMoist® white cake mix' fails to even register on my participants' tumblrs only underlines these microblogs' independent semiotic existence. It can even be said that the nostalgic community's, and Wallflower's in particular, repurposing of signs and signifiers provides a valuable empirical continuation to Andy Warhol's creation of a 'space for the return of what modernism represses: image, representation, popular/low culture, kitsch and every other imaginable 'impurity'. For Warhol, the very notion of originality was suspect. Having started his career as a commercial artist, he borrows or steals images from the consumer culture that surrounds him' (Taylor, 1992, p. 17; Wallflower is incidentally an Andy Warhol admirer and 'The world fascinates me' was M's tumblr motto for a while).

The case is similar with the majority of the media files that the bloggers use to populate their tumblrs, which is to say that these digital artefacts rarely bare an immediate commercial identifier (those that do are sometimes cropped, blurred, made unidentifiable, etc.). The purpose they are used for is, again, to calibrate and continuously to stylize the broader 'nostalgic' communal discourse, with each hypermediated element functioning like just another colour on a painter's easel (a fragrance bottle, a detail from a dress, a close-up of a human's face, all occupying the same level of signification as an impressionistic painting, a piano sonata, or a quote by Rilke or Fitzgerald): digital content that might be re-combined, felt, expressed and arranged as part of something deeper, something beyond the sum of its parts. Such postmodern collage is not necessarily intended to be in some way resistant to the commercial or ideological origins of the source material. Nor do the bloggers pay particularly conscious attention to these somewhat intrinsic aspects of their craft, characterised as it is by a nonchalantly proficient digital literacy; and yet this craft enables them to claim agency and to a degree autonomy by exercising the complete freedom to do, quite simply, as they like.

How far this all seems from the usual 'curatorial' histories, debates and cultural studies of recent years (e.g., O'Neill, 2012; Rugg & Sedgwick, 2007). It still seems to me that, no matter how reflexive, collaborative or dialogical, or even critical of the 'self-regarding' tendencies of their own (artistic) field to 'overstate the significance of the individual curatorial position' (O'Neill, 2012, p. 2), these critical discussions continue to revolve largely around the seemingly ineluctable issue of how and with what effects art is mediated. And while credible voices (e.g., Charlesworth, 2007; Hylton, 2007) do question the neo-managerial 'bureaucratization' of art, the continued privilege of academic, state or institutional interests in art, or the professionalisation of the artistic field as such, together with its increased regularisation and exposure to market forces, few voices from within the discipline actually step outside the canonical literature to allow for viable connections to be made to phenomena such as those encountered on Tumblr (e.g., Krysa, 2006, p. 14; Gere, 2010, p. 5).

Yet it is evident from the case study examples above that the young nostalgics do filter, understand, share and ultimately 'curate' a wide variety of material, including (but not always of) an artistic nature or origin. Thus Tumblr can also be understood as a collaborative, (trans)personal/(trans)media archival space. While investigating the processes of maintaining and visiting these tumblrs, my study focused on outlining the sensory, emotive, affective, experiential and performative avenues that crisscross my participants' archives. These, when understood as 'interchange and free play between virtual images and material artefacts', or as a process conducive 'to more democratic, collective and active experience[s]', could arguably be used to create what Michelle Henning, in discussing the emerging literature in the field, suggests would be a more '"elastic", "delirious" or "exploded" museum: a more anarchic and playful museum without walls' (Henning, 2013a, p. 1; see also Henning, 2013b).

Even with the boundaries between audience, authorship and the curated 'objects' themselves overlapping (be they ideas, songs, images, anonymous dialogues, symphonies or daguerreotypes), we can perhaps still dream of artistic institutions collaborating some day with services such as Tumblr. Imagine, for example, plasma screens connected to specific tumblr flows and placed in various rooms (or public gardens; or city streets), perhaps according to some collaborative curatorial algorithms (e.g., based on #hashtags or independently curated aesthetic user bases). This would arguably bring a nuclear transformation to Malraux's vision, for it would be a truly democratic (trans-critical/trans-artistic) version of his 'museum without walls [...] miniatures, frescoes, stained glass, tapestries [...], "details" and even 'statuaries', all becoming, through photography (and Tumblr) not only dynamic 'colour plates', to be arranged, rearranged, played with, not only 'moments of art' (see Malraux, 1978, pp. 44–6), but moments of 'life' itself. Such installations might even provide concrete examples of Rancière's (2009) otherwise quite opaque proposition: 'not the transmission of the artist's knowledge or inspiration to the spectator. It is the third that is owned by no one, but which subsists between them, excluding any uniform transmission, any identity of cause and effect' (p. 15); or, again: 'the third level: the assemblage of data and the intertwining of contradictory relations [which] are intended to produce a new sense of community' (p. 58).

As Jean-Paul Martinon (2013) alludes to in his playful, subtle, yet deeply philosophical argument (pp. 1-13), one possible way forward could be to differentiate between curating professionals and 'The Curatorial', the latter understood in a similar vein to that of Tumblr's aforementioned expressive potential:

> a jailbreak from pre-existing frames, a gift enabling one to see the world differently, a strategy for inventing new points of departure, a practice of creating allegiances against social ills, a way of caring for humanity, a process of renewing one's own subjectivity, a tactical move for reinventing life, a sensual practice of creating signification, a political tool outside politics, a procedure to maintain a community together [...] the measures to create affects, the work of revealing ghosts, a plan to remain out of joint with time [...] a sharing of understanding, an invitation for reflexivity, a choreographic mode of operation, a way of fighting against corporate culture, etc. (Martinon, 2013, p. 4)

Seen in this light, the Tumblr infrastructure, and the young nostalgics in particular, show striking similarities with Martinon's bravest invocation, that of Stéphane Mallarmé's unfinished, somewhat Babylonian project C'est (Engl. *This is*), a two-hour synesthetic spectacle combining 'magic, a small parade, some ballet, a recital, the execution of an alchemical ritual, the calculation of a mathematical formula, the reading of sacred texts, some mime, the contemplation of a crystal chandelier and a carefully planned fireworks display', all of it orchestrated from behind the scenes by 'an "Operator" (half priest, half comedian) [...] with the help of 24 "Assistants"' (p. 1). Being familiarized with my participants' archives, where virtually all of the elements above can be found in one form or another, Mallarmé's vision feels deeply liberating. For, as Martinon notes, the great symbolist's scenes (not unlike my own participants' Curatorial impulses and collections) are: expository (displaying the work of others); multi-temporal (conjoining the past with the present); multi-artistic in their 'constellation of meaning'; possessing no hero, they are also 'seemingly egalitarian', 'viewer-centered', 'experiential and participatory'; they do not feel like an 'exhibition', but more like a 'manifestation'; furthermore, they are 'multi-sited', with 'no centre of significance', and they allow no 'pre-determined rules, grammar or syntax', opening themselves to 'the unpredictable'; finally, lacking a prescribed plot or a pattern, no single perspective or point of view prevails, and thus they retain a political potential that can be both formative and educational (see Martinon, 2013, pp. 2–3).

Conclusions

At their very core, tumblrs remain spaces in which individuals add, or redirect, content. However, invariably throughout my interviews, the purpose and the literal act of 'expression' comes up as an essential component, if not the core motivation behind the blogs. All participants feel that their tumblrs 'reflect parts of their personality', with many of them identifying very strongly with the content, layout, style and mood of their websites.[6] Unlike more conventional, text-based social networking sites (e.g., online profiles), where young people 'write themselves into being' (see boyd, 2008, pp. 28-31), these largely anony-mous tumblrs benefit from a special kind of co-creative expressive potential, enabling their users to interactively and imaginatively preserve a sense of agency, identity and community.

In this sense, and as far as the original, still expanding Tumblr infrastruc-ture is concerned, these microblogging mechanics, with their perpetual states of user-centred, user-dependent representational fluxes and interactions, con-tinue to exist in a highly idiosyncratic digital ecology that significantly aug-ments 'the autonomy of communicating subjects vis-à-vis communication corporations, as the users become senders and receivers of messages' (Castells, 2008, p. 4). With no formal hierarchy other than the one created by every user in their individual dashboard preferences, and with relatively little commercial information being displayed, circulated or sold, the way this flow of data functions — both structurally and philosophically — points to individuals who are, to use Jenkins' terminology, increasingly more active and selective rather than passive or inert, becoming unpredictable and 'migratory' sources of cultural connectedness, and displaying little to no loyalty to the monolithic corporate networks of one type or another that enable their specific mode of collaborative production (see Jenkins, 2006, pp. 18–19).

Nevertheless, despite Tumblr's radical potential, caution continues to be advisable. Digital 'pessimists' have, of course, long disputed that many social networking services, by transforming individual/private qualitative informa-tion (e.g., shopping preferences, travel destinations, biographical input) into quantitative public data that can be sold to and processed by third parties, give rise to pertinent concerns over unregulated commerce, surveillance and a cen-tralization of power that is far less democratic or unpredictable than users or early optimistic theorizers tended to believe (see Turow, 2012; Jakobsson & Stiernstedt, 2010; Dijck & Nieborg, 2009; Fuchs, 2015, p. 378). Tumblr remains, for better or worse, a private enterprise, and while David Karp's commitment to the integrity of his brainchild seems extraordinary, many other dangers, from bankruptcy to corporate incompetence or greed, can lead to the medium's degradation.

Overall, however, while optimists may indeed overestimate individuals' creative powers and their potential for anti-corporate dissent and constant cultural migration in networked media, it should also be noted that the pessimist argument tends not to transcend the fact that issues of power centralization, cultural displacement and corporate domination are inherent within capitalist modernity and intrinsic to most organised forms of mass communication ('technology is always, in a full sense, social', necessarily dependant on 'complex and variable connection[s] with other social relations and institutions' – Williams, 1981, p. 231). The question should therefore not be whether these problems exist in digital manifestations — they certainly do — but rather inquire as to whether the new tools, platforms and possibilities for personal expression can add sufficient cultural value, psychological satisfaction, and, to use Williams' (1980) vocabulary, allow for enough individual 'direct autonomous composition' (p. 62) so as to effectively consolidate the network-based social-economic evolutions sketched out by optimistic models such as that proposed by Benkler (2006). In the young nostalgics' case, I have argued, Tumblr did indeed seem to provide all of these things, perhaps even enabling the creation of that elusive, liberating and communal-centered activity 'that combines the intelligence and the action of the multitude, making them work together' (see Hardt & Negri, 2000, pp. 302–3).[7]

Notes

[1] Please note that, when capitalised, I will use the noun 'Tumblr' to refer more generally to the platform/enterprise, while 'tumblr(s)' will be used to signify the actual blogs.

[2] Even the fact that Yahoo! took a $230 million write-down on the business (essentially admitting they had overpaid for it), while also abandoning its sales integration effort — the move, pushed by Mayer in early 2015 and cancelled a year later, is reported to have created confusion and power struggles between Tumblr's and Yahoo's teams (Kim, 2016) — seemed to reinforce the same point. With Karp's authority seemingly intact, it remains to be seen whether Yahoo!'s plan to make Tumblr one of the 'three pillars' behind its comeback plan (see Oreskovic, 2016) will be kept by Verizon.

[3] For example, despite attempting to include male participants in my study, it was largely females who replied and who were willing to participate in the research. As the feminine aspects of these tumblrs play a key role in

their semiotic and cultural construction — these young women often use Tumblr to 'recuperate' or 'curate' the emotion outside its male-centered psycho-historical and artistic contexts, thus raising interesting gender issues that I was unable to fully explore in this article — this has not negatively impacted on the relevancy of my findings. Nonetheless, future efforts can and should focus on recruiting male members of the nostalgic community, as inter-gender comparisons would prove valuable.

4 Wallflower herself acknowledged this issue during our interview, explaining her recent attempts to mitigate it: 'It's a very big problem with Tumblr. First when I started [with] Tumblr, I didn't know that. I didn't think that I had to write the author, to make a source link, but then over the time I understood that I had to include the author of the photo, and I always, always link the source material, always. When you click on the blog, when you click on the picture, you go at the source of the photo, *maybe not always the author*, but maybe [an]other blog that I found.'

5 In the specific case of Luna, although she did not expressly mention any traumatic or problematic nuances related to her ethnic background, her status as a Syrian emigrée in the Netherlands might even underline the affective permutations, indeed emotionally recuperative valences of nostalgia — in this sense, the emotion's role in developing alternative narratives of history for victims of (post)colonial/postcommunist abuse or displacement has been tentatively described in a recent study (see Ladino, 2005).

6 On 17 June 2012, I extracted from one of my participant's blogs (Charlotte) a 'viral' textual image (it had been noted by no less than 185,153 tumblr users); although I was unable to locate the original source, it merits citing: 'A person's tumblr tells a lot about them. It shows what kind of images they see in their head, who they love, who they hate, even what they think about other people. But most of all – has all the words they never said to people, all the words they couldn't have said but should have said'.

7 Note that this is precisely why I have opted for a qualitative, relatively small-scale analysis of one particular Tumblr community/phenomenon. My adherence to the 'digital optimism' paradigm should only be considered in this particular context. While my case studies may indeed outline the positive communicational/expressive potential that Tumblr technology has, while the platform may even be a necessary ingredient in this alchemy, it is evidently not a sufficient one — the users' conscious input and the judicious expressive/aesthetic calibration of their tumblrs make the journals what they are. On its own, Tumblr is little more than computer language (though a very well written one) and hardware; it could never, in itself, become primordial cause, means and message behind the nostalgic community (or any other community) per se. Like Williams, I too dislike such technically deterministic claims, while nonetheless maintaining a certain optimism in regard to the future of this type of technology, or rather to its

human potential and its applications in wider — civic, artistic, therapeutic, educational — spheres. [NB: Particularly unwieldy links have been shortened using Google's URL shortener (http://goo.gl)].

References

Arnold-de-Simine, S. (2013). *Mediating Memory in the Museum: Trauma, Empathy, Nostalgia*. Houndmills: Palgrave Macmillan.

Arvidsson, A. (2006). *Brands. Meaning and Value in Media Culture*. London: Routledge.

Barthes, R. (1977). The Death of the Author. In *Image – Music – Text*. Trans. and ed. by Heath, S. London: Fontana Press.

_____. (1991). *Mythologies*. Trans. by Lavers, A. New York: The Noonday Press.

_____. (1997). *The Eiffel Tower and Other Mythologies*. Trans. by Howard, R. Berkeley, CA: University of California Press.

Baudrillard, J. (1981). *Simulacra and Simulation*. Trans. by Glaser, S. F. Ann Arbor, MI: University of Michigan.

Benkler, Y. (2006). *The Wealth of Networks: How Social Production Transforms Markets and Freedom*. New Haven, CT: Yale University Press.

Bercovici, J. (2013). 'Tumblr: David Karp's $800 Million Art Project'. *Forbes*, 2 January. Retrieved from http://goo.gl/LXpmC.*

Betters, E. (2015). 'What's the point of Snapchat and how does it work?' *Pocket-lint.com*, 26 December. Retrieved from http://goo.gl/NEd99S.

Boundas, C. V. (2006). 'What Difference Does Deleuze's Difference Make?' In Boundas, C. V. (Ed.). *Deleuze and Philosophy*. Edinburgh: Edinburgh University Press

boyd, d. (2008). 'Why Youth ♥ [heart] Social Network Sites: The Role of Networked Publics in Teenage Social Life.' Buckingham, D. (Ed.). *Youth, Identity, and Digital Media*, pp. 119–42. Cambridge, MA: MIT Press.

Boym, S. (2001). *The Future of Nostalgia*. New York: Basic Books.

Bruno, G. (2002). *Atlas of Emotion: Journeys in Art, Architecture and Film*. London: Verso.

Brustein, J. (2013). 'Yahoo! Hopes to Profit From Tumblr Without Ruining It'. *Business Week*, 20 May. Retrieved from http://goo.gl/U6xMNo.

Castells, M. (2008). *Communication Power*. Oxford: Oxford University Press.

Charlesworth, J. J. (2007). Curating Doubt. In Rugg, J., & Sedgwick, M. (Eds.). *Issues in Curating Contemporary Art and Practice*. Chicago, IL: University of Chicago Press.

Cheung, W. Y. et al. (2013). Back to the future: Nostalgia increases optimism. *Personality and Social Psychology Bulletin*, 39(11), 1484–96.

Cook, P. (2012) Labours of Love: In Praise of Fan Websites. *Frames*, 1(1). Retrieved from http://framescinemajournal.com/article/labours-of-love-in-praise-of-fan-websites

Davis, F. (1979). *Yearning for Yesterday: A Sociology of Nostalgia*. New York, NY: Free Press.

Dewey, C. (2015). 2015 is the year that Tumblr became the front page of the Internet. *The Washington Post*, 23 December. Retrieved from https://goo.gl/oJljlG.

Dijck, J. van & Nieborg, D. (2009). Wikinomics and its discontents: A critical analysis of web 2.0 business manifestos. *New Media & Society*, 11(5), 855–74.

Dixon, C. [TechCrunch] (2011). David Karp: Why I Started Tumblr | Founder Stories [Video file]. Retrieved from https://goo.gl/BFjLfd.

Dodman, T. W. (2011). Homesick epoch: Dying of nostalgia in post-Revolutionary France. Unpublished PhD. Chicago, IL: University of Chicago.

Edwards, J. (2013). Here's Tumblr's total revenue for 2012 — and how it will make a profit in 2013'. *Business Insider*, 2 January. Retrieved from http://goo.gl/rfKUjR.

Firat, A. F., & Dholakia, N. (2016). From consumer to construer: Travels in human subjectivity. *Journal of Consumer Culture*. Published 15 January online. Retrieved from http://goo.gl/s4lCp0.

Foucault, M. (1979). What is an author? In J. Hanari (Ed.). *Textual Strategies: Perspectives in Post-Structuralist Criticism* (pp. 141-160). Ithaca, NY: Cornell University Press.

Fritzsche, P. (2004). *Stranded in the Present: Modern Time and the Melancholy of History*. Cambridge, MA: Harvard University Press.

Friz, A., & Gehl, R. W. (2015). "Pinning the Feminine User: Gender Scripts in Pinterest's Sign-Up Interface" (2015 May 5). Media, Culture and Society (forthcoming). Retrieved from http://ssrn.com/abstract=2602954.

Fuchs, C. (2015). *Culture and Economy in the Age of Social Media*. New York: Routledge.

Gauntlett, D. (2015). *Making Media Studies: The Creativity Turn in Media and Communications Studies*. Peter Lang: New York.

Geertz, C. (1973). *The Interpretation of Cultures: Selected Essays*. New York, NY: Basic Books.

Gere, C. (2010). Research as art. In H. Gardiner & C. Gere. (Eds). *Art Practice in a Digital Culture*, pp. 1–8. Farnham: Ashgate.

Goriunova, O. (2012). New media idiocy. *Convergence: The International Journal of Research into New Media Technologies*. Published online 25 September. Retrieved from https://goo.gl/D6bsXN.

Gunkle, D. (2016). *Of Remixology. Ethics and Aesthetics after Remix*. Cambridge, MA: MIT Press.

Hardt, M., & Negri, A. (2000). *Empire*. Cambridge, MA: Harvard University Press.

Henning, M. (2013a). The virtual artefact: Social media and the play of the image (unpublished, revised). *Artefacts, Culture and Identity*. Annual Conference of the International Society for Cultural History, Istanbul, Turkey, September 11-14 2013. Retrieved from http://goo.gl/pcwxIn.

Henning, M. (2013b). With and Without Walls: Photographic Reproduction and the Art Museum. In Henning, M. (Ed) *The International Handbooks of Museum Studies Volume 3: Museum Media: Part 4: Extending the Museum* pp. 507–602, Hoboken, NJ: John Wiley & Sons

Hepper, E. G. et al. (2012). Odyssey's end: lay conceptions of nostalgia reflect its original Homeric meaning. *Emotion*, 12, 102–19.

Hesmondhalgh, D. (2013). *The Cultural Industries*. 3rd Ed. London: Sage.

Hylton, R. (2007). 'Thoughts on Curating'. In Rugg, J., & Sedgwick, M. (Eds.). *Issues in Curating Contemporary Art and Practice*. Chicago, IL: University of Chicago Press.

Jakobsson, P., & Stiernstedt, F. (2010). 'Pirate of Silicon Valley: State of Exception and Dispossession in Web 2.0'. *First Monday*, Vol. 15, No. 7 (HTML rendering). Retrieved from http://goo.gl/vBT5VL.

Jameson, F. (1991). *Postmodernism, or the Cultural Logic of Late Capitalism*. London: Verso.

Jenkins, H. (2006). *Convergence Culture*. New York: New York University Press.

Jenkins, H. (2013). *Textual Poachers: Television Fans and Participatory Culture*. Classic Edition. New York: Routledge.

Karp, D. (2016). 'Coming soon: Money from your Tumblr'. David's Log (personal blog). Retrieved 3 December 2016 from https://goo.gl/GOGf4U.

Kim, E. (2016 February 14). 'Yahoo is ditching a plan that caused turmoil within Tumblr'. *Business Insider*. Retrieved from http://goo.gl/4UiIyR.

Krysa, J. (2006). *Curating Immateriality: The Work of the Curator in the Age of Network Systems (DATA Browser 03)*. Autonomedia.

Ladino, J. (2005). Longing for wonderland: nostalgia for nature in post-frontier America. *Iowa Journal of Cultural Studies*, 5(5) (HTML rendering). Retrieved from http://goo.gl/fsP7d.

Lasch, C. (1991) *The True and Only Heaven: Progress and Its Critics*. New York, NY: W. W. Norton

Malraux, A. (1978). *The Voices of Silence*. Trans. by Gilbert, S. Princeton, NJ: Princeton University Press.

Martinon, J. P. (2013). 'Introduction'. In J.P. Martinon (Ed). *The Curatorial: A Philosophy of Curating*. London: Bloomsbury.

McCoy, T. (2015 February 27). The inside story of the "White Dress, Blue Dress" drama that divided a planet. *The Washington Post*. Retrieved from https://goo.gl/BYG5qj.

O'Neill, P. (2012). *The Culture of Curating and the Curating of Culture(s)*. Cambridge, MA: MIT Press.

Oreskovic, A. (2016). Yahoo just admitted that it overpaid for Tumblr. *Tech Insider*, 2 February. Retrieved from http://goo.gl/Cu3yaE.

Perez, S. (2016). Tumblr to introduce ads across all blogs. *TechChrunch*, 27 July. Retrieved from https://goo.gl/XCx1M7.

Pickering, M., & Keightley, E. (2006). The modalities of nostalgia. *Current Sociology*, 54(6), pp. 919–41.

Rancière, J. (2009). *The Emancipated Spectator*. Trans. by. Elliott, G. London: Verso.

Reeve, E. (2016). The secret lives of Tumblr teens. *New Republic*, 17 February. Retrieved from https://goo.gl/DiSbxz.

Rifkin, A. (2013). Tumblr is not what you think. *TechCrunch*, 18 February. Retrieved from http://goo.gl/pGs03.

Rose, G. (2007). *Visual Methodologies: An Introduction to the Interpretation of Visual Materials*. London: Sage.

Routledge, C. et al. (2013). Nostalgia as a resource for psychological health and well-being. *Social and Personality Psychology Compass*, 7(11), 808–18.

Rugg, J., & Sedgwick, M. (Eds.) (2007). *Issues in Curating Contemporary Art and Practice*. Chicago, IL: University of Chicago Press.

Stewart, S. (1993). *On Longing: Narratives of the Miniature, the Gigantic, the Souvenir, the Collection*. Durham, NC: Duke University Press.

Tan, G. (2013). Tenth grade tech trends. *Posthaven*. [Blog entry]. Retrieved from http://goo.gl/UFtEI.

Taylor, M. (1992). Reframing postmodernisms. In Berry, P., & Wernick, A. (Eds). *Shadow of Spirit: Postmodernism and Religion*. New York: Routledge.

Thornton, S. (1995). *Club Cultures. Music, Media and Subcultural Capital*. Cambridge: Polity Press.

'Tumblr Ads and You' (2016). Official Tumblr webpage. Retrieved from https://goo.gl/uutnfP.

Turow, J. (2012). *The Daily You*. New Haven, CT: Yale University Press.

Walker, R. (2012). Can Tumblr's David Karp embrace ads without selling out? *The New York Times*, 12 July. Retrieved from http://goo.gl/GhmNiV.

Walters, E. (2016). What Verizon's acquisition of Yahoo means for Tumblr and Flickr. *Paste Magazine*, 27 July. Retrieved from https://goo.gl/aXW8QZ.

Wernick, A. (1991). *Promotional Culture: Advertising, Ideology and Symbolic Expression*. London: Sage.

West, N. (2000). *Kodak and the Lens of Nostalgia*. Charlottesville, VA: University of Virginia Press.

Wildschut, T. et al. (2010). Nostalgia as a repository of social connectedness: The role of attachment-related avoidance. *Journal of Personality and Social Psychology*, 98, 573–86.

Williams, R. (1980) Means of Communication as Means of Production. In *Problems in Materialism and Culture: Selected Essays*, pp. 50-63. London: Verso.

Williams, R. (1981). Communications technologies and social institutions. In Williams, R. (Ed.). *Contact: Human Communication and its History*, (pp. 225–38). London: Thames and Hudson.

———. (2003). *Television: Technology and Cultural Form*. London: Routledge Classics (e-Library).

Wilson, J. L. (2005). *Nostalgia: Sanctuary of Meaning*. Lewisburg, PA : Bucknell University Press

CHAPTER NINE

Expertise and Collaboration: Cultural Workers' Performance on Social Media

Karen Patel

Birmingham City University

Introduction

The idea of the 'expert' is often associated with people who are called upon to provide comment, analysis and critique. In science in particular, experts are the 'voice' in news media about issues of interest to the public (Wynne, 1992). In the arts, the experts are often critics (Bourdieu, 1996; Bennett, 2010) or cultural intermediaries (Taylor, 2013), for example those working in advertising (Nixon, 2014) or consultancy (Prince, 2014). What about experts who aren't critics or intermediaries, i.e. the creators and artists themselves?

I find that expertise is often taken for granted in accounts of cultural work; experts are just experts – they are considered to be more knowledgeable than non-experts, but how? Why? The following quote by Leila Jancovich, in her work on participatory arts programmes, is an example of this:

> While some professionals defined their backgrounds as providing invaluable arts expertise, many of the public participants questioned

How to cite this book chapter:
Patel, K. 2017. Expertise and Collaboration: Cultural workers' performance on social media. In: Graham, J. and Gandini, A. (eds.). *Collaborative Production in the Creative Industries*. Pp. 157–176. London: University of Westminster Press. DOI: https://doi.org/10.16997/book4.i. License: CC-BY-NC-ND 4.0

the knowledge of the professionals, referring to them as self-appointed experts. This was supported by the fact that many of the 'experts' interviewed, acknowledged that they knew little about arts practice outside their specialism. (Jancovich, 2015, p. 7)

What exactly makes someone an expert in the arts? Just because someone is less familiar with subjects outside of their field, how does that mean they're not an expert in their specialism, as Jancovic is suggesting?

My analysis of artists' performance of expertise on social media suggests that expertise is a social process, and it is performed on social media in a platform-mediated way among artists who negotiate between competition and collaboration. Pierre Bourdieu's *The Rules of Art* (1996) and Howard Becker's *Art Worlds* (2008 [1984]) are respectively accounts of competition and collaboration in the art world and both position art-making as a social process, which I argue also helps to conceptualise expertise, too, as a social process.

Social media platforms allow opportunities for cultural workers to find work and build a reputation (Suhr, 2015) but they are also sites for people to perform expertise. Drawing from the empirical work I have carried out on a group of artists I suggest that expertise tends to be performed on social media through the input and endorsement of other people, which contributes to a consensus about someone's expertise and helps to define whether they can be deemed an 'expert'. Ultimately, expertise is important in cultural work because the ability to communicate and demonstrate your expertise is essential in order to secure work (Andres and Round, 2015; Jones, 2002) in a competitive cultural industries job market where there is an 'oversupply of labour' (Banks and Hesmondhalgh, 2009, p. 420).

My empirical work consisted of an analysis of samples of social media posts from 19 independent UK artists working in fine art, digital art, writing, music and crafts. I drew from Candace Jones's (2002) signalling expertise framework for the analysis, to identify particular expertise signalling strategies by the artists. Jones describes signalling as activities which showcase someone's identity through prior projects, competencies and relationships, which 'convey information to others as a form of strategic action' (p. 209). I adapted the framework for the analysis of social media, incorporating elements such as retweets, mentions and imagery used on social media to account for its various affordances which shape how expertise is performed on platforms.

Artists were looked at specifically to explore Bourdieu's (1996) idea of the *illusio* in relation to arts workers and their performance of expertise on social media, and what this can tell us about contemporary cultural work. The *illusio* is a 'collective belief in the game' which is 'fundamental to the power of consecration, permitting consecrated artists to constitute certain products, by the miracle of their signature (or brand name) as sacred objects' (p. 230). This consecration is a process involving those in power. What about the *illusio* in the social media age, where any artist can have a public profile, call themselves an expert, and display cultural products which could potentially reach millions of people? From my analysis, there are suggestions that on social media, the status and power of artists' online associations are crucial in their performance of expertise.

While Bourdieu's conception of the art world suggests a competitiveness among artists, Howard Becker's (2008) *Art Worlds* paints a more collaborative, congenial picture. In my analysis of artists' social media posts I find evidence of this too, where artists would often 'retweet' and help promote the work of fellow artists and craftspeople, who are essentially their competitors. This suggests that expertise is a social process, and artists perform their expertise on social media through a negotiation between competition and collaboration. This builds on current accounts of cultural work, as well as accounts of expertise.

In the following section I'll outline the scholarly work done on expertise, to help us understand how expertise could be most usefully conceptualised.

What is expertise?

There is no universal definition for what expertise or an expert is, and the notion of the 'expert' is increasingly problematic 'in a world where socially distributed expertise and knowledge production (e.g. peer-to-peer "lay thinking" as facilitated by the internet) is widespread' (Wilson, 2010, p.372). Arnoldi (2007) defines expertise as 'the product of a symbolic attribution of status and authority, changing over time' (p. 50). Schudson (2006) describes an expert as 'someone in possession of specialized knowledge that is accepted by the wider society as legitimate' (p. 499). This echoes Stephen Turner's (2001) view that experts not only need the skills and knowledge, but also recognition from audiences, to be considered expert.

This idea of expertise as socially constituted is apparent in the field of Science and Technology Studies (STS) from which much of the original literature around the philosophy of expertise stems. Scholars in STS sought to investigate the sociology of science, for example Brian Wynne (1992) who highlighted the erosion of public trust in scientific experts and questioned the legitimacy of these experts after the Chernobyl fallout, where the expertise of the 'lay' sheep farmers proved valuable yet was largely ignored by scientists. This questioning of the legitimacy of expertise is discussed by Ulrich Beck (1992) in *Risk Society,* where public trust in experts was undermined during the 1980s and early 1990s by not only mistakes and inaccuracies, but also the incorrect perception of the public by experts as 'engineering students in their first semester' (p. 59). This led to less public trust in experts, and increased mass media exposure by experts has been argued to contribute to a de-legitimisation of expertise overall (Beck, 1998; Luhmann, 2000; Arnoldi, 2007). What about the legitimacy of expertise performed in more contemporary contexts on social media? What form does it take? And how does it link to the context of 'social' interaction where highly collaborative dynamics are at stake? My work in this chapter provides some insights here in relation to artists.

Scholars in STS have tried to unpack exactly what an expert is, with no agreed consensus. Hubert and Stuart Dreyfus (1986) described expertise as an everyday competence and an effective ability to use expert skills and knowledge to improvise in difficult situations – an embodied human performance. Collins and Evans (2006) propose a SEE (Studies of Expertise and Experience) approach, which classifies three types of expertise: no expertise, interactional (experience or practice based) expertise and contributory (knowledge based) expertise. However, the authors admit there are boundary problems with these categorisations, and their conception of experience-based expertise has been criticised by Addis (2013) for placing too much emphasis on the embodied ability of the individual rather than the input and role of others in expertise, using peer review and examination as examples where other people are crucial for expertise.

Following this, expertise is best understood as a social relation, 'where a particular actor has authority over another actor through their possession of a particular form of knowledge: the way a doctor has authority over the patient' (Prince, 2010, p. 6). According to Prince, this results from the expert's situation within a community's knowledge culture. There are parallels here with Pierre Bourdieu's ideas of the *illusio*.

Expertise in cultural work

The *illusio* is applied by Bourdieu in the *Rules of Art* (1996), where he describes it as a consensus about artists which is fundamental to the elevation of those artists over others. The bourgeoisie in the nineteenth-century art world were influential in this 'elevation' and consecration of artists. Even though such artists would eventually be able to live from just their signature or brand name on their work because they had come to be known as the 'experts' through these power relations, Bourdieu highlights the importance of consensus in the consecration of artists, arguing that the individual, artistic 'genius' is socially constituted and not solely arising from individual talent or special gifts.

Another conceptualisation of the art world comes from Howard Becker (2008) in *Art Worlds*. Whilst not particularly referring to expertise, Becker highlights the importance of reputation in the art world and how this too is socially constituted. The term 'Art World' is used by Becker:

To denote the network of people whose cooperative activity, organized via their joint knowledge of conventional means of doing things, produces the kind of art works that the art world is noted for. (p. xxiv)

Art Worlds demonstrates how the influence of others, particularly distributors, critics and consumers, are integral to reputation building. Like Bourdieu, he critiques the myth of the individual, artistic genius and acknowledges the role of people who appear more entitled to speak on behalf of the art world than others. Becker argues that such roles, and subsequent values about how art is to be judged, are formed through a social process where consensus is crucial. In turn, these people are important in the building of an artist's reputation. In a departure from Bourdieu's emphasis on power and power relations, Becker's conception of the production of art places much more emphasis on the division of labour in the process and the amount of collaboration and co-operation involved.

More recent accounts cultural work describe it as precarious (Gill and Pratt, 2008) extremely competitive (Bilton, 2007) and highly individualised (McGuigan, 2010), but these types of conditions were synonymous with the experiences of artists anyway (Forkert, 2013). What about the experiences of artists in the social media age? The increased popularity of social media platforms in recent years has opened up cultural production to almost everyone who can access it, resulting in a proliferation of 'amateur' cultural production, collaborative co-creative production (Banks, 2009) with subsequent concerns about the inferior quality of cultural products (Keen, 2007) and undermining of professional ethics and values (Kennedy, 2015). Social media too is a competitive space which is increasingly profitable for people who know how to use it for their benefit, whether it be through blogging (Duffy, 2016), selfies on Instagram (Marwick, 2013) or generating Facebook 'likes' (Gerlitz and Helmond, 2013). What about the experiences of artists in this space? What is the role of collaboration here, specifically among artists? This chapter provides insights into how artists utilise social media for the benefit of their career.

There is relatively little work about expertise in contemporary cultural work. Russell Prince (2010) identifies an 'emerging expert system' in the UK creative industries where a small community of people have realigned their practices to situate themselves within government in order to influence cultural policy. However, these people are not cultural workers involved directly in production, but cultural intermediaries (such as critics and consultants) and CEOs of media companies. Candace Jones (2002) draws on the work of Erving Goffman (1959) to conceptualise how expertise is signalled in creative industry careers, arguing that signals are important for conveying one's knowledge and expertise in the competitive creative industries job market. Jones devises a framework for analysing expertise signals, which I adapted for my social media analysis and will discuss in the next section.

Approach

To analyse the social media posts of the 19 UK artists, I used a version of Jones' signalling expertise framework (see Patel, 2015) to take into account the specific features of social media, such as platform structures, interactions and affordances. The framework consists of three primary elements, (with my adaptations in brackets): institutional context (i.e. the context of the user, their background and career trajectory), signalling content (the aesthetic style of social media text and images, exhibiting the requisite skills in both their social media posts and presentation of their art, and career relevant connections and interactions on social media) and signalling strategies (using social media affordances such as retweets to enhance status, the type of relationships pursued and how they are manifest on social media, and strategic approaches to impression management on social media). This framework is useful for such an analysis because it specifically focuses on expertise among creative industries workers, however Jones did not test the framework empirically. After amending the framework for social media analysis, the signalling expertise framework becomes a useful tool not only conceptually, but also methodologically.

The 19 artists were found mostly by looking through online artist directories, specifically Arts Derbyshire, Art in Liverpool and New Art West Midlands. I selected artists who appeared to use social media regularly for professional purposes, so for each artist I visited their individual social media profiles and looked at the last time they posted and how frequently they posted. If they had posted at least twice in the past week, I approached them. I also approached artists that I had met at events, or were suggested to me by my own contacts. For each participant, I collected (via screenshot) 10 days' worth of posts from the social media sites they most frequently used; the most common being Twitter, Facebook (pages) and Instagram. The amount of posts collected varied among users, ranging from over 100 posts from one participant to 10 for another so I made some adjustments to the amounts I collected for each participant during the data collection process. Rather than analysing each post individually, I analysed each users' posts in groups of 3 or 4 because I found a lot of posts exhibited similar forms of signalling content. Once all posts were analysed using the signalling content criteria, this helped me work out the user's signalling strategy and institutional context.

Ethical considerations

In the screenshots that follow in this chapter, you will see that I don't conceal the identity of my participants. All participants mentioned here have given consent for their online identities and social media posts, which includes retweets, to be featured in this discussion.

The 'publicness' of people's information on the Internet is a primary ethical concern. Even though social media profiles are freely available and people choose to make them public, it doesn't necessarily mean they are 'there for the taking' to be used for research (Henderson et al, 2013). As argued by boyd and Crawford: 'just because it is accessible doesn't make it ethical' (2012: 671). Users may be aware they are using a public forum but some may not fully understand the implications of what they post, or how far it could reach (Marwick and boyd, 2011). For my approach, I decided that being transparent with my participants and asking their permission to use their social media posts was the best option. Allowing them the flexibility to choose which level of anonymity they prefer reduces some of the ethical concerns about the 'publicness' of social media.

Using screenshots is also an unusual practice in social media research, as posts are often extracted through data mining methods (boyd and Crawford, 2012). However that was not suitable for this study, which relies on the close analysis of each individual's posts. In addition, taking screenshots is an effective way of presenting the full context of the post that the platform allows, such as the numbers of retweets and likes for each tweet, Facebook and Instagram likes and comments, and most importantly for artists in particular, the images posted.

Displaying endorsements and positive reviews

From the analysis, the most prominent theme was the crucial role of other people and institutions in artists' performance of expertise online. This is partly demonstrated in how artists shared endorsements made about them, and also through mutual aid and collaboration within the artistic community, which I will discuss later.

A practice which was most evident on Twitter, most of the artists in my sample used the retweet and 'quote' functions of Twitter to share posts they were mentioned or featured in by others. This particularly centred on their participation in events, but also in direct association to their work. Eimear, a mixed media artist, tweeted first about an exhibition she was participating in:

Figure 9.1: Eimear exhibition tweet.

Then after the show, she retweeted positive comments:

Figure 9.2: Eimear retweets.

Robyn, a fine artist, also retweeted mentions about her residency in Wales:

Figure 9.3: Robyn residency tweet.

Robyn also covered this residency extensively by herself on Twitter. These retweets focused on events and exhibitions, and by retweeting the comments and tweets of others, they are adding to coverage of the event on their own Twitter profile, an example of the 'reputation building' signalling strategy in Candace Jones' (2002) signalling expertise framework.

Another form of public endorsement sharing came in the form of 'positive reviews'. For example the below retweet by Colette, an artist in Liverpool:

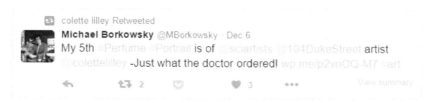

Figure 9.4: Colette retweet.

Not only is this a public endorsement of Colette but also of the art gallery she co-founded. Tweets such as this are a form of 'positive review' which are crucial for people who use social media and other online environments to make a living (Suhr, 2015). Positive reviews were also evident in the Facebook and Instagram comments of Cherie, another artist in Liverpool:

Figure 9.5: Cherie Instagram picture of gallery.

For Cherie, her interaction with customers helped to amplify the positive review, as the user she was speaking to replied with even more positive comments. This is part of what Jones (2002) calls an 'impression management' signalling strategy.

The most important form of public endorsement for an artist would come from a high profile individual or institution, and there were a couple of examples among the artists of this endorsement being amplified by them. Being associated with or acknowledged by higher profile individuals and companies is important for one's career, and this is illustrated by Bourdieu's idea of the *illusio*. Bourdieu talks about how powerful individuals were able to elevate and consecrate some artists over others, through a social process of consensus. That, to some extent is still the case because the more renowned an endorser is, the more power they have to elevate an artist over others on social media. A high profile individual or institution can show endorsement simply by tweeting about that artist and their work, and this is what I understand as a public endorsement. In the case of the artists within my sample, two in particular, Abi and Phil, displayed the endorsement of high profile companies. Abi, an artist and author, was mentioned by her publisher, which she retweeted and added a comment:

Figure 9.6: Abi quote of publisher.

Phil, a music composer, often tweeted about his work and where it is featured:

Figure 9.7: Phil's tweets about his work.

While Phil didn't retweet, he mentioned those organisations in his tweets to associate himself with them. Using mentions in tweets about higher profile work is an example of the 'amplification' of signals as part of the 'status enhancement' element of signalling expertise. The specific functions of Twitter such as mentions and retweets allow this amplification to occur in a public way with just a click.

Not everyone within the sample associated with others in the ways described here, for example Colin, who rarely retweeted others and posted only his own work on Facebook, Twitter and Instagram, sometimes with an offer to buy prints or a discount code. Compared to the other participants, he appeared to have the highest profile, with thousands of followers across all platforms and hundreds of likes for each post. He appeared to have less of a need to share the endorsements of others.

These acts of retweeting and sharing are most common with Twitter, because the platform structure allows it. Only when posts are created by the user, such as in the case of Cherie who took her photo and put it on Instagram, can the associations occur through other means such as likes and comments. This demonstrates how the functions of the platform can be fundamental to how expertise is performed on social media.

So, while the *illusio* can help us to understand the importance of influential people and institutions in artists' performance of expertise, the analysis revealed an activity which problematises Bourdieu's conception of the competitive, individualistic art world, and this was expressed through mutual aid and collaboration within the artistic community.

'Mutual aid' and collaboration among the artistic community

'Mutual aid' is a concept applied to the cultural industries by de Peuter and Cohen (2015) to describe the development of 'bottom-up infrastructures to support independent work' (2015, p. 306) in the context of worker resistance in the cultural industries, 'where workers, often through new labour organizations that exist outside the bounds of traditional trade unions, are lobbying for social protections and higher pay and exerting collective pressure to reclaim autonomy over their crafts and their lives' (2015, p. 305). While their specific example doesn't relate directly to this work, the idea of mutual aid is useful to describe the displays of mutual support among the artistic community, visible on social media, in contemporary cultural work where discourses of individualism and enterprise prevail in a precarious labour market.

Mutual aid is used by de Peuter and Cohen to describe the collaboration between cultural workers to improve labour conditions. By working together, cultural workers have increased powers for collective bargaining. For this research, the idea of artists collaborating and working towards a common goal is a useful way of conceptualising the activities of the artists I observed. In my analysis, I found numerous examples of artists sharing the work of other artists, even those who appeared to be in direct competition with them. Why would they do this? The concept of mutual aid helps us understand that such collaboration brings benefits to all artists involved, and as I'll demonstrate in this section, on social media these benefits include more exposure for their work and the formation of mutually beneficial associations, which both contribute to the artists' performance of expertise.

This type of activity among artists is evident in Howard Becker's (2008) account of the art world, which describes artists as supportive and collaborative rather than competitive. Becker, importantly, also describes the role of 'folk' art – done by 'ordinary people in the course of their ordinary lives, work seldom thought of by those who make or use it as art at all, even though, as often happens, others from outside the community it is produced in find artistic value in it' (2008, p. 246). He illustrates this with the example of women quilt makers, who make them as family members and neighbours, not as artists. These types of activities can now be monetised through social media and websites such as Etsy, where a particular 'handmade' community has formed which has contributed to the revival of craft work (Luckman, 2015). Some of the participants I observed make and sell their work through Etsy, and it was within this group that I found many examples of retweeting and sharing other artists' work-artists they are also in competition with. Below, Abi sells her own art through Etsy and yet she regularly retweets the work of other makers, often with a positive comment:

Figures 9.8a, b: Abi retweets of crafts.

Lisa, a writer, often praised work of other writers:

Figure 9.9: Lisa: supportive tweets.

The second tweet features an anthology called *A Winter's Romance*, which includes a story by Lisa. Yet, she is tweeting about this anthology not by mentioning her own work, but the contribution of another writer in the anthology by posting a mini positive review.

Lisa and Abi appear to be retweeting the work of people who are essentially their competitors; they are helping to promote their competitors' work by sharing it on their own Twitter profile. This is an example of reciprocity, which is a common practice on social media as a form of mutually beneficial online social relation (Chia, 2012) driven by the idea that people will eventually be rewarded for their own engagement. In Abi's case, her reward for retweeting others' work is an enhancement of her own profile by telling her followers a little more about herself, through the work of others. Lisa in particular was involved in a collaboration with other writers which seemed mutually beneficial for all, because by mentioning fellow writers in the anthology it increases the chances of them returning the favour either immediately or at another point in the future. This reciprocity is a collaborative mechanism that reinforces the artists' performance of expertise on social media, and would be more effective for reaching more people than an artist simply posting their own work, without interacting with others. While these artists are sharing the work of their competitors, the benefits of collaboration outweigh the potential threat from competition.

There were other forms of mutual aid and collaboration also in evidence on social media. Maria, a textiles artist, tweeted an open call and publicly mentioned it to two other artists who she felt may be interested; an altruistic act and an example of artists supporting each other.

These acts of endorsement and 'mutual aid' on social media potentially problematise the notions of individualistic, competitive artistic work described by Bourdieu (1996) and repeated in subsequent accounts of cultural work in neoliberal times, for example by Jen Harvie (2013), who describes the 'artpreneur', working 'privately for her own advantage, she models neoliberalism' (p. 63). Such discourses of individualism, competitiveness, workaholism and blurring between personal and professional life are well documented in cultural work (see Hesmondhalgh and Baker, 2011) with Melissa Gregg (2014) highlighting how this is exacerbated by new technologies. Alice Marwick (2013) argued that social media applications foster an individualistic subjectivity and encourage competition, but my findings suggest this isn't necessarily the case for these artists.

For them, social media platforms allow new opportunities for work, collaboration and mutual aid among both 'professional' and 'amateur' artists. The platform-specific features within Twitter allow these artists to share each other's work, with positive comments through the 'quote' function (as Abi did) or by including other artists in posts through @ mentions. Where there is collaboration between artists, as with Lisa and the anthology, she posted and commented on the work of others within that anthology as a way of simultaneously promoting her work and that of the other writers, reinforcing the possibility of reciprocal re-posting and retweeting to further amplify and increase the potential audience for the work. This mutual aid on social media is also a part of the collaboration.

Figure 9.10: Maria sharing opportunity retweet.

Within my sample, these acts of mutual aid and support were displayed most frequently among the female participants, and between them and fellow female artists. Susan Luckman (2015) notes the resurgence in the 'craft economy' particularly among middle class women, who choose to work from home and set up craft businesses on Etsy which fit around the demands of parental and domestic responsibilities. While Luckman usefully highlights the isolation and stress these women face, who juggle managing their businesses, their identities (particularly online) and their families, she does not pay much attention to the possibilities offered by running these online businesses, and the potentially positive social connections formed between female makers and artists which can be facilitated through social media and sites such as Etsy. Further research could examine this in more depth, by interviewing female artists in relation to how they use social media, particularly in terms of collaboration and mutual aid.

Conclusion

The aim of this chapter was to find out how expertise is performed on social media by artists, and what this means for collaboration in cultural work. I tested the applicability of Pierre Bourdieu's *illusio,* a concept which suggests that in the art world, positive consensus about an artists' expertise is crucial for that artist to be consecrated, or elevated, among others. I aimed to work through this concept on social media interactions and posts by artists, as part of their performance of expertise, because the idea of the *illusio* is a competitive, individualistic conception of the art world, compared to more collaborative accounts such as Howard Becker's *Art Worlds.*

Through my analysis, I found evidence of both competition and collaboration in artists' performance of expertise on social media. The *illusio* highlights the role of powerful people and organisations in elevating artists to prominence. If artists are associated with well-known people or companies on social media, that potentially increases their exposure, elevates their status and significantly enhances their performance of expertise. Also important for these artists are positive reviews from customers, clients and peers, which are regularly retweeted and shared. This builds on work about online evaluation (Reagle, 2015; Gandini, 2015) and I suggest this is a more specific type of evaluation, because on sites such as Twitter and Facebook such positive or negative reviews can be carefully curated by the artist, who can choose whether or not to share it to their own profile.

I conceptualised evidence of collaboration using the idea of mutual aid (de Peuter and Cohen, 2015). On social media, this was apparent through artists' retweeting and sharing of each other's work on social media, even though they are potential competitors for work. This appears to be a more congenial, altruistic practice, what Howard Becker described in *Art Worlds* – where collaboration is essential for artists to create and sell their work. Mutual aid is a useful concept to describe cultural workers helping each other in this way. What also needs to be considered on social media are some of the particular norms of social relation, such as reciprocity, where users participate with some expectation of receiving some form of return or reward for their engagement.

An effective performance of expertise is what enables artists to gain work and make a living, and social media platforms are a relatively free and potentially wide-reaching way to do this. From my analysis, I argue that the artists using social media for the performance of expertise negotiate between promoting their own work, and forming potentially beneficial online associations with other artists in their area. While associating with high-profile companies and people is important for artists' performance of expertise, collaboration is equally crucial too, because the associations formed with other artists can lead to increased exposure of each other's work on social media through reciprocal sharing and mutual aid. I also found evidence of mutually beneficial collaborative production in the anthology Lisa was involved in. This collaboration enabled Lisa to promote her anthology by posting and commenting on the contributions of others.

The evidence of collaboration and mutual aid in my analysis also offers a departure from more individualistic conceptions of social media activity, particularly self-branding (Hearn, 2008; Page, 2012; Marwick, 2013) and self-promotion (Scharff, 2015). Such ideas imply an inward-looking and self-centred approach to social media performance, and while of course the artists in my sample are performing expertise for their own benefit, they are often raising the profile of other artists at the same time.

A final consideration is the role of social media *platforms* in these practices of performing expertise. It is important to remember that social media platforms have particular temporal and structural qualities which affect the way people use them, and how information is received from them. Ultimately, these platforms are designed to harvest people's information to make money (Andrejevic, 2011; Arvidsson and Colleoni, 2012). Skeggs and Yuill (2015) argue that platforms and the algorithms that run them are ideological; they are structured in certain ways and can be changed by developers at any time to continue to serve the interests of owners and corporations.

These corporations and their platforms shape the way that expertise is performed on social media, and the way it is received by users. Artists in my study negotiate this as part of their work, and I argue that platforms are crucial to consider in contemporary accounts of cultural work. Artists need to get their work noticed in order to sell their work, get commissions and make a living. Social media is a relatively cheap way for artists to perform their expertise and get their work noticed, and platforms for some of them are central to this. Sometimes, this is done through collaborations, and these collaborations can be facilitated through the Internet and particularly social media, an efficient way to network and connect with fellow artists all around the world and participate in collaborative projects often from the comfort of their own home. Corporation-owned platforms, then, are central to this, and the algorithms and platform structures mediate collaborations and performances of expertise, ultimately, to benefit the corporations. User data is sold to marketing companies, platforms are designed to deliver advertisements, and the users themselves need to agree to terms and conditions in order to continue benefitting from the 'free' platforms. How do artists negotiate these trade-offs? The corporations ultimately benefit, but most of the artists in my sample also benefit from platforms, so does that make it okay? Any future research which involves social media should be more critical of platforms and platform owners.

While this chapter provides some important insights into contemporary cultural work, collaboration, expertise and social media methods, further work is required to explore the experience of female artists in particular in relation to collaboration and the performance of expertise, and how expertise is performed on social media by people working in other competitive sectors, drawing from the methods utilised in this chapter.

References

Addis, M. (2013). Linguistic competence and expertise. *Phenomenology and the Cognitive Sciences*, 12 (July 2013): 327–36. DOI: https://doi.org/ 10.1007/ s11097-011-9211-5

Andrejevic, M. (2011). The work that affective economics does. *Cultural Studies*, 25(4–5): 604–20. DOI: https://doi.org/10.1080/09502386.2011.6 00551.

Andres, L., & Round, J. (2015). The creative economy in a context of transition: A review of the mechanisms of micro-resilience. *Cities*, 45: 1–6. DOI: https://doi.org/10.1016/j.cities.2015.02.003.

Arnoldi, J. (2007). Universities and the public recognition of expertise. *Minerva*, 45(1): 49–61. DOI: https://doi.org/10.1007/s11024-006-9028-5.

Arvidsson, A., & Colleoni, E. (2012). Value in informational capitalism and on the Internet. *The Information Society*, 28(3): 135–50. DOI: 10.1080/01972243.2012.669449.

Banks, J. (2009). Co-creative expertise: Auran Games and Fury – A case study. *Media International Australia*, 130, 77–89. DOI: https://doi.org/10.1177/1329 878X0913000110.

Banks, M., & Hesmondhalgh, D. (2009). Looking for work in creative industries policy. *International Journal of Cultural Policy*, 15(4): 415–30. DOI: https://doi.org/10.1080/10286630902923323.

Beck, U. (1992). *Risk Society: Towards a New Modernity*. London: SAGE.

_____. (1998). Politics of Risk Society. In *Politics of Risk Society*, J. Franklin (Ed.). Cambridge: Polity.

Becker, H. (2008). *Art Worlds 25th Anniversary edition*. Berkeley, CA: University of California Press.

Bennett, T. (2010). Sociology, aesthetics, expertise. *New Literary History*, 41(2): 253–76.

Bilton, C. (2007). *Management and Creativity: From Creative Industries to Creative Management*. Oxford: Blackwell Publishing.

Bourdieu, P. (1996). *The Rules of Art: Genesis and Structure of the Literary Field*, translated from French by S. Emanuel. Cambridge: Polity Press.

boyd, D., & Crawford, K. (2012). Critical questions for Big Data. *Information, Communication & Society*, 15(5): 662–79. DOI: https://doi.org/10.1080/1 369118X.2012.678878.

Chia, A. (2012). Welcome to me-mart: The politics of user-generated content in personal blogs. *American Behavioral Scientist*, 56(4): 421–38. DOI: https://doi.org/10.1177/0002764211429359.

Collins, H.M. and Evans, R. (2002). The third wave of science studies: Studies of expertise and experience. *Social Studies of Science*, 32(2): 235–96. DOI: https://doi.org/10.1177/0306312702032002003.

de Peuter, G., & Cohen, N. S. (2015). Emerging Labour Politics in Creative Industries. In K. Oakley & J. O'Connor, (Eds.) *The Routledge Companion to the Cultural Industries*. London: Routledge, pp. 305–18.

Dreyfus, H. L., & Dreyfus, S. E. (1986). From Socrates to Expert Systems: The Limits of Calculative Rationality. *Technology in Society* Vol. 6(3): 217–233

Duffy, B. E. (2016). The romance of work: Gender and aspirational labour in the digital culture industries. *International Journal of Cultural Studies* 19(4): 441–57. DOI: https://doi.org/10.1177/1367877915572186.

Forkert, K. (2013). *Artistic Lives: A Study of Creativity in Two European Cities*. Farnham: Ashgate Publishing.

Gandini, A. (2015). Online social influence and the evaluation of creative practice: A critique of klout. In H.C. Suhr (Eds.) *Online Evaluation of Creativity and the Arts*. London: Routledge, pp. 150–68.

Gerlitz, C., & Helmond, A. (2013). The Like Economy: Social buttons and the data-intensive web. *New Media & Society*, 15(8): 1348–65. DOI: https://doi.org/10.1177/1461444812472322

Gill, R., & Pratt, A. (2008). In the social factory? Immaterial labour, precariousness and cultural work. *Theory, Culture & Society*, 25(7-8): 1–30. DOI: https://doi.org/10.1177/0263276408097794.

Goffman, E. (1959). *The Presentation of Self in Everyday Life*. New York, NY: Doubleday.

Gregg, M. (2014). Presence Bleed: Performing Professionalism Online. In M. Banks, R. Gill and S. Taylor, (Eds.) *Theorizing Cultural Work: Labour, Continuity and Change in the Cultural and Creative Industries*. London: Routledge, pp. 122–35.

Harvie, J. (2013). *Fair Play: Art, Performance and Neoliberalism*. Basingstoke: Palgrave Macmillan.

Hearn, A. (2008). 'Meat, Mask, Burden': Probing the contours of the branded 'self'. *Journal of Consumer Culture*, 8(2), 197–217. DOI: https://doi.org/10.1177/1469540508090086

Henderson, M., Johnson, N. F., & Auld, G. (2013). Silences of ethical practice: Dilemmas for researchers using social media. *Educational Research and Evaluation*, 19(6): 546–60. DOI: https://doi.org/10.1080/13803611.2013.805656.

Hesmondhalgh, D., & Baker, S. (2011). *Creative Labour: Media Work in Three Cultural Industries*. London: Routledge.

Jancovich, L. (2015). The participation myth. *International Journal of Cultural Policy*, (May 2015): 1–15. DOI: https://doi.org/10.1080/10286632.2015.1027698.

Jones, C. (2002). Signaling expertise: How signals shape careers in creative industries. In M. Peiperl, M. Bernard & A. Anand, (Eds.) *Career Creativity: Explorations in the Remaking of Work*. Oxford: Oxford University Press, pp. 209–28.

Keen, A. (2007). *The Cult of the Amateur: How Blogs, MySpace, YouTube, and The Rest of Today's User-generated Media Are Destroying Our Economy, Our Culture, and Our Values*. London: Nicholas Brealey Publishing.

Kennedy, H. (2015) No Learning, No Spec: Spec Work Competitions and the Spec Movement. In H.C. Suhr (Eds.) *Online Evaluation of Creativity and the Arts*. London: Routledge, pp. 112–28.

Luckman, S. (2015). *Craft and the Creative Economy*. Basingstoke: Palgrave Macmillan.

Luhmann N. (2000). *Art as a Social System*. Stanford, CA: Stanford University Press.

Marwick, A. E., & boyd, D. (2011). I Tweet Honestly, I Tweet Passionately: Twitter Users, Context Collapse, and the Imagined Audience. *New Media & Society*, 13 (1): 114–33. DOI: https://doi.org/10.1177/1461444810365313.

Marwick, A. E. (2013). *Status Update: Celebrity, Publicity, and Branding in the Social Media Age*. New Haven, CT: Yale University Press.

McGuigan, J. (2010). Creative labour, cultural work and individualisation. *International Journal of Cultural Policy*, 16 (3): 323–35. DOI: https://doi.org/10.1080/10286630903029658.

Nixon, S. (2014). Cultural intermediaries or market device? The case of advertising. In J.S. Maguire and J. Matthews, (Eds.) *The Cultural Intermediaries Reader*. London: SAGE, pp. 34–42.

Page, R. (2012) The linguistics of self-branding and micro-celebrity in Twitter: The role of hashtags. *Discourse & Communication*, 6(2): 181-201. DOI: https://doi.org/10.1177/1750481312437441.

Patel, K. (2015) The performance of expertise on social media by creative and cultural workers. Presented 19 June at Reframing Media/Cultural Studies, University of Westminster. Retrieved from https://www.academia.edu/18642850/The_Performance_of_Expertise_on_Social_Media_by_Creative_and_Cultural_Workers._Cultures_in_Disarray_Kings_College_

London_11_Jun_2015_and_Reframing_Media_Cultural_Studies_ University_of_Westminster_19_Jun_2015.

Prince, R. (2010). 'Fleshing out' expertise: The making of creative industries experts in the United Kingdom, *Geoforum*, 41(6): 875–84.

_____. (2014). Economies of Expertise: Consultants and the Assemblage of Culture. *Journal of Cultural Economy* (ahead of print): 1–15. DOI: https://doi.org/10.1080/17530350.2014.974654.

Reagle, J. (2015) Revenge Rating and Tweak Critique at Photo.net. In H.C. Suhr (Ed.) *Online Evaluation of Creativity and the Arts*. New York, NY: Routledge, pp. 20–40.

Scharff, C. (2015). Blowing your own trumpet: Exploring the gendered dynamics of self-promotion in the classical music profession. *The Sociological Review*, 63(S1): 97–112. DOI: https://doi.org/10.1111/1467-954X.12243.

Schudson, M. (2006). The trouble with experts–and why democracies need them. *Theory and Society*, 35 (5–6): 491–506. DOI: https://doi.org/10.1007/s11186-006-9012-y.

Skeggs, B., & Yuill, S. (2015). The methodology of a multi-model project examining how Facebook infrastructures social relations. *Information, Communication & Society*, 4462(October): 1–17. DOI: https://doi.org/10.1080/1369118X.2015.1091026.

Suhr, H.C. (2015) Introduction: Toward an Interdisciplinary Understanding of Online Evaluation of Creativity and the Arts. In H.C. Suhr (Ed.) *Online Evaluation of Creativity and the Arts*. New York, NY: Routledge, pp. 1–19.

Taylor, C. (2013). Between culture, policy and industry: modalities of intermediation in the creative economy. *Regional Studies*, (November 2014): 1–12. DOI: https://doi.org/10.1080/00343404.2012.748981.

Turner, S. (2001). What is the problem with experts? *Social Studies of Science*, 31(1): 123–49. DOI: https://doi.org/10.1177/030631201031001007

Wilson, N. (2010). Social creativity: Re-qualifying the creative economy. *International Journal of Cultural Policy*, 16(3): 367–81. DOI: https://doi.org/10.1080/10286630903111621.

Wynne, B. (1992). Misunderstood misunderstandings: Social identities and public uptake of science. *Public Understanding of Science*, (1): 281–304. DOI: https://doi.org/10.1088/0963-6625/1/3/004.

CHAPTER TEN

Girls Rock! Best Practices and Challenges in Collaborative Production at Rock Camp for Girls

Miranda Campbell
(Ryerson University)

Introduction

On a sunny Sunday in July 2013, Rock Camp for Girls Montreal (RCFG) was at renowned local recording studio Hotel2Tango. Saturday night at RCFG featured the showcase concert in which six bands made up of girls ranging in age from 10-17 performed. During the five-day summer camp leading up to the showcase concert, the campers learnt an instrument, formed a band, and wrote an original song together. Some of them had never picked up an instrument before the camp. At the Sunday recording session, the previous night's nerves and excitement have quieted, and the atmosphere is calm and cozy. One volunteer has brought bagels and cream cheese, and another has baked a pie. Campers snack and hang out, waiting their turn to record. Some watch Demi Lovato videos on YouTube on the computer in the lounge. In the recording studio, volunteers help campers with their set up, one asking her band if

How to cite this book chapter:
Campbell, M. 2017. Girls Rock! Best Practices and Challenges in Collaborative Production at Rock Camp for Girls. In: Graham, J. and Gandini, A. (eds.). *Collaborative Production in the Creative Industries.* Pp. 177–196. London: University of Westminster Press. DOI: https://doi.org/10.16997/book4.j. License: CC-BY-NC-ND 4.0

everyone feels comfortable. The recording engineer who has volunteered his time to work with RCFG communicates with campers from his booth through their headphone monitors, and I am tickled to see one camper's eyes light up in amazement as she hears his voice in her headphones. After the last band is done recording, we wait for parents to pick up the last campers, and the recording engineer leaves, telling us to close the door behind us.

This opening anecdote of the concluding day and recording session at the summer camp suggests some of the potential of moving towards more collaborative modes of production such that women and in particular young girls may have increased participation in the music industry. However, the presentation of this cozy scene belies the underlining challenges, not only of organizing a summer camp with a set goal of content production, but also of moving from individual-based to collaborative modes of production more generally. Here, I operationalize the concept of the 'community of practice' (CoP) (Lave & Wenger, 1991; Wenger, 1998, 2010) in order to analyse these possibilities and challenges. RCFG might be understood as an alternative CoP that forwards collaborative modes of cultural production with clear and explicit means of participation, in opposition to the individualised navigation of informal and often inequitable routes of accessing cultural production in creative industries employment. Primarily working with Wenger's (1998) main characteristics of CoPs of mutual engagement, joint enterprise, and shared repertoire, in this case study of RCFG, I chronicle how these characteristics set up RCFG as an alternative CoP, as the camp seeks to reconfigure the exclusionary nature of these characteristics in more traditional CoPs, in particular in terms of gendered participation in music scenes. The sense of mutual engagement, joint enterprise, and shared repertoire at RCFG can be read to stem from the desire to foster female empowerment and widen access to music scenes, but these characteristics of RCFG as an alternative CoP can also be odds with existing policy structures, as well as individual desires and rationales for participation at the camp, posing challenges for the implementation of the tenets of RCFG on a broader scale.

Miell and Littleton note that the rise of interest in creative collaboration stems from a desire to support these initiatives and create improved opportunities for creative work: 'whilst there is an agreement about the value of trying to establish supportive contexts for collaboration, there is also a recognition that any attempts at intervention need to reflect the requirements and preferences of particular groups and communities. There is no simple agreed formula that can be applied to promote creativity' (2004, pp. 1–2). In what follows, rather than attempt to determine a normative CoP 'formula', I instead seek to articulate the particular requirements and preferences of RCFG as a CoP, and question how and if these requirements/preferences could be implemented on a wider level.

Theoretical context: Creative industries and communities of practice

As a concept, CoPs have been forwarded to capture horizontal 'learning by doing' in the company of other, more seasoned practitioners. While the concept was originally articulated through examples of craft-based modes of employment, including midwifery and tailoring, it has been used to map the characteristics of a wide array of groups and locales, such as virtual and online communities, second-language learners, and more formalised workplaces, including those in the creative industries (Cox, 2005; Contu, 2013). Though the organizing features of CoPs vary across iterations, emphasis on learning as it relates to identity formation through a community remains a key theme across conceptualizations. The earliest outline of CoPs, developed by Lave and Wenger (1991), forwards the concept of 'legitimate peripheral participation', which outlines how newcomers to a community are integrated and socialised within that community through observation and by initially taking on simple, low-risk tasks, before gradually taking on a more central role. Though this model of CoPs might suggest an apprenticeship type-model of learning, the proposed concept emphasises informal rather than formalised routes into the community, driven by the task at hand rather than set agendas. Wenger's later (1998) articulation of CoPs presents a definition of the concept in more precise terms, suggesting that CoPs are formed through mutual engagement, joint enterprise, and shared repertoire (pp. 72–3). As such, CoPs are united by and driven by a clear purpose or joint enterprise that is sustained over time through the relationships and norms of mutual engagement, and that produces a common set of resources, or a shared repertoire.

The CoP concept might be readily applied to work in the creative industries, as routes into employment in these fields are often informal or based in networks (Campbell, 2013; Oakley, 2006). Wenger's work has been critiqued for its inattention to power dynamics and structural forces that constrain individual agency and ability to gain access and learning through a CoP (Cox, 2005). These critiques have also been made of work in the creative industries more generally, as the informal and network-based modes of entry reproduce and exacerbate dominant patterns of workplace inequity. Conor, Gill and Taylor (2015) provide an overview of how the creative industries have been championed as seemingly open employment avenues for all based in merit and talent, but in fact have less equitable employment profiles than labour markets on the whole. As an alternative CoP, RCGF seeks to create access and forward collaboration in order to widen participation in male-dominated music scenes.

Though gender imbalance in music scenes have long been noted, in 2015 this inequity came to the forefront, as seen in the viral edits of British music festival posters, which were photoshopped to remove all the bands that did not have any female members (BBC News, 2015). The results were visually shocking: the posters went from having dozens of bands listed down to handfuls. The experiment has been reproduced for Canadian and American music festivals, resulting in similarly empty posters (Cannon, 2015; Teo, 2015). In 2016, the Canadian Juno Awards nominees for artist of the year, album of the year, rock album of the year, rap recording of the year and dance recording of the year, were all men. On Twitter, female Canadian musician Grimes took note of the absence of women nominees in these categories, as well as for 'engineer or producer of the year etc.', and linked the lack of recognition with lack of participation: 'I can't help but feel that if women were equally rewarded for technical work they would feel inclined to participate more' (Thiessen, 2016). In response to the Juno nominations, Amy Millan of the band Canadian band Stars started the hashtag #JunosSoMale, referencing the #OscarsSoWhite hashtag, which highlighted the lack of racial diversity in the 2016 Oscar nominations (Bell, 2016). Given this continued problem of gender inequity in the music industry, I will investigate below how the mutual engagement, joint enterprise, and shared repertoire of RCFG might foster conditions to forward greater inclusion of women in music scenes.

Historical context: Riot Grrrl and female-led music scenes

The existence of girls' rock camps may be one of the most long-lasting legacies of riot grrrl, an alternative and subcultural movement of the 1990s that initially centered around Olympia, Washington but diffused nationally and internationally, and that sought to claim space for women in the music industry through female-led bands, but also through taking control of the means of production and dissemination (Downes, 2007; Marcus, 2010). Riot grrrl was a response to male-dominated punk scenes: though these scenes may have intended to provide resistance to mainstream musical practices, they often reproduced hegemonic gender norms that created unsafe conditions for the participation of women (Gottlieb & Wald, 1994; Kearney, 1997; Leonard, 1998). Hesmondhalgh's (1999) analysis of 'indie' as a musical genre notes that the legacy of punk rock as a movement was a form of music that set out to organise itself around an alternative set of operating principles, and '[transcend] romantic notions of musical creativity' (p. 37) and move away from the 'cultural myth' of 'the isolated genius [as] hero' (p. 35) and from musical practices based in 'competitive individualism' (p. 55). Hesmondhalgh notes, however, that even within communities intending to operate with counter-hegemonic practices, exclusionary barriers to participation reasserted themselves, and ultimately bands associated with the indie movement reproduced conventional norms associated with rock and roll musical performance, with 'bands consisting of four or five young men playing guitars and drums' (p. 46).

In his articulation of CoPs as 'social learning systems', Wenger (2010) suggests that entering into a CoP 'translates into a regime of accountability' or 'a way to honor the history of learning of that community' (p. 187). As a musical formation, punk famously abandoned the notion of in-depth accountability as a rite of passage into musical production, instead suggesting that learning three chords is sufficient for starting a band (Laing, 1985). Battle's analysis of the Montreal music scene underscores 'the left-leaning, progressive and community-minded politics of indie music scenes in general, and particularly, those in the Montreal indie music community' (2009, p. 85). Nonetheless, Battle also notes the inaccessible and elitist nature of this scene (p. 109), suggesting that even when a regime of accountability is problematized by a CoP, other exclusionary barriers to participation may be erected.

Riot grrrl not only saw the rise of female-identified people playing in bands, such as Bikini Kill, Bratmobile, Heavens to Betsy, and so on, but more broadly gave rise to teen girl empowerment with a do-it-yourself feminism centered around cultural production that 'can be seen in the emergence of a polymorphous infrastructure of grrrl-related cottage industries that include the production of not just music, but zines, stickers, crafts, mixed tapes, and alternative menstrual products' (Piano, 2003, p.254). Though the riot grrrl movement pointed towards the widespread involvement of girls in acts of creativity and the creation of networks around these forms of cultural production (Huq, 2006), rather than adulation of performers in bands, media focus became centered on key individuals, in particular Kathleen Hanna of Bikini Kill, as figureheads or spokespeople for the movement, eventually leading to a refusal of riot grrrls to engage with the media and to the demise of the movement under the banner of the riot grrrl name (Marcus, 2010). Ali (2012) comments on the intention of Hanna and others in the movement to work towards a model of rooting the individual within a community framework, invoking Sarah Hoagland's (1988) concept of *autokeny*.

Though CoPs might offer a lens to foreground the self within this community framework, the focus in Wenger's work remains on the individual's learning and trajectory into the community, rather than on an alternative, community-based mode of identity. Wenger's (1998) articulation of CoPs emphasises the characteristic of sustained mutual engagement, yet sustaining a community-based or collaborative model of identity poses challenges. Chronicling the rise of third-wave feminism (in which riot grrrl can be situated), Heywood and Drake (1997) comment on the difficulty of sustaining community-oriented models of the feminist self within the larger individual-centric culture: 'despite our knowing better, despite our knowing its emptiness, the ideology of individualism is still a major motivating force behind many third wave lives' (1997, p. 11). Despite the demise of riot grrrl as a network of female-led bands, Schilt and Giffort (2012) profile other indicators of the longevity of riot grrrl, as women involved in this movement have founded and volunteered with local girls rock camps, which can be seen to continue some of the community-focused mode of the riot grrrl movement through a dual focus on collaboration and personal empowerment at these camps.

Research methods

RCFG has existed since 2009, and emerged out of the movement of girls' rock camps initiated by the Rock 'n' Roll Camp for Girls founded in Portland, Oregon in 2001. Girls' rock camps now exist across the globe: Girls Rock Alliance, the international coalition of rock camps, includes more than 50 camps. I was involved with RCFG as a volunteer coordinator and member of the Board of Directors from 2011–13, and my case study of this organisation is based in participant observation, in particular at the 2013 summer camp, as well as semi-structured interviews with volunteers. Participant observation involves the researcher in a dual role: engaging in activities while also observing them (Spradley, 1980, p. 54). This type of methodology and dual role brings specific ethical concerns and necessitates openness and transparency with the intent to observe, as well as the purpose and impact of the research (Dewalt & Dewalt, 2002; Jones, 1996). Prior to the beginning of the RCFG 2013 summer camp, I sought approval from the organisation's Board of Direction to conduct research. After the Board voted in favour of my proposal, I distributed a 'Letter of Information' to volunteers and parents of campers via email (access to these email lists was granted by the Board). This 'Letter of Information' notified participants in the summer camp of my intent to conduct research with the summer camp. The letter to volunteers also stated that they may be contacted for interviews about their experiences.

The joint enterprise (Wenger, 1998) of RCFG as a summer camp might be the focus on campers collectively writing an original song in bands, but more broadly, the joint enterprise of RCFG can also be understood as the feminist project of creating more inclusive music scenes and widening access to musical production through the maintenance of an alternative CoP. Discussing the 'duality' of CoPs as a balance of creative and constraining forces, Wenger (1998) identifies a participation/reification duality, arguing that participation in practices produces reified artifacts. In my analysis here, I draw on the RCFG *Volunteer Handbook* as a reified artifact that both reflects and shapes the mode of participation of volunteers and campers at RCFG.

Rock Camp for Girls Montreal as collaborative CoP: Widening access and participation

The RCFG model is based in female mentorship for girls, with all technical and musical instruction being led by female-identified and gender non-conforming people. In my interviews with RCFG volunteers, many of these volunteers referenced existing dynamics in the music industry and their own experiences of marginalization as driving forces behind their desires to volunteer their time with the organization. As such, these experiences form one of the bases of joint enterprise in the CoP. One volunteer, Alex,[1] comments:

In the world we live in, there is a low number of successful minority figures in the music industry. Whether you identify as a girl, as queer, as transgender, as black, etc., I believe it is hard to find a place in such a heteronormative and "masculine" industry. For instance, I constantly face discrimination and judgment when doing something as simple as buying a guitar in a music store. I do believe that the music industry should be a safer space and a more open-minded and diversified sphere. Rock Camp for Girls definitely plays an important part in such a movement and I want to be a part of it (Alex, personal communication, 2013).

Though one premise of RCFG is to address this lack of visibility and participation of female musicians, RCFG works towards the goal of empowerment through music rather than mastery of an instrument or performance itself. Technical skill can often be a mechanism of exclusion from participation in music scenes, and rather than only offer a corrective that merely seeks to repair this skill deficit, RCFG also seeks to foster alternative means of participation.

Collaborating with others is one part of working towards this goal of widening access and participation to musical production. RCFG's mandate states that the camp 'fosters the promotion of self-esteem, skill-building and critical thinking skills for girls through collaborative music composition and performance. We supplement the music component of Rock Camp for Girls Montreal with workshops based on feminist and anti-oppression frameworks that provide girls with a space for critical examination and empowerment' (Rock Camp for Girls Montreal, 2014). Youth will inevitably enter into musical production with various levels of knowledge and expertise. Media education scholars have sought to address pervasive competitive individualism in cultural production, and advocate moving towards collaborative modes of production when working with youth as a means to widen access to cultural production, such that it can be more equally spread (Buckingham & Sefton-Green, 1994; Jenkins, 2009; Sefton-Green & Sinker, 2000). Buckingham (2003) notes the difficulties of setting up a school curriculum that moves away from the Romantic notion of the individual creator, suggesting that collaborative production might be 'desirable and necessary' but is also accompanied by challenges as students 'come to the classroom with different levels of expertise and knowledge about the media, and with different motivations towards production.' Foremost of the challenges that Buckingham addresses is gender, citing the example of boys intimidating or excluding girls with specialist musical expertise or knowledge (pp. 129–30).

While rock and independent or counter-cultural forms of music sometimes operate around insider knowledge and subcultural capital, RCFG is based in explicitness and clarity in order to demystify music and music-making in the attempt to create an inclusive environment in which everyone feels comfortable to participate and contribute. Miell and Littleton (2004) comment that 'inherent in contemporary approaches to collaborative creativity is an emphasis on studying the processes involved rather than a sole focus on examining the quality of the product of creative endeavours' (p. 1), and this movement from product to process is also found in the operations of RCFG in the attempt to create conducive conditions so that all girls at the camp feel empowered to participate. Fostering these conducive conditions can also be read as the joint enterprise of the camp: while volunteers facilitate the creation of this environment, the camp also seeks to bring campers on board such that there is a shared investment in the creation of this inclusive environment.

Typically, the first day of camp features a group agreement exercise, where campers suggest parameters of conduct for the week-long camp in order to create a welcoming and respectful environment for everyone. Campers all agree to these parameters, and these terms are posted in the camp space to serve as reminders. In community-based settings, group agreements are used to foster co-operation, to create a safe space, and to make the maintenance of this safe space the responsibility of the group rather than the responsibility of facilitators (Girls Action Foundation, 2009; Seeds for Change, 2013). Though the campers lead the suggestions for the group agreement, a volunteer facilitates this session and sometimes needs to intervene. Jesse chronicles that:

> I remember last year, one of their suggestions was, "don't listen to Justin Bieber", and I sort of flagged that one when I saw it, and said, "well, I don't know if we can all agree [to not] listen to Bieber, because I happen to like Justin Bieber, and that's ok. And I'm sure lots of other people here also like Justin Bieber. So it's important that you can express your opinions about these things, but you don't make other people feel bad about their personal preferences." And they were a little "ok, yeah." And it's that sort of thing that we set from day one that I think contributes to the idea of a safe space (Jesse, personal communication, 2013).

This example of Bieber initially being denigrated in front of the group points to the need for intervention when creating an inclusive space rather than merely allowing campers to self-facilitate. While Wenger (2010) characterizes much of the learning in CoPs as horizontal, occurring between peers, he also suggests the need for 'vertical accountability' in the maintenance of CoPs, such as 'decisional authority' and 'policies and regulation'. He comments 'another common mistake is to demonize vertical accountability and romanticize local engagement in practice. A self-governed community is not heaven. It can reproduce all sorts of undesirable things, such as racism or corruption' (p. 192). The RCFG *Volunteer Handbook* also sets out explicit policies to create inclusive conditions, including a camp rules that prohibit racist, homophobic, or otherwise discriminatory behavior or song lyrics.

The RCFG *Volunteer Handbook* also has suggestions for talking about music in an inclusive way by referring to types of sounds like 'a fast song, a slow song, a heavy song, a noisy song' rather than genres or bands that can 'make some campers with less musical experience feel alienated or not as cool' (Rock Camp for Girls Montreal, 2012, p.37). This inclusive language problematises the notion that CoPs will necessarily have or create a shared repertoire (Wenger, 1998). Rather than organizing itself around a common musical repertoire of genres or examples of music, and seek to bring newcomers into this shared knowledge, RCFG seeks to sanction diverse levels of musical knowledge and experience. As such, this inclusive language can be seen as part of the shared repertoire of the camp rather than an accrued knowledge of musical history or musical skills. Though skill development does happen during the summer camp, this is limited in scope due to the week-long duration. Indeed, the *Handbook* stresses there is no 'correct' way of playing music, suggesting 'encouraging the player to find her own way' rather than demonstrating how the instrument should be played (p. 36).

This inclusive language also shapes the suggestions for volunteers about how to talk about the song that the campers are writing together. Though musical instruction might advocate finding one's own way rather than mastery of a skill, there is also a desire for 'everyone [to be] on the same page' (p. 37) in the songwriting process. The *Handbook* suggests that campers collectively name different parts of the song with references like 'the zombie verse' or the 'spaghetti verse' so all band members can contribute to the songwriting process. Large flipchart paper is a common teaching tool at RCFG, so that everyone knows where the band is in the composition and performance process. These mechanisms that attempt to get everyone in the band involved suggest a move away from a model of a principal individual songwriter who comes to rehearsal with parts of a song already written or a model of the vocalist being responsible for lyrical composition. The RCFG model suggests that any or all band members might be involved in any stage of the songwriting process.

Though RCFG has the word 'rock' in its title, the above list of different types of songs or sounds suggest a broader definition of musical production at RCFG, and the camp actively encourages the exploration of other genres of music, suggesting that 'it's not "Rock Camp" in the sense of "rock n' roll" as much as the idea that "girls rock"!' (p. 39). In the band I worked with in 2013, the two vocalists were heavily invested in angelic, soprano singing, while the bass player professed her love for death metal. The happy medium that was struck in this band was that the bass player would do backing vocals in the style of 'death growls' or deep guttural grunts, producing a song that intermittently mixed different genres together. Apart from death metal, exploration of other musical genres at RCFG primarily means an openness to pop music. While much of the understanding of countercultural or alternative spaces comes with a preconceived notion of an opposition to mainstream or commercialized forms of production, the RCFG model of collaboration is based in meeting people where they are at and validating existing interests.

McRobbie and Garber's (1975/2006) analysis of what has been termed the 'bedroom culture' of girls suggests that giving visibility to the activities of girls within youth and subculture studies means engaging with girls' commercial and pop-oriented music sensibilities. These commercial and pop sensibilities continue to be associated with feminine musical interests, and continue to be denigrated in the twenty-first century (Bray & Kiek, 2013; Pelly, 2013). At RCFG, pop music is often mobilised as part of the shared repertoire of existing musical knowledge, and is incorporated in music instruction. Jaime, who volunteered as a keyboard instructor in 2013, chose to teach how to play the keyboard through having her group play along to Carly Rae Jepsen's 'Call Me Maybe.' She comments:

> It surprised me, my first year at Rock Camp, how poppy everything was … But it makes sense, because that's what those campers are listening to, right? The reason that we chose ["Call Me Maybe"], we chose it on the second or third day, we chose it just because it was so prominent at camp, and people were using it in workshops … That Carly Rae Jepsen song is fun, because it has a really prominent riff that is the tune of the song. So you don't really hear the guitars so much. You hear this really prominent keyboard riff, and it's actually only three notes. And you can actually play it just with one hand. So it's easy for the campers to figure out. We just help them. And then we could listen to the song and we could all play along. (Jaime, personal communication, 2013)

Here, the simplicity of the songwriting – a sometimes maligned feature of pop music – is cited as leading to empowerment due to the ease of playing and learning something that is abundantly present in the contemporary musical landscape.

Though pop music may be prominent at RCFG, this does not mean that rock has been abandoned. Jesse comments that vocals are taught through collective singing, and as such it is important to choose songs that:

> everyone knows or kind of knows or one they can listen to and be like, "yeah, I like that" … One of the songs we did in my first year was "Cherry Bomb" by the Runaways, and they love that. It's a really rocking, attitude … it's anthemic. They can scream along with that. We also do "I Love Rock N Roll", Joan Jett—a lot of Joan Jett happening in vocals. We did Lady Gaga, "Telephone". (Jesse, personal communication, 2013)

Through the week of camp, vocalists also work on learning a song at home to bring and perform for their vocal instruction group. Asked what type of songs campers pick, Jesse states:

> they are almost always top 40 type radio songs. Songs that they hear at home, on YouTube … One of them sang 'Part of Your World' from *The*

Little Mermaid last year; I couldn't even handle that. I was crying the whole time. So music soundtrack type of songs.

Giffort's (2011) case study of Girls Rock! Midwest found that volunteers recognise 'multiple ways of being feminist and doing feminism' (p. 579), and put a feminist approach into practice through 'doing' feminism with empowering activities rather than 'telling' about feminism. Similarly, in this vocal instruction example, a camper's decision to bring in a song from Disney – hardly a bastion of feminist consciousness raising – is celebrated rather than critiqued. The purpose of RCFG is not to suggest to campers that the music they already know is artificial, commercial, inauthentic, or inferior, but rather to celebrate and validate their interests while broadening them with workshops like 'Girl Rock History', about the history of women in music across genres.

Pop music also spills over into the way that music is sometimes created by bands at RCFG, and in some cases, may reconfigure what 'original' might mean in terms of musical composition. Mentoring her band, Morgan, a band coach, comments:

> We were stuck trying to find some kind of chorus, and one of the suggestions that I made to my band is that in my own writing practice, when I get stuck, sometimes it helps for me to have a place-holder lyric or melody until I figure something else out, so I suggested that maybe they use something like that to hold the place until they found something that they liked or they thought would work, and then [Lady Gaga's "Paparazzi"] was what they came up with. I think that for them, for many of them, pop music is the point of access into music, because it's so available, right. I think it was great. I was like, "by all means" (Morgan, personal communication, 2013).

Through the week of RCFG, this band sang the chorus of 'Paparazzi' while they were writing their own song, eventually changing the lyrics but keeping some of the vocal phrasing and melody of Lady Gaga's piece. At RCFG, the expanded and reworked notion of shared repertoire can be read as an attempt to create inclusion in the CoP, while in more traditional CoPs, shared repertoire may act as an exclusionary mechanism. Wenger (2010) comments 'learning as the production of practice creates boundaries, not because participants are trying to exclude others (though this can be the case) but because sharing a history of learning ends up distinguishing those who were involved from those who were not' (p. 182). Though Wenger suggests there is an 'unavoidability' of boundaries of practice, at RCFG, part of the terms of the joint enterprise is expanding what a shared repertoire or boundary of practice might typically look like in music scenes rather than assuming they are unavoidable, as a shared history of learning has historically led to the exclusion of women from these scenes.

Challenges in collaborative modes of cultural production at Rock Camp for Girls Montreal

Though validating interests and an openness to working with existing material to reconfigure concepts of originality might be means to foster greater collaboration, access, and inclusion within a CoP, this model is not without its challenges. Some of these challenges are interpersonal. At RCFG, band coaches facilitate an environment where the entire band participates in the decision-making process regarding songwriting, but a predisposition towards collaborating is not always universally found across the campers. Charli, a band coach, comments on her experience of working with bands in which one member is blocking decision making, 'just saying no to everything and wanting to have all the ideas and absolutely blocking every other possible option', and then having to work creatively to allow this camper to see 'the necessity for collaboration and for making compromises, whether this is speaking with the camper one-on-one or getting the band to allow the camper who is blocking to work on certain parts of the songwriting alone.' Working with the youngest group in particular, made up of 10-year olds, Charli says:

> I would try to get the campers to come up with one thing that they wanted to be in the song and then we would work together, with the group, to find things that the other people could play while they were playing that thing that they liked, so it was like each person contributing something they felt was pretty cool and special. (Charli, personal communication, 2016)

This requires 'lots of patience, both from me and from the campers' amidst an environment of 'people losing their patience, or not listening.' Hesmond-hlagh and Baker note the sex segregation in creative industries work where men occupy more prestigious creative roles and women are assigned work that is seen to have a 'need for consensual and caring communication, and coordination' (2015, p. 34). Here, with Charli's description of the effort required to achieve consensus, we might observe that these qualities are neither innate not necessarily found across all girls, which poses difficulties in working collaboratively. While the joint enterprise of the camp might be defined as collaborative songwriting while also creating more inclusive conditions in music scenes more broadly, competing individual desires may still manifest in these collectively-driven enterprises.

Working collaboratively is also challenging with competing interests and desires with regards to how time might be spent during the summer camp. Charli comments:

> [songwriting] is hard, because a lot of the time a lot of the campers would spend their whole year looking forward to camp and they would become very invested in how the song was turning out, they

had a lot of hopes about how it was going to be. (Charli, personal communication, 2016)

Returning to the keyboard instructor Jaime's decision to use 'Call Me Maybe' as a teaching tool, Jaime also comments that:

Of course not everybody likes that kind of music, and there's always one camper in the group who is going to be totally resistant to the pop music, and is more into stuff that I've never heard of, or punk ... more obscure stuff. That's an older camper, usually. But then there's not a whole lot we can do to accommodate their tastes. Just in my experience, those campers who are not really into the pop, and they'll just be kinda cool, and "no, I don't want to do Carly Rae; I'm more into this really obscure punk band." But then they don't want to suggest anything either. So I'm like, "you're going to go along; we're going to practice this." So it's not the most inclusive pedagogy, but we only have 45 minutes, so we just have to pick a song and learn it. (Jaime, personal communication, 2013)

Though pop music may have a prominent role at RCFG and a prominent role in the lives of the campers, it is not a universal meeting ground where everyone feels included. We also see this in the Bieber backlash in the example from the first day of camp above. Thornton (2005) suggests that subcultural capital manifests itself through asserting power through knowledge and tastes, and this dynamic can be at play at RCFG in spite of an explicit intention of acceptance and inclusion in the joint enterprise.

These competing interests with regards to how time is spent is also challenging for the formation of sustained mutual engagement in the CoP. Though RCFG organises various activities year-round, and many campers return to the camp year after year, the summer camp is only a seven-day event, and only five of these are spent on learning an instrument, forming a band, and collaboratively writing a song. In his discussion of UK-based music youth arts programs, Rimmer (2009) gives an overview of the divergence between the policy structures that give rise to these programs and which are often focused on performance and other quantifiable outputs that can be used for program evaluation and assessment on the one hand, and on the other hand young people's interests in joining and participating in these programs, which may not stem from a desire to compose and perform an original song.

To date, RCFG has been self-funded, and does not need to meet government funding requirements to produce a certain output. At RCFG, it would seemingly be accepted if a band wanted to perform a cover song or didn't want to perform at all. The pressure of time and output remain at RCFG, even if they are not externally mandated. Charli remarks that 'campers would have anxiety attacks about not being able to finish in a week.' Campers not only sometimes struggle with collaborative songwriting but also sometimes struggle with overcoming stage fright and the internalised need to be perfect that many young girls feel, but only have five days to do so. Charli notes that 'there's internal barriers to looking stupid or not being good enough to justify drawing attention to yourself. I feel like that is very girl-specific.' Vocalists in particular are:

> most likely to feel scared to even start, scared to make any sound at all because the sound would be the wrong sound. They'd prefer to stay in this fantasy space where they would talk about what it was going to be like but would never feel comfortable to take the risk of going there. And so the work would be to break down their barriers and help their group encourage them until they felt comfortable. (Charli, personal communication, 2016)

This limited time at RCFG and at-times large task that forms the joint enterprise may compromise the formation of shared sense of sustained mutual engagement amongst the campers.

Collaborative cultural production and intellectual property

Beyond these interpersonal and time challenges, collaborative modes of production that favour a model of cultural hybridity may be at odds with intellectual property laws that govern musical production and dissemination. These issues notably emerge with multi-million dollar lawsuits or other high profile cases when musicians feel others have used their material without permission or acknowledgement (Grow, 2015; Kreps, 2015; O'Connor, 1999), but these issues also emerged in RCFG's small-scale and community-based mode of collaborative production. Morgan, the band coach who worked with the band whose composition involved reworking a Lady Gaga song, notes that this issue of permission to use others' material arose in band discussions, and resulted in a discussion on the evolution of music history through appropriation of existing forms:

> I think all music is just building upon existing patterns, to use that pattern and incorporate it in a new way. I think that sometimes we get really caught up in the idea of originality, particularly when it comes to pop music. I think that's often one of the biggest criticisms of pop music, is that it all sounds the same, or whatever, it follows a particular formula, but I think the formula is just a base to jump off from. The campers were a little bit concerned about, "well, aren't we ripping this off?" And then we ended up having a conversation about how, where does pop music come from? Contemporary pop music. It comes from rock and roll; it comes from blues; it comes from jazz. All of these things are just building on top of each other anyway. We ended up having this really great conversation about music history. (Morgan, personal communication, 2013)

RCFG as a whole would generally support this philosophy, insofar as the camp supports its campers in their musical journeys and musical exploration generally. Indeed, the first day of RCFG typically features a 'Superstar Songwriting' workshop that seeks to demystify songwriting and show campers that it is possible to write and perform a song in a compressed amount of time. In this activity, workshop leaders model how to choose a song, find its karaoke track on YouTube, and rewrite its lyrics to express a new theme. This workshop is connected with the feminist mandate of the camp of empowerment through learning by doing and being able to create while using critical thinking, as campers are encouraged to consider the message of their chosen song and rewrite the lyrics to reflect a more positive theme.

As the ephemeral process of the five-day camp gets fixed on tape in the recording process, this approach to songwriting that validates making use of existing forms enters the industrialised and monetised area of cultural dissemination. RCFG initially intended to sell these recordings for fundraising purposes for the camp, but the recording engineer who was volunteering his time intervened in this process, raising questions about the potential distribution of revenues earned from the sale of these CDs. The recording engineer asked if the bands would be entitled to some of the profits, if the bands could also sell their songs, and if they did, if they would be obligated to give some of their revenues back to RCFG. He raised the possibility of one of the songs becoming a YouTube sensation and selling 20,000 downloads through the RCFG website. Though difficulties of both reaching an audience in a crowded digital environment and earning a sustainable income as a small-scale cultural producer have been noted (Byrne, 2012; Hesmondhalgh & Baker, 2011; Taylor, 2014), this possibility of 20,000 downloads is not altogether absurd. Beyond these concerns of revenue sharing, the recording engineer asked if the fundraising CD might compromise the sense of mutual engagement through joint enterprise at the camp should the bands felt they were being 'used' to create content that RCFG would use for its own means. Over time, these discussions eventually led to the development of a non-exclusive licensing agreement, so that the terms of RCFG using campers' songs would be clear and mutually agreed upon; the organisation also stepped back from the idea that the songs would be sold for its fundraising purposes, and instead would use the material for the purpose of promoting the camp.

In the licensing agreement that RCFG uses, campers have to attest that 'works are original works and that these do not infringe upon any copyright belonging to any third party.' While the camp works to foster collaboration and sanctions reworking existing forms, these philosophies are at odds with intellectual property laws. Chanock (2009) notes that 'the world of property law seeks one true version or definition of matters which the world of cultural studies acknowledges to be subject to plasticity, hybridity, and change. Bringing these two worlds together is a formidable challenge' (p. 187). Discussing the learning that happens in CoPs, Wenger (2010) asserts that 'learning produces a social system' and that this learning forms a 'practice that can be said to be the property of the community' (p.181). The reality of collective ownership is, however, much murkier in intellectual property structures. In her discussion of divergence between small-scale/independent music labels and existing copyright structures, Piper (2010) notes that 'community interest, inclusion, altruism and action out of a non-monetary interest play little role' in copyright laws (p. 425), but these concepts may be important to a small-scale and collaboratively-based mode of cultural production, including the community-minded project of RCFG.

The 2012 revision to the Canadian Copyright Act makes provisions to sanction 'user-generated content' (UGC) such as fan fiction or other forms creative reworking of existing content. This revision specifies that the user-generated content must be 'non-commercial' in nature to be exempted from copyright infringement. Murray and Trosow (2013) comment that 'as a practical matter, this may be a difficult distinction, as the commercial / non-commercial nature of use might shift over time. What happens is the UGC begins as a wholly non-commercial project, such as school project or a hobby activity, and it subsequently enjoys a measure of success?' (p. 146). This possibility could potentially apply to a RCFG production, starting as a non-commercial summer camp project that reworks an existing form, and that could go on to enjoy commercial success. Concerning the copyright structures that surround UGC moving into a commercial arena, Murray and Trosow remark that 'we will have to watch how the practice develops in this area' (p. 147). Though a CoP might favour horizontal or collaborative learning through joint enterprise, the broader reality of the larger culture remains individually driven in terms of property law structures.

Conclusion

In 1975, McRobbie and Garber argued in defense of the bedroom culture of girls, suggesting that studying commercial interests could be a way for the field of subculture studies to register the activities of girls, as these subjects lacked visibility in a field focused on the spectacle of supposedly resistant activities of young men. More than 40 years later, the musical interests of young girls may still be overlooked and denigrated as overtly commercial. Working with rather than against these commercial interests is part of how RCFG seeks to foster collaboration, but this process is not without its challenges, as existing policy structures collide with practice, and the realities of a week-long summer camp with a set goal of content production may limit the transformative potential of creating alternative communities.

Though CoPs may have been conceptualised as spaces of horizontal learning, these communities may reinforce rather than dismantle dominant structural forces of power and inequity. This pattern is also found in the creative industries, which have been championed as more accessible employment routes based in talent, but in fact exacerbate labour market inequities. As an alternative CoP, RCFG's sense of mutual engagement, joint enterprise, and shared repertoire aims to foster a model of collaboration that is less male-centric and potentially more open and inclusive. As such, this collaborative model in the CoP seeks to widen participation to include more girls and young women in musical production. In a still starkly male and individual-centric music industry, RCFG's practices offer some possibilities for opening pathways for women to take centre stage. However, collaborative modes of production alone cannot intervene to remove systemic barriers to entry to creative work or address lack of equity in the creative industries writ large; as such, continued work needs to be done at the policy level and in the creative industries to move towards greater gender equity.

Acknowledgements

The author gratefully acknowledges the support from research assistant Anna Frey and Ryerson University's Faculty of Communication and Design's SRC Conference Travel Fund to present this paper at the Creative Industries and Collaborative Production conference at Middlesex University.

Notes

[1] Pseudonyms have been used for Rock Camp for Girls Montreal volunteers. In keeping with Rock Camp for Girls' Montreal's emphasis on moving towards gender-neutral language (e.g. using the term 'campers' rather than 'girls'), an effort has been made by the author to choose gender-neutral names as pseudonyms.

References

Ali, N. (2012). From riot grrrl to Girls Rock Camp: Gendered spaces, musicianship and the culture of girl making. *Networking Knowledge* 5(1): 141–60.

Battle, S. (2009). "The Beginning After The End": Independent Music, Canadian Cultural Policy and the Montreal Music Scene. M.A. thesis, Concordia University.

BBC News. (2015). How these music festival line-ups look without all-male bands. Retrieved from http://www.bbc.co.uk/newsbeat/article/31629520/how-these-music-festival-line-ups-look-without-all-male-bands.

Bell, J. (2016). 2016 Juno nominations spur #JunosSoMale hashtag. Retrieved from http://www.cbc.ca/news/trending/amy-millan-junos-so-male-1.3430457.

Bray, E., & Kiek. M. (2013). Is pop music sexist? Canadian musician Grimes thinks so. Retrieved from http://www.independent.co.uk/arts-entertainment/music/features/is-pop-sexist-canadian-musician-grimes-thinks-so-8609503.html.

Byrne, D. (2012). *How Music Works*, San Francisco, CA: McSweeney's.

Buckingham, D. (2003). *Media Education: Literacy, Learning, and Contemporary Culture*, Cambridge, UK: Polity Press.

Buckingham, D., & Sefton-Green, J. (1994). *Cultural Studies Goes to School: Reading and Teaching Popular Media*, London: Taylor and Francis.

Campbell, M. (2013). *Out of the Basement: Youth Cultural Production Practice and in Policy*, Montreal: McGill-Queen's University Press.

Cannon, K. (2015). What Coachella and 6 other music festival lineups would look like without men. Retrieved from http://www.sheknows.com/entertainment/articles/1080274/coachella-and-other-music-festival-lineups-with-the-male-acts-removed-photos.

Chanock, M. (2009). Branding identity and copyrighting culture: orientations towards the customary in traditional knowledge discourse. In C. Antons (Ed.) *Traditional Knowledge, Traditional Cultural Expressions and Intellectual Property Law in the Asia-Pacific Region*, The Netherlands: Wolters Klumer, pp. 177–94.

Conor, B., Gill, R., & Taylor, S. (Eds.) (2015). *Gender and Creative Labour.* Oxford: Wiley-Blackwell.

Contu, A. (2014). On boundaries and difference: Communities of practice and power relations in creative work, *Management Learning* 45(3), 289–316.

Cox, A. (2005). What are communities of practice? A comparative review of four seminal works. *Journal of Information Sciences.* Vol 31. (6).

Dewalt, K., & Dewalt, B. (2002). *Participant Observation: A Guide for Fieldworkers*, Walnut Creek: AltaMira.

Downes, J. (2007). Riot grrrl: The legacy and contemporary landscape of DIY feminist cultural activism. In N. Monem (Ed.) *Riot Grrrl: Revolution Girl Style Now*, London: Black Dog Publishing, pp. 12–51.

Giffort, D. (2011). Show or tell? Feminist dilemmas and implicit feminism and Girls' Rock Camp, *Gender & Society* 24(5): 569–88.

Girls Action Foundation. (2009). Creating a group agreement. In *Amplify Toolkit: Designing Spaces and Programs for Girls*, Montreal: Girls Action Foundation.

Gottlieb, J., & Wald, G. (1994). Smells Like Teen Spirit: Riot grrrls, revolution and women in independent rock. In A. Ross and T. Rose (Eds.) *Microphone Fiends: Youth Music and Youth Culture*, London: Routledge, pp. 250–74.

Grow, K. (2015). Robin Thicke, Pharell lose multi-million dollar 'Blurred Lines' lawsuit. Retrieved from http://www.rollingstone.com/music/news/robin-thicke-and-pharrell-lose-blurred-lines-lawsuit-20150310.

Heywood, L., & Drake, J. (Eds.). (1997). *Third Wave Agenda: Being Feminist, Doing Feminism*, Minneapolis, MN: University of Minnesota Press.

Hesmondhalgh, D. (1999). The institutional politics and aesthetics of a popular music genre, *Cultural Studies* 13(1): 34–61.

Hesmondhalgh. D., & Baker, S. (2011). *Creative Labour: Media Work in Three Cultural Industries*, Abingdon: Routledge.

_____. (2015). Sex, Gender and Work Segregation in the Cultural Industries. In B. Conor, R. Gill, and S. Taylor (Eds.) *Gender and Creative Labour*, Oxford: Wiley-Blackwell, pp. 23–36.

Hoagland, S. (1988) *Lesbian Ethics, Toward New Value*. Paolo Alto, CA: Institute of Lesbian Studies.

Huq, R. (2005). *Beyond Subculture: Youth and Pop in a Multi-Ethnic World*, London: Routledge.

Jenkins, H. (2009). *Confronting the Challenges of Participatory Culture: Media Education for the 21st Century*, Chicago, IL: MacArthur Foundation.

Jones, R. (1996). *Research Methods in the Social and Behavioral Sciences*, Sunderland: Sinauer Associates.

Kearney, M. (1997). The missing links: Riot grrrl-feminism-lesbian culture. In S. Whiteley (Ed.) *Sexing the Groove: Popular Music and Gender*, London: Routledge, pp. 207–29.

Kreps, D. (2015). Tom Petty on Sam Smith Settlement: 'No Hard Feelings, These Things Happen.' Retrieved from http://www.rollingstone.com/music/news/tom-petty-on-sam-smith-settlement-no-hard-feelings-these-things-happen-20150129.

Laing. D. (1985). *One Chord Wonders: Power and Meaning in Punk Rock*, Philadelphia, PA: Open University Press.

Lave, J., & Wenger, E. (1991). *Situated Learning: Legitimate Peripheral Participation*, Cambridge: Cambridge University Press.

Leonard, M. (1998). Paper planes: Travelling the new grrrl geographies. In T. Skelton and G. Valentine (Eds.) *Cool Places: Geographies of Youth Cultures*, London: Routledge, pp. 101–18.

Marcus, S. (2010). *Girls to the Front: The True Story of the Riot Grrrl Revolution*, New York: Harper Perennial.

McRobbie, A., & Garber, J. [1975] (2006) . Girls and Subculture. In S. Hall and T. Jefferson (Eds.) *Resistance Through Rituals: Youth Subcultures in Post-War Britain* (2nd ed.), London: Routledge, pp. 177–88.

Miell, D., & Littleton, K. (Eds.). (2004). *Collaborative Creativity: Contemporary Perspectives*, London: Free Association Books.

Murray, L., & Trosow, S. (2013). *Canadian Copyright: A Citizen's Guide*, Toronto: Between the Lines.

Oakley, K. (2006). Include us out—Economic development and social policy in the creative industries, *Cultural Trends* 15(4): 255–73.

_____. (2009). The disappearing arts: Creativity and innovation after the creative industries, *International Journal of Cultural Policy* 15(4): 403–13.

O'Connor, C. (1999). The Verve sued again over 'Bitter Sweet Symphony.' Retrieved from http://www.mtv.com/news/511079/the-verve-sued-again-over-bitter-sweet-symphony.

Pelly. J. (2013). Grimes speaks out in defense of Beyoncé, 'Gangham Style,' and Mariah Carey. Available at http://pitchfork.com/news/49448-grimes-speaks-out-in-defense-of-beyonce-gangnam-style-and-mariah-carey.

Piano, D. (2003). Resisting Subjects: DIY Feminism and the Politics of Style in Subcultural Formations. In D. Muggleton and R. Weinzierl (Eds). *The Post-Subcultures Reader*, Oxford: Berg, pp. 253–65.

Piper, T. (2010). An 'Independent' View of Bill C-32's Copyright Reform. In M. Geist (Ed.) *From "Radical Extremism" To "Balanced Copyright": Canadian Copyright and the Digital Agenda*, Toronto: Irwin Law, pp. 423–46.

Rimmer, M. (2009). 'Instrumental' playing? Cultural policy and young people's community music participation, *International Journal of Cultural Policy* 15(1): 71–90.

Rock Camp for Girls Montreal. (2012). *Volunteer Handbook*, Montreal: Rock Camp for Girls Montreal.

Rock Camp for Girls Montreal. (2014). Mission and mandate. Retrieved from http://girlsrockmontreal.com/about/mission-and-madate.

Schilt, K., & Giffort, D. 'Strong Riot Women' and the Continuity of Feminist Subcultural Participation. In P. Hodkinson and A. Bennett (Eds.) *Ageing and Youth Cultures: Music, Style and Identity*, London: Bloomsbury

Seeds for Change. (2013). *A Consensus Handbook: Co-operative Decision Making for Activists, Co-ops, and Communities*, Lancaster: Seeds for Change.

Sefton-Green, J., & Sinker, R. (Eds.). (2000). *Evaluating Creativity: Making and Learning by Young People*, London: Routledge.

Skillset. (2010). *Women in the Creative Media Industries*, London: Skillset.

Spradley, J. (1980). *Participant Observation*, New York, NY: Holt, Rinehart and Winston.

Taylor, A. (2014). *The People's Platform: Taking Back Power and Culture in the Digital Age*, Toronto: Random House.

Teo, M. (2015). Here's what Canadian festival posters look like with the all-male acts removed. Retrieved from http://www.aux.tv/2015/03/heres-what-canadian-festival-posters-look-like-with-the-all-male-acts-removed.

Thiessen, B. (2016). Grimes blasts Juno Awards for lack of women nominees. Retrieved from http://exclaim.ca/music/article/grimes_blasts_juno_awards_for_the_lack_of_female_nominees.

Thornton, S. (2005). The Social Logic of Subcultural Capital. In K. Gelder and S. Thornton (Eds.) *The Subcultures Reader*, London: Routledge, pp. 200–9.

Wenger, E. (1998). *Communities of Practice: Learning, Meaning and Identity*, Cambridge: Cambridge University Press.

_____. (2010). Communities of Practice and Social Learning Systems: The career of a concept, in C. Blackmore (Ed.) *Social Learning Systems and Communities of Practice*, London: Springer Verlag, pp. 179–98.

CHAPTER ELEVEN

Work In The Creative Economy: Living Contradictions Between the Market and Creative Collaboration

Ashley Lee Wong

(School of Creative Media, City University of Hong Kong)

Introduction

In today's neoliberal creative economy, many of us wear several hats and take on different identities in the pursuit of multiple jobs, projects and roles in a fragmented and precarious labour market. The emergence of what has become know as the creative economy coupled with the financial crisis in the late 2000s has led to the diminishing of the welfare state and especially arts funding under successive governments in the UK. There are now fewer full-time positions and a marked rise in self-employment, where a so-called 'creative class' are celebrated as the new 'model entrepreneurs' (Gill and Pratt, 2008, p. 2). This market-driven mentality devolves the financial risks of producing creative work in this sector to the individual, while the traditional workers' safety net of the welfare state slips from under their feet. Flexibility of the labour market is viewed as desirable for those who want more control over their time, yet it

---

How to cite this book chapter:

Wong, A. L. 2017. Work In The Creative Economy: Living Contradictions Between the Market and Creative Collaboration. In: Graham, J. and Gandini, A. (eds.). *Collaborative Production in the Creative Industries.* Pp. 197–215. London: University of Westminster Press. DOI: https://doi.org/10.16997/book4.k. License: CC-BY-NC-ND 4.0

allows businesses to exploit freelancers without the need to provide social security including pensions, sick pay and holidays. Creative industries discourses promote cultures and models of collaboration in order to create a supportive co-working network on the one hand (in the neo-liberal context previously described, where there is less state support), but also for business efficiency, flexibility and profit on the other (Banks, Conor and Mayer, 2015, preface). This chapter outlines some of the general ways in which concepts of collaboration are employed across the creative industries, before contrasting these with the particular example of how this practice is explored reflexively and critically by independent artists and their collective processes.

The motivation and primary example of this chapter comes in the form of an auto-ethnographic reflection on my own working practices, employed as head of programmes and operations at a commercial creative start-up based around the distribution of digital artworks, but also as the founder of an independent art/research collective. Both forms of work have their own values and language and both also discuss ideas of collaboration in different ways. This chapter attempts to parse concepts of collaboration to critically approach new models of work that might open possibilities towards a different kind of future.

Creative beginnings

I completed my studies in Digital Image/Sound and the Fine Arts at Concordia University in Montreal, Canada in 2006. At the time I was already organising events independently with artists and musicians. My events became platforms for art with an experimental curatorial approach. These typically took place in disused spaces or venues and brought together a community of multidisciplinary artists working across media arts, video, music and performance to create collaborative events. At the time, I was naive to the role that artists play in the gentrification of cities, as first noted by Richard Florida (2002). Artists occupy disused areas which they revitalise with minimal means and bring new value by creating productive communities. However, the flip side that Florida is less concerned with is that property rents increase as a consequence and local communities are incrementally pushed out by property developers eager to build luxury flats and new (or often repurposed) commercial spaces. Though the events we organised were temporary, the areas in Montreal where they took place would later become gentrified as artist communities tend to be the first to identify and revitalise forgotten areas of the city.

Following my studies, I moved to Hong Kong to work in a media art space called Videotage and I continued to develop independent projects and curate events under a project called LOUDSPKR (www.loudspkr.org). My events were always produced on a shoestring budget and normally just broke even, with any profits going to the artists. The intent was never to turn it into something that I could earn a living from – it was always about community, shared experience, experimentation and play. It was a great learning experience, however, the long-term sustainability of the projects was always a concern. At the time I didn't have a clear idea of what I wanted to do in terms of translating this experience into a career, but I wanted it to include elements of working with artists and creating platforms for sharing their work. These independent projects were a 'labour of love', undertaken in the hope that one day it would be possible to pursue them full-time.

Miya Tokumitsu (2014) discusses the idea of Doing What You Love (DWYL) as an expectation of work for people of my generation, where '[W]ork becomes divided into two opposing classes: that which is lovable (creative, intellectual, socially prestigious) and that which is not (repetitive, unintellectual, undistinguished).' In creative work, in particular, we are willing to sacrifice our free-time, work more for less, pursue unpaid internships and often work for free in exchange for the preeminent currency of the creative economy: recognition. Tokumitsu explains that DWYL is an ideological tool of capitalism that presents conditions of exploitation in a favourable light to the exploited, or in other words, presents work – particularly creative work – as advantageous to the socially disadvantaged. Through promotion of lifestyle, recognition and fame, the creative industries makes jobs desirable and at the very same time creates the conditions for self-exploitation and exploitation by employers. We may love the work, but we hate the stress and lack of financial security. It is difficult to find stability in a highly competitive environment where one constantly has to promote oneself in order to secure the next job. Angela McRobbie (2011) identifies the roots of the present situation in the UK in the emergence of the creative economy under New Labour, where the first generation of students graduated from art school with few job prospects and large amounts of debt. Young creative graduates have little choice but to attempt to turn their passions into a career in a 'talent-led economy' (McRobbie, 2011, p.7) which promotes individualism and competition. The nature of creative work in this scenario becomes 'permanently transitional' (McRobbie, 2002, p. 97), as workers skip from project to project without any long-term job security. I soon realised how this reality had become my own, even as I rejected participating in competitive industry.

In 2008 I moved to London to begin an MA in Culture Industry at Goldsmiths, University of London, to help put my work into perspective. It was also the beginning of the economic crisis, which had a large impact on the independent projects I was working on. The London I discovered was already saturated with artists and events. I did not want to compete with them or contribute to that already dense space. My work is always a response to the city: the people and possibilities (as well as the constraints) of a place. I felt more constraints than possibilities and it did not feel appropriate to continue the work in the same way. In times of economic crisis, we enter a space of withdrawal: there were more pressing issues at hand that needed to be addressed before we could really experiment freely again. At the same time, Goldsmiths taught me to see the culture industry critically and understand my role within it as a cultural producer. I was contributing to the Creative Economy whether I liked it or not – to remain idle and passive was not an option and I began developing a new project which took a different form from the experimental events I was organising.

Precariousness

Soon after graduating I started an art/research collective called DOXA (www. doxacollective.org) with my collaborator Yuk Hui. We began organising a series of discussion events on 'Re-imagining Culture' which brought together artists, activists and collectives to discuss issues around the funding cuts to the arts, free and precarious labour, internships, and to find new models and strategies for cultural work in the current economic climate. We pursued projects not for the love of the work, but because we felt we could not continue our creative work in the same way and needed to take a step back to address our conditions of work first and foremost to find other ways of living and working together. Our creative practice became a research-, politics- and community-based form of work, bringing together groups with common concerns. We were informally organised and worked on a project-by-project basis due to limited time and resources. Our work critiqued the role of art in a market economy and the ways in which it was being appropriated into the neoliberal logics of the creative economy – through processes of gentrification and the branding of the city as well as the exploitation of the 'free' creative labour of artists. We were starkly aware of our own working conditions and role within an increasingly neo-liberalised economy – but we also had the desire to change it. Within the realms of the art world our work could be considered a form of 'socially engaged art' practice that, in Greg Sholette's overview (2015), 'attempts to bring about a system-wide reboot' (p. 98).

At the time of producing events with DOXA, I was also working freelance for arts organisations and creative start-ups. It was low paid but it allowed me the flexibility to pursue my independent work on the side. I worked for an Arts Council-funded organisation called Sound and Music producing digital projects and online video content. The organisation's funding was soon cut and projects dried up. I also worked in marketing for an online music start-up (now defunct) where I was essentially a paid intern for almost a year, but this also allowed me to take time off unpaid to attend residencies abroad. At the same time there were fewer opportunities and full-time jobs available in a labour market that became increasingly casualised as government cuts to the arts began to bite. I found myself in a typically precarious situation: Where precarity, as Rosalind Gill and Andy Pratt (2008) note 'signifies both the multiplication of precarious, unstable, insecure forms of living and, simultaneously, new forms of political struggle and solidarity that reach beyond the traditional models of the political party or trade union.' (p. 3) Workers have fewer protections and social security as employers shift more towards freelance and temporary workers over full-time workers. Freelancers are naturally more precarious and require new political organisations to mobilise and defend worker's rights. It becomes more difficult to point fingers and to collectively mobilise when everyone has different and quite likely multiple employers. The financial burden is placed on our individual shoulders – though the system would say we have only ourselves to blame – or are there ways to find solidarity and instigate change in spite of these circumstances? The Carrot Workers Collective and Precarious Workers Brigade in the UK and Arts+Labour in the US are just a few groups working to defend labour rights for precarious workers within the arts and beyond. The work of DOXA continues to explore alternative models for collaboration as a means to address the precarious conditions of cultural work. It is long-term and ongoing as – symptomatically – we have limited means and time to organise whilst balancing other work.

Survival

In order to resist precariousness, I had to move outside of my field in the arts into the commercial creative industries, which includes marketing, PR and advertising. My first full-time position in the UK was in a creative agency in Shoreditch that developed mobile experiences for brands. It was my first time working in a commercial environment and I had little experience beyond my independent projects and non-profit work within the arts sector. I consciously chose not to pursue work in the arts given the cuts to funding, and the few low-paid jobs available at the time. I was not willing to pursue unpaid internships, due to the necessity to earn a livable wage. Survival became a priority as I needed to pay off student debts and find a more stable living situation before having the means to return to my independent work. In addition to debt, I also had minimum income requirements for my visa which I had to meet in order to stay in the country as someone from outside the EU. I was amongst the last of the applicants to receive the post-study work visa (now abolished) which allowed me more time to stay and work in the UK. These circumstances pushed me to find work in the commercial sector outside of my field. I made a conscious decision to attempt to separate work and life, where work is strictly something I do for a living, and any creative work I pursue is not under pressure to support my living. Working in the agency, I witnessed young designers and creatives working until midnight and on their weekends to complete jobs for clients on time. They were paid decently but were put – and put themselves – under high pressure. They loved producing creative content for high-profile brands, yet the flexibility of the working conditions also meant there was little work-life balance. In line with Mark Banks' (2014) discussion of the pleasures and possibilities of cultural work, I observed colleagues routinely 'being in the zone' ('BITZ'): 'the optimal fusion of the productive mind and laboring body … while simultaneously normalising the self-exploiting surrender of body and soul to the economic principle.' (pp. 242–9)

Collaboration in the realm of the creative agency meant having a network of creative friends who have a wide range of skills from design, web, animation, photography, music etc. in order to source talent to realise a wide range of projects for brands. Socialising and making friends also becomes a way of finding someone to help on a project or finding new work. Being involved in the East London community most people work in the creative industries, often as freelancers and are highly networked as both their work and social lives become entwined. One's network also becomes one's brand and value that one brings to a company and also determines the jobs you get as a freelancer. Pandering to client expectations becomes a skill you have to learn to ensure that their money has been well spent. I quickly realised I didn't enjoy work in agencies, which have become a form of the contemporary factory for creative workers that churn out products and campaigns. I stayed only six months before seeking work elsewhere.

Following this period, I found a job at an online start-up called Sedition (www.seditionart.com) that distributes art in digital formats for display on screens and devices. It brought together my interest in art, technology and new models and platforms for art. Working full-time meant I had to put my independent projects aside for evenings and weekends. It was a step closer to bringing the work I do for a living and work that I love together. At the start-up, I started out as a community manager – managing the social media, promoting new artist launches and coordinating marketing events and projects. I had obligations to work full-time at a desk as a waged labourer, selling my time and body to a business. After work, I had little energy to pursue independent work with DOXA, though we have managed to produce projects, albeit over a much longer time scale. Juggling different modes of work are reflected in the practices, values and approaches to the work.

Reputation economy: Collective process vs. brand building

As a long-term project, the work of DOXA is something that does not have to produce profit or succeed as a business. It is a platform for developing and sharing ideas within a community to imagine and approach another future. These are projects and ideas that we could always return to when we find the means. The project is free to evolve with people and time as DOXA or as another entity for a different set of concerns that may be more pertinent to the times in a shifting economy. We can straddle different modes of thinking and working, but also understand the role it plays in our lives and our personal investments within them. On the one hand, working independently we struggle to find resources – we want to resist the market imperative for free labour yet our work with DOXA is always given freely. At times we have encountered disputes with collaborators who have expected payment for participating in an event when none of us were paid except the designer of the poster for our event. To organise independently and informally requires trust and understanding that the work we are doing is not for personal gain. Regardless, we are generating value and building a reputation for ourselves by placing our names on promotional materials for events and listing them on our CVs as achievements. These were never the intentions, but we nonetheless find ourselves as participants in what Alessandro Gandini (2015) terms the 'reputation economy' (13).

Working in a creative digital tech start up brings the imperative for recognition and the value of reputation to the foreground as the pre-eminent means for creating a market and generating profit. My role at the start up was to promote new artworks and artists and leverage the names of renowned artists like Tracey Emin, Damien Hirst, Yoko Ono to sell the business through our online channels including social media, email, affiliate partnerships and events. I was using the reputation of artists as a currency to sell the idea of the platform as a new way to collect and value the artworks that were for sale. It's about who you know and the reputation of artists and institutions that you partner with, and leveraging contacts and building strategic alliances that would mutually benefit our brands. For instance, we would actively seek out partnerships with high-profile museums and institutions like London's Institute of Contemporary Art and Serpentine Galleries (and even give extra to the partnership in exchange for the association). Through the partnerships we would be validated by an established institution – essential as a relatively new start-up. At the same time, I could also build my personal profile as a professional in the arts: the job gave me the opportunity to work with artists whom I would otherwise not be able to access. Alison Hearn (2010) argues that 'reputation' is conditioned and, arguably, constituted by cultural and economic institutions that have the power to authorize and direct attention, and transmute that attention back into value.' (p. 423). Referring to the work of Adam Arvidsson and Nicolai Peitersen (2009), she describes the ways in which reputation has become the 'new standard of value' in the digital age. The reputations of artists are also built on their track record of exhibiting in recognised institutions; critics and art historians validate their work and in so doing establish its value within the art market. The processes of the start-up place emphasis around the necessity of building value by association through strategic partnerships with cultural institutions and the marketing of high-profile artists. All of this seeped into the need to develop my own personal brand as a professional in the industry.

On the one hand, with our independent work recognition is not the aim but rather a derivative of presenting work in the public realm. Many artists choose to disavow ownership in support of more collaborative models of practice and produce work under an anonymous collective name. For instance, *Reena Spaulings* is a collectively-authored novel by New York artist collective Bernadette Corporation (Corporation, 2005), written by multiple individuals providing a range of perspectives about a fictional character. The many individual contributions are brought together under the collective's name. However in the commercial art market, authorial recognition is valued as the means of validating an artist's work and determining its value. It plays a role in marketing and building of brands to develop strategic associations with well-known institutions. Despite resisting the competitive individualisation that is so central to the reputation economy, at times we are compelled to claim ownership and quantify the value of our personal contribution when it comes to payment, fees or protecting our 'intellectual property'. It becomes an issue when independent work becomes self-sustaining, and deciding who has the privilege to take the credit to be allowed to work on the projects full-time without relying on other sources of income. In addition to our collaborative projects we continue to use our individual names on published articles and other texts.

Intellectual property vs. free culture

The creative industries generate revenue from intellectual property and proprietary content that is protected and sold to ensure profits go to those who hold the rights. In the same way, the start-up sells artworks as high-resolution videos and images that are distributed as digital limited editions. The works come with a digital certificate of authenticity which has the signature of the artist and edition number. In a sense going against the nature of the Internet where files are infinitely reproducible, the platform creates a false scarcity in which only a limited number of works are available for purchase. Employing forms of digital rights management (DRM) including watermarks on artwork previews which are removed after the work is purchased, works cannot be downloaded (to avoid any free distribution of the work online) but are delivered so they can be viewed on any device through the browser or using one of the free apps for iPhone, Android and Samsung Smart TV. The certificate of authenticity confirms that the user is the owner of that original edition from the artist (rather than an illegitimate copy). It reinforces the idea of original ownership and the value of limited works by notable artists. We have direct relationships with the artists and have contracts with them to distribute their work. The arrangement opens up a number of possible new revenue streams with a 50:50 net revenue share with the artist, though the artist retains the copyright to their work. As Sarah Brouillette (2009) has written, 'commercial value requires aesthetic value that only accumulates through disavowal of commerce, such that autonomy and market determination are an intimate dialectical pair.'(844)

In contrast to independent art circles there is a different kind of value circulating in free culture (Lawrence Lessig, 2004) and the open source movement – which values keeping creative content and software open to be used and altered to allow ideas to evolve and thrive, particularly with online work which can be easily shared. For artists who value free culture, this creates a problem in terms of how to make a living from selling one's work when it's available online for free. By protecting the proprietary artwork, the start-up creates a model for artists to sell works in a limited format and create value through scarcity and also secondary sales through the trade platform. Once works have been sold out, they can be re-sold on the trade platform for any price. In many cases, the value will increase since they are no longer available for sale as such. Since so much content online is available for free, the start-up creates a means to sell digital artworks and secure its authenticity and value. Going against free culture, the works cannot be downloaded or removed from the platform. They are held securely in the Vault in your account. They are copyrighted works by artists – who might legally take you to court for any unauthorised use of their work.

With DOXA all our work is distributed online for free. We publish our texts and PDFs online which are free to be downloaded and viewed. Our interest is to share the knowledge globally to others who might find our work useful or enlightening when addressing the same questions. We support copyleft values where work is distributed freely, yet any derivatives must be distributed under the same conditions.

Open source software is distributed using licenses such as the GPL (General Public License) where anything incorporating open source software must itself be licensed as free software under the same terms. This enforces an ethic of sharing in the software development community and supports keeping knowledge open (as opposed to closed and proprietary). By keeping code open, a global community can contribute and continue to build and improve the code without limitations. It is still possible for commercial companies to use open source software, which is made available for free by charging for customer support and hardware. Open source is connected to the idea of the commons in the sharing of knowledge and resources that is not privately owned. Originally pertaining to natural resources, the digital commons relates to open access to knowledge (i.e. Wikipedia) and free use of digital assets including images, music, and videos. The copyleft movement and Creative Commons creates more flexible licensing for the use of creative works as a step towards a digital commons (Berry, 2008). Artists have explored the notions of the commons extensively in recent years. For example, Ele Carpenter's ongoing project Embroidered Digital Commons (2005–16) (Lacetti, 2006) invites people to embroider and stitch a lexicon around the digital commons as a shared language for understanding the term.

Enclosures of the commons occur in the privatisation of shared resources where we are required to pay for access to content and information. It can be said the limitations on the use of the artworks on the platform where they cannot be downloaded or freely used but only legitimately purchased with the certificate of authenticity marks the enclosure of creative work and limits access to those who can afford to purchase them (though works on the platform are more affordable than works in the traditional art market ranging from as low as £5 up to £1,000). Works can only be viewed with a watermark overlaid on the

Figure 11.1: Paolo Cirio, *Daily Paywall* (2014). Newsprint and plastic news-rack, dimensions variable. Image courtesy of the artist.

video prior to purchase and in lower resolution. Watermarks do not appear on purchased artworks, which are available in high-resolution formats.

Artists have responded critically to these online enclosures, which are contradictory to the liberatory promise of the Internet in which information can be so readily available and distributed. An example would be paywalls for news websites like the *Financial Times* and *The Economist* which limit access without payment of a subscription fee. Artist Paolo Cirio created a project called *Daily Paywall* (2014) in which he hacked the paywalls of these news sites and made the articles available for free as a means to circumvent the enclosures on knowledge in today's digital economy. Readers could earn $1 for responding to quizzes on the featured articles as a reversal of economies. In a discussion on the digital commons with urban theorist Tim Waterman, he states: 'the commons will never be fully enclosed, because capitalism is dependent upon the commons to create value that it then marketises and financialises.' (Catlow and Waterman 2015). Waterman sees possibilities for resistance as the commons is lived and enacted. He says, 'It's not at all a contradiction to say that what is common is simultaneously enclosed, exploited, and liberatory. It's a matter of tipping the balance so that the creation of the commons outpaces its negation.' (Ibid)

Working commercially in a start-up and giving my labour freely as part of a research collective I am acutely aware of how these seemingly contradictory logics can co-exist. Artists can still distribute their work online for free, yet sell a version of the work on a canvas or digital frame in a gallery. On the one hand I necessarily have to invest my efforts in protecting intellectual property and ensuring payment for creative work, on the other hand I contribute work to the commons to be freely accessed by all – but with no remuneration in the case of my free labour and self-exploitation. In addition to the open and closed models of creative work, there are also horizontal and vertical models of organisation to consider.

Horizontal vs. vertical

Like most commercial businesses today, the start-up is organised hierarchically with a CEO, senior staff and junior staff. Though as a start-up it is much more flexible and roles and responsibilities are much more fluid and there a fewer layers of management where one may take on many responsibilities as part of a small team. When I started working at the start-up, I had a domineering, micro-managing boss who was relentless and very difficult with members of the team which reinforced the traditional power divides within the company. Many staff members were hired and fired at a fast rate due to clashes with the CEO. Hierarchies are reflected through pay and responsibilities. Members of the team report to the head of their department and respond to tasks handed down from their manager. There can be a level of competition to get the promotion and pay rise or stock shares. Cost cutting reduced the size of the team and the hierarchies are less drastic, but they still continue to exist.

This is in stark contrast to DOXA, where we choose to organise horizontally. Setting up the collective we researched flat models of organisations such as cooperatives, where ownership is shared, and pay and responsibility is equally distributed. Cooperatives promote peer learning where employees learn from each other and take on different roles in the company. With a long history dating back to the seventeenth century, cooperatives began primarily within the agricultural, insurance and banking industries but can be also applied to creative businesses. An example is Calverts, an art and design cooperative operating in East London for over thirty years. We invited them to present at an event titled: *Towards an Economy Of The Commons* at Chisenhale Gallery in 2010. Director Sion Whellens (cited in Wong, 2009–12, p. 150) describes cooperatives as 'an organization of men and women who come together to address their common social, cultural and economic needs.' As a flat organisational model, each member or employee of Calverts is a 'director' yet simultaneously has the responsibility of answering the phone - a task normally taken care of by lower level office administrators. As a small business, they operate with about 10 full-time members who are equally invested in the work and share the use of the equipment for their personal creative projects. Members, who generally stay in the organisation for 10 years, share knowledge and skills through apprenticeships and help new staff step-up to their various roles. As an organizational model, Whellens described seven principles of a cooperative, which include:

1. An open and voluntary membership;
2. Democratic organisation (one member one vote);
3. Members in economic relationship with each other;
4. Autonomy from institutions, governments and corporations;
5. A model of education i.e. helping each other develop and learn professionally and in practice;
6. Cooperation with other cooperatives to create a larger economy of cooperatives around the world to develop a global movement and;
7. A mandate to provide sustainable development within the communities in which they operate.

Cooperatives present a model that is fair for their workers who have a say in the running of the business and receive have equal pay to all others in the company. Though often only able to operate successfully on a small scale, there are examples of larger cooperatives including Suma, a vegetarian and organic food wholesaler with over 140 employees / owners. For Brett Scott cooperatives are premised on 'risk-sharing between those who participate in the venture, and also common access to the common pool of what is created in the process' (quoted in Sharp, 2014). In a neoliberal economy where risk is increasingly placed on the individual with little social security, the cooperative redistributes risk across a support network, reducing the precariousness and associated anxieties individuals might otherwise experience.

Today tech companies are appropriating more horizontal management models like Agile which are often implemented within hierarchically organised companies. Agile is a business methodology that is widely used in IT businesses as a means to assist in effective self-management of technical teams where communication between each team member is made easier and issues are made visible in order for the team to respond to quickly and efficiently. It is management practice that supports close team working and communication, sharing of skills through pair programming, and constant reflecting on progress to make appropriate changes along the way in conversation with the primary stakeholder. The way of working is iterative and collaborative and intended to improve the productivity of project teams. In his recent exhibition *Products For Organising* at Serpentine Galleries, artist Simon Denny looks at corporate organisational structures including Agile and Halocracy (a horizontal, self-organising management structure) and draws links to hacker culture.

Management structures and methodologies have evolved to be more open and allow for levels of self-management where digital artisans or knowledge

Figure 11.2: Simon Denny: Products for Organising; Installation view, Serpentine Sackler Gallery; 25 November 2015 – 14 February 2016. Photograph © 2015 readsreads.info

workers feel more in control and capable of self-realisation – a mode of production that promises seemingly unalienated work. Tiziana Terranova (2000) has observed that '[K]nowledge workers need open organizational structures to produce, because the production of knowledge is rooted in collaboration...' She claims that '[T]he fruit of collective cultural labor has been not simply appropriated, but voluntarily channelled and controversially structured within capitalist business practices.' (Ibid, p. 39). Models of collaboration and self-organisation existing in what might be deemed the 'authentic' cultural labour of hackers and artists are adopted in order to draw value from knowledge workers – but with productivity, efficiency and ultimately profit in mind. Though many tech start-ups strive towards a flat management model, they are still relatively rare (Kastelle, 2013) and many still operate hierarchically particularly as they grow larger. Several notable horizontally organised tech companies like Valve (Warr, 2013) and Github (Finley, 2014) have also revealed the invisible hierarchies that continue to emerge in a workplace, which resemble the social dynamics of high school cliques.

Despite the blurring between horizontal and vertical now in the contemporary work environment, my experience in the creative tech start-up is still very strictly hierarchical, despite being a small team. At DOXA we have no formal structure. We strive to be collaborative and do not instill hierarchies. However, hierarchies do naturally emerge even amongst individuals – between those who are older, more experienced or more outspoken. It is possible to practice models of consensus decision-making, though we are too informally organised to develop fully as a cooperative. It is however a case study we'd like to explore and develop for future projects.

Conclusion

Those of us involved in creative work in the digital economy are pushed to work multiple jobs and living an existence within contradictory values, investing our resources across commercial and non-commercial worlds. We willingly give our time and put our minds and bodies to work at all moments of the day, to the point where the separation between work and life breaks down. We are caught between practices of self-branding, protection of intellectual property, negotia-tion of competitive hierarchies, sharing of knowledge and resources, and the collaborative production of value that benefits the many over the few. We can also see the ways in which the industry appropriates ideas of collaboration and how neoliberalism cannot exist without the commons as it operates to mon-etise and financialise it.

Anton Vidokle discusses the dilemmas faced by artists and explores the possible economies for artists to support their work and living. He writes that 'art is suppressed under the specter of bohemia, condemning artists to a precarious and often alienating place in the day-to-day relations that hold other parts of society together.' Artists can alternatively take the route of Andy Warhol and embrace the market economy by promoting their own brand and artwork as commodity, but then they have their work 'regarded as mere craft'. Other artists will fall back on finding sponsors/patrons to support and legitimise their practice. He says, '[w]e are perfectly capable of being our own sponsors, which in most cases we already are when we do other kinds of work to support our art-work. This is something that should not be disavowed, but acknowledged openly. We must find the terms for articulat-ing what kind of economy artists really want.' Vidokle recognises the value of balancing 'other kinds of work' to support one's art practice and to avoid allowing art becoming profitable as it is promoted in the creative economy. Many artists and cultural workers (like myself) will seek work within the industry to support independent practice. Other avenues such as education or academic fields have similar values to art practice,in contrast to pursuing work in the commercial industries, that might outrightly contradict an indi-vidual's own independent practice.

Increasingly we see artists reflexively interrogating these issues. For instance, in Maria Eichhorn's exhibition, *5 weeks, 25 days 175 hours* at Chisenhale Gal-lery, she asks the staff to take the five-week duration of the exhibition off work

Figure 11.3: Hito Steyerl, *Strike*, 2010. Image courtesy of the Artist and Andrew Kreps Gallery, New York.

and close the gallery. The project questions contemporary labour conditions in which leisure and free time is taken at the workplace and so ancillary staff are freed from their duties to explore their non-work interests whilst still being paid (Searl, 2016). The project suggests that the traditional weapon of labour – the strike – continues to offer scope for resistance against the demands of work. Yet the artwork also demonstrates why this traditional mode of resistance has receded in the creative economy. Hito Steyerl (2015) discusses the artist's strike where the current art economy relies on the physical presence of the artist. She explains that the artist's strike makes little sense when 'No one working in the art field expects his or her labour to be irreplaceable or even mildly important anymore. In the age of rampant self-employment or rather self-unemployment the idea that anyone would care for one's specific labour power seems rather exotic.' An artist strike could take the form of absenteeism in which a prop is used as a placeholder as a reminder of the absence of the artist which may otherwise go unnoticed.

The artist collective AutoItalia produced a project called *On Coping* in which artists shared their strategies in dealing with the current demands of the economy. Strategies include exploring hobbies as affordable therapy, processes of taking care of the self, and identifying pressures, absences and loopholes in one's life. Therapies are a way of coping with the situation, but do not resolve them. It eases the pain in a way that yoga and meditation have become popularised as relief to our stressful lives. *On Coping* brings together artists to discuss their precarious and financially strained conditions and their creative approaches to coping. Additional propositions for the future of work are presented in Accelerationist theory which advocates technology as the primary means of liberating humans from the dictatorship that work has on our lives.

Writers like Paul Mason, as well as Nick Srnicek and Alex Williams, approach ideas of post-capitalism which support the idea of full automation – where machines take over certain jobs and humans need to work less and less. This will be coupled with a universal basic income provided by the state which would abolish poverty. Mason (2015) believes the shift towards post-capitalism will be supported by free collaborative economies where information and resources are free and abundant. Srnicek and Williams envision '...building a post-work society on the basis of fully automating the economy, reducing the working week, implementing a universal basic income and achieving a cultural shift in the understanding of work.' (2015, p. 111) As the Left has lost the imagination for the future, these theorists attempt to posit a position we can take forward. There are many considerations when thinking about full automation particularly the kinds of work we expect machines to take over (including care work) and the risks of increasing machine intelligence to also self-create and self-update, yet the proposition of eliminating work and liberating us from our work identities frees us to imagine the possibilities of what we could do and desire for the world. Though full automation is still projected far into the future by several decades or more, it presents us a vision to collectively work towards starting at the present.

For the moment, as we can only speculate on a post-work world, we must continue our work in building the commons through models of sharing knowledge and resources, as well as by experimenting with ways of working cooperatively together. We may have to continue creating a separation between our for-profit and non-profit work that we do to support our living, but to continually defend the commons and understand the ways in which we are exploited in the neoliberal creative economy so as to limit the damage – to ourselves but just as importantly to the communities we work among. There are ways in which we can move towards another future, by pursing the important work that we do (outside the work we do to survive). These different economies can co-exist as we find models between the commercial and non-commercial work as we have in the current climate to find the means to pursue the work we truly value. We can fight for fairer contracts and government support for freelancers and precarious workers, and lobby for a universal basic income (soon to be trialled in Ontario, Canada) (MacDonald, 2016; Segal, 2016). Above all it is necessary to create time and space to find new ways of living and working that might enable us to approach alternative visions of the future in an economy that is fairer for all.

References

Arvidsson, A. and N. Peitersen. (2009). *The Ethical Economy*, online version. Retrieved from http://www.ethicaleconomy.com/info/book.

Auto Italia. (2015). On Coping: A Reading For Liverpool. [Art Programme].

Banks, M. (2014). 'Being in the Zone' of cultural work. *Culture Unbound: Journal of Current Cultural Research*, 6: 1, 241–62

Banks, M., Conor, Bridget, and Mayer, Vicki. (Eds.) (2015). *Production Studies, The Sequel!: Cultural Studies of Global Media Industries*. London and New York: Routledge.

Barbrook, R. and Andy Cameron. (2008). The Californian Ideology, *Mute* Vol. 1, No. 3. Retrieved from http://www.metamute.org/editorial/articles/californian-ideology.

Berry, David M. (2008). *Copy, Rip, Burn: The Politics of Copy Left and Open Source*. Pluto Press.

Brouillette, S. (2009) Creative labour and auteur authorship: Reading *Somers Town. Textual Practice* Vol. 23(5): 829- 847 Carpenter, Ele. (2005-). Embroidered Digital Commons [Digital artwork].

Catlow, R. and Tim Waterman. (2014). Situating the digital commons.: A conversation between Ruth Catlow and Tim Waterman. Furtherfield, 28 October. Retrieved from http://furtherfield.org/features/interviews/situating-digital-commons-conversation-between-ruth-catlow-and-tim-waterman.

Cirio, Paolo. (2014). Daily Paywall [online artwork]. Available at: https://www.paolocirio.net/work/daily-paywall/

Corporation, Bernadette. (2005). *Reena Spaulings*. MIT Press

Denny, Simon. (2016). *Products for Organising*. London: Serpentine Galleries.

Ellis, Carolyn Tony E. Adams & Arthur P. Bochner. (2011). Autoethnography: An Overview. Forum: Qualitative Social Research. Vol. 12, 1, Art. 10. Retrieved from http://www.qualitative-research.net/index.php/fqs/article/view/1589/3095.

Finley, K. (2014). Why workers can suffer in bossless companies like Github. *Wired*, 20 March. Retrieved from http://www.wired.com/2014/03/tyranny-flatness.

Florida, R.L. (2002). *The Rise of the Creative Class: And How It's Transforming Work, Leisure, Community and Everyday Life*. New York: Basic Books.

Gandini, A. (2015). Digital work: Self-branding and social capital in the freelance knowledge economy. *Marketing Theory*. pp. 1–19.

Gill, R. and Andy Pratt. (2008). Precarity and cultural work, in the social factory? Immaterial labour, precariousness and cultural work. *Theory, Culture & Society*. Los Angeles, London, New Delhi, and Singapore: SAGE, Vol. 25 (7–8): 1–30.

Hearn, A. (2010). Structuring feeling: Web 2.0, online ranking and rating, and the digital 'reputation' economy. *Ephemera Journal*. Retrieved from http://www.ephemerajournal.org/sites/default/files/10-3hearn.pdf.

Holman Jones, Stacy. (2005). Autoethnography: making the personal political. In Norman K. Denzin & Yvonna S. Lincoln (Eds.), *Handbook of Qualitative Research* (pp. 763–91). Thousand Oaks, CA: Sage.

Kastelle, T. (2013). Hierarchy Is overrated. *Harvard Business Review*, 20 November. Retrieved from https://hbr.org/2013/11/hierarchy-is-overrated.

Klein, Naomi. (2008). *The Shock Doctrine: The Rise of Disaster Capitalism.* London: Penguin.

Laccetti, J. (2006). Open Source Embroidery. Furtherfield. Available at: http://furtherfield.org/interviews/open-source-embroidery

Lazarrato, M. (2006). Immaterial Labour, in Paolo Virno and Michael Hardy (eds.) *Radical Thought In Italy: A Potential Politics*, Minneapolis: University of Minnesota Press.

Lessig, L. (2004). *Free Culture: How Big Media Uses Technology and the Law to Lock Down Culture and Control Creativity.* New York, NY: Penguin.

MacDonald, Fiona. (2016). A Canadian province is about to start trialling universal basic income. *ScienceAlert*, 10 March. Retrieved from http://www.sciencealert.com/a-canadian-province-is-about-start-giving-everyone-a-universal-basic-income

Mason, Paul. (2015). The End Of Capitalism Has Begun. *Guardian,* 17 July. Retrieved from http://www.theguardian.com/books/2015/jul/17/postcapitalism-end-of-capitalism-begun.

McRobbie, A. (2002) From Holloway to Hollywood: happiness at work in the new cultural economy. In P. du Gay & M.Pryke (Eds.) *Cultural Economy: Cultural Analysis and Commercial Life*, London: Sage, pp. 97–114.

_____. (2011). Key concepts for urban creative industry in the UK. Retrieved from http://research.gold.ac.uk/6052/1/october%25202011%2520Wd0000023%5B1%5D.pdf.

Newsinger, J. (2015). A cultural shock doctrine? Austerity, the neoliberal state and the creative industries discourse. *Media, Culture and Society.* 37: 2, pp. 302–13.

O'Brien, Dave. (2014) *Cultural Policy: Management, Value and Modernity in the Creative Industries.* London and New York: Routledge.

Searl, A. (2016). Nothing to see here: the artist giving gallery staff a month off work. *Guardian*, 25 April. Retrieved from http://www.theguardian.com/artanddesign/2016/apr/25/nothing-to-see-here-maria-eichhorn-chisenhale-gallery.

Segal, Hugh D. (2016). *Finding a Better Way: A Basic Income Pilot Project for Ontario.* Massey College, University of Toronto. Retrieved from https://www.ontario.ca/page/finding-better-way-basic-income-pilot-project-ontario.

Sharp, D. (2014). Hacking the future of money: interview with Brett Scott. *Shareable*, 29 April Retrieved from http://www.shareable.net/blog/hacking-the-future-of-money-interview-with-brett-scott (accessed 20 February 2016).

Sholette, G. (2015). Delirium and resistance after the social turn. *Field: A Journal of Socially-Engaged Art Criticism.* Spring 1: 95–138.

Srnicek, N. and Alex Williams. (2015). *Inventing the Future: Postcapitalism and a World Without Work.* London: Verso.

Steyerl, H. (2015). The terror of total dasein: Economies of presence in the art field. *Dis Magazine.* Retrieved from http://dismagazine.com/discussion/78352/the-terror-of-total-dasein-hito-steyerl.

Terranova, T. (2000). Free labor: producing culture for the digital economy. *Social Text,* 63, Vol, 18, No. 2, Durham, NC: Duke University Press, pp. 33–58.

Tokumitsu, M. (2014). In The Name of Love. *Jacobin Magazine,* Issue 13: Alive In Sunshine, 13 January. Retrieved from https://www.jacobinmag.com/2014/01/in-the-name-of-love/.

Vidolke, A. (2013) Art without market, art without education: Political economy of art. *e-flux journal #43* - March

Warr, p. (2013 July 9). Valve's flat management structure 'like high school'. *Wired.* Retrieved from http://www.wired.co.uk/article/valve-management-jeri-ellsworth.

Wong, A. (2009–12). AMASS: towards an economy of the commons. *Reviews in Cultural Theory.* Vol.2.3: On the Commons. Edmonton: University of Alberta.

About the Editors and Contributors

The Editors

Dr James Graham is Senior Lecturer and Convenor of the Promotional Cultures Research Group in the Faculty of Arts and Creative Industries, Middlesex University, London.

Dr Alessandro Gandini is Lecturer in Digital Media Management and Innovation in the Department of Digital Humanities, Kings College, London, UK.

The Contributors

Dr Carolina Bandinelli is Teaching Fellow in Digital Culture at the Department of Digital Humanities King's College, London and Senior Researcher for the AHRC project CREATe at Goldsmiths London.

Dr Miranda Campbell is Assistant Professor in the School of Creative Industries, Faculty of Communication and Design, Ryerson University, Ontario, Canada. She is the author of *Out of the Basement: Youth Cultural Production in Practice and in Policy* (2013).

Dr Jamie Clarke is Senior Lecturer and co-course leader of media culture and production at the School of Business, Law and Communications, Southampton Solent University, UK.

Dr Alberto Cossu is a postdoctoral researcher in the Department of Social and Political Sciences at the University of Milan.

Rosamund Davies is Senior Lecturer, Media and Creative Writing, Department of Creative Professions and Digital Arts, University of Greenwich, UK.

Dr Leora Hadas is is Teaching Associate, Department of Culture, Film and Media, University of Nottingham, UK. Her work has been published in *Cinema Journal, European Journal of Cultural Studies*, and *Critical Studies in Media Communication*

Dr Jacob Matthews is Associate Professor in Information and Communication Sciences at the Culture and Communications department of Paris 8 University, and member of the Cemti research lab. He is co-author of *Le web collaboratif* (2010)with Philippe Bouquillion.

Dr Dinu Gabriel Munteanu is a member of the Faculty of Media and Communication, Bournemouth University, UK. He has a background in psychology and the liberal arts. His recent research focuses on memory, digital curation, imagination and the arts.

Karen Patel is a PhD researcher at the Birmingham School of Media, Birmingham City University, UK.

Ashley Lee Wong is a Doctoral Researcher at the School of Creative Media, City University of Hong Kong, Head of Programmes and Operations at the online platform Sedition and co-founder of the DOXA collective (www.doxacollective. org).

Index

CPSIA information can be obtained
at www.ICGtesting.com
Printed in the USA
LVHW022145220921
698455LV00008B/317